Lawless

Lawless

A LAWYER'S UNRELENTING FIGHT FOR JUSTICE IN A WAR ZONE

KIMBERLEY MOTLEY

ALLEN&UNWIN

First published in the United Kingdom by Allen & Unwin in 2019. This paperback edition published in the United Kingdom by Allen & Unwin in 2020

Allen & Unwin
c/o Atlantic Books
Ormond House
26–27 Boswell Street
London WC1N 3JZ

Phone: 020 7269 1610
Fax: 020 7430 0916
Email: UK@allenandunwin.com
Web: www.allenandunwin.com/uk

A CIP catalogue record for this book is available from the British Library.

Paperback ISBN 978 1 76063 318 9
E-Book ISBN 978 1 76063 396 7

Printed in Denmark by Nørhaven A/S

10 9 8 7 6 5 4 3 2 1

For my beloved Deiva, Seoul, and Cherish.
I hope that one day you'll understand.

CONTENTS

PROLOGUE

Court is in session on the Spanish island of Mallorca. I'm sitting with my client, a young British man accused of selling drugs on the neighbouring island of Ibiza, when my phone vibrates in my pocket. I quietly slide it out and read the message sent by another client, Laila, who was recently kidnapped from Vienna to Afghanistan.

"I don't know if they have guns," the message says.

I scan the courtroom. It's not good form for lawyers to send text messages while the court is in session, but Laila needs a quick reply. I begin to type, casually, trying not to draw any attention to myself.

"Are you wearing the black clothes?"

I hit send and get an instant response.

"Yes."

"When you get in the car, we have a burqa for you. Put it on."

"Okay."

I think back to the first time I saw a burqa in 2008 when I arrived in Afghanistan. I had found the ghoulish blue head-to-toe coverings both terrifying and maddening; a visible sign of the oppressive culture of misogyny that was rife in the country. Ironic, then, that I'm now using the burqa to try to free Laila.

I listen as our witness is being questioned by the prosecutor. If found guilty, my client is facing nine years in a Spanish jail and a lifetime stain on his record as a convicted drug dealer. I turn to him and offer a reassuring smile. He listens nervously as the prosecution continues their cross-examination.

"Relax," I whisper.

I watch the prosecutor as he works our witness. Our witness is consistent, assured, confident. Good man, I think to myself. He's answering all the aggressive questions perfectly. Just as I would answer if I were in his position. I try to concentrate, but my mind keeps darting back to Laila. What is she doing? I wonder.

Keeping my phone out of the sight of the judges, I check it again. Nothing at first, but then it vibrates in my hand, almost making me jump. I open the text. It's from one of my guys; they're outside the house in Afghanistan where Laila has been imprisoned for months. The coast was as clear as it was going to get.

I text Laila again.

"The gate is unlocked. The car is outside. Get in it."

I send the message. I can feel my heart rate rising. Another text.

"I'm scared."

"I know. Get in the car Laila."

One of the judges from the three-judge tribunal eyes me disapprovingly from the bench. I smile back and return my focus to the witness. My phone buzzes again.

"I can't," texts Laila.

Fuck.

Like many trafficked victims whom I've rescued over the years, Laila is showing signs of psychological confinement. She has a small opportunity to escape, but fear has taken over. Frozen in Afghanistan, she was terrified to make a move. I have an idea.

"Do you have the headphones with you?"

"Yes."

"In two minutes go to the bathroom. Put the headphones on. I'll send you a voice note."

I had had a sleepless week, what with locating Laila, setting up her rescue and preparing for the trial in Mallorca. And now, for the first time in six days, when we only have a few precious minutes to rescue this young woman, she's lost her nerve. If we don't act now, she'll disappear to Pakistan and we may not find her again. It's now or never.

Back in the courtroom the prosecutor droned on with her cross-examination. I start coughing. I cough as hard as I can until the whole court has stopped what it's doing and everyone is looking at me. I hold up my hand as I cough harder. A little concerned, the judge who stared at me earlier raises an eyebrow as if to say, "Are you okay?"

"We are going to take a quick break," she says, eyeing me suspiciously, but also probably hoping I'm not going to cough up a lung.

I nod to her, wait for the judges to leave the court, then run out of the courtroom to the bathroom, locking the door behind me.

"Laila," I say, into the phone, "listen to me very carefully. You have five minutes to get in the fucking car. If you don't, we will be gone forever. I will not look for you in Pakistan. I will not help you anymore. I will never answer your calls. Five. Minutes."

In the ten years I've been based in Afghanistan, I've represented multiple clients from different countries with vastly different backgrounds, who have had challenging legal issues, many in intensely dangerous situations. I know this territory now like the back of my hand, and although for me it has become just another day's work, I know that for Laila every second could be the difference between life and death.

My phone vibrates.

"Ms Motley, please don't leave." Laila texts.

I text back.

"Four minutes."

1

THE PLAYLIST

In 2007 I was living and working in Milwaukee, Wisconsin. Milwaukee is where I grew up. It's where I went to school. It's where I started my life with my husband, Claude, and it's where we had our three kids, Deiva, Seoul and Cherish. I know Milwaukee better than I know myself. Although that doesn't mean I have to like it.

Ever since I was a kid, Milwaukee has been the most segregated city in the United States.[1] It's a place that incarcerates more black men than any other city in the US so that now more than 50 per cent of black men in their thirties and early forties have been incarcerated in some type of state prison.[2] In 2018, Milwaukee was deemed the worst place in America to raise a black child.[3]

These may seem like just another set of grim urban statistics to you, but they are more than just numbers to me. They represent the experiences I've had my whole life.

I grew up in the projects. When I was seven, my best friend was a girl named Janine. I would go to her house every day to play, and I can still remember her mother, a beautiful woman who was always kind to me. I remember how sometimes she would bake us cookies. One night I was lying in bed when suddenly the street was lit up by the lights of ambulances and police cars. The sirens rang out and I could hear voices shouting outside my window.

The next day I found out that Janine's mother had been murdered by her father. She had tried to get away, banging on people's doors, crying for help, but no one opened up their door for her. Her husband beat and stabbed her to death in the street and threw her body in the green dumpster that I passed when I walked to school every day.

When I was nine, my two brothers and I were playing baseball in the neighbourhood playground and an older teenager came over to borrow our bat. He took the bat from us and beat the shit out of another kid in the middle of the street right there in front of us.

That is Milwaukee. It's the city where I was born and raised. It's a city that I love and hate. It's the city that made me who I am and prepared me for whatever the world could throw at me.

Despite growing up in the projects, not going to college was never an option. Not with my Korean mother and African-American military father. Even though I had my heart set on other things, they expected me to go to college to get a degree. Still, it wasn't until I was twenty years old and pregnant with Deiva that I decided to focus on getting a paralegal degree so I could find a job that earned enough to provide for her.

I have always had an interest in the law. When I was two, my father was nearly killed in a car accident while he was working, but not only did his then employer, General Electric (GE), refuse to pay compensation for the disabilities he suffered as a result of the accident, they actually fired him. He was forced to sue. The case rumbled on for years and at times was the main focus of life in our house. Eventually it went to court and he lost. That transformed life for us because, while we weren't rich before the accident, we were definitely poor after it. We even had to give away our dog.

After earning my paralegal degree, I finished my Bachelor's degree in criminal justice and then went to graduate school and law school at two different universities simultaneously, graduating in May 2003. I wasn't yet sure in what area of law I wanted to practise, but I'd tell people "anything but criminal law" because I had grown up in that world and seen enough of it to last a lifetime. But when the Milwaukee Public Defender's Office visited our campus and I started talking to one of their recruiters, she convinced me that I was well suited for the work and offered me a job. Already pregnant with my second child, Seoul, it seemed easy to say yes.

Becoming a public defender is for a lot of people the first time they're introduced to poverty. It can be quite a culture shock. In order to be a lawyer worth your salt, you have to know the law but also how to deal with people who might be very different from anyone you've ever met. So as soon as I started working at the Milwaukee Public Defender's Office I could tell I was unusual. While for most of my peers, this was the first time that they'd seen criminal activity up close, I'd been conditioned to it since I was a little kid.

It takes a special person to be a really good public defender, to be that kind of advocate, because it's more than a job, it's a lifestyle. Unfortunately, it didn't take long before I began to feel that that lifestyle wasn't what I wanted. I felt increasingly like I had to choose between being a good lawyer and having a good life. I'm not saying that I had to be super-wealthy, but it frustrated me that I couldn't do my job well and also live a full life outside of it. Our system in the US just doesn't allow for people to do that work, represent poor people and have enough time or money to support a family.

Like most public defenders, I was overwhelmed with cases. I was required to represent somewhere between 200 and 250 people per year, which meant there was little time to go to the office or have meetings or to do any of those other things you might think a lawyer does with her day. My days began with dropping off my eldest daughter and son, Deiva and Seoul, at school and my youngest daughter, Cherish, at child care. I then spent the rest of my time running between the court and the jail.

The day I met David was a pretty typical day.

I had dropped off the kids that morning and had been bouncing from court to court. Or, as in David's case, fronting up to argue bail.

The way our Public Defender's Office worked was that we took bail hearings on a rotating basis, so when you're on you argue bail for everyone arrested that week. Whoever they might be, whatever they've done, you try to make some kind of reasonable argument no matter how hopeless. I've literally stood up in a bail hearing and argued that the fact my client has actually showed up, albeit in handcuffs, is sitting in court politely and promises that he won't run (this time) are positive factors that the judge should consider when setting bail. You do what you can.

So the day I met David I'd arrived at court and knew I had around ten minutes to see what we might use to convince the court not to incarcerate him. To be honest, I was on autopilot because I'd seen ten Davids already that day. Or so I thought.

Something about David's file was unusual. He was still in high school; I could use that and argue that he was less of a flight risk. He had no prior record, which definitely helped, and he also had a part-time stable job—another bonus. Before I'd even considered the details of his case I had figured this kid had a good shot at being released on bail.

David was a seventeen-year-old black kid who was preparing for his prom. To get himself looking his best, David went to get a haircut at the local barber shop. He sat down in the barber's chair, and while the guy was cutting his hair the other guys were shooting the breeze like guys in barber shops do. Then one of the guys pulled out a gun that he'd just bought from some guy on the street.

Everyone was excited at the sight of the gun. They started laughing and joking about it as the barber removed the clip and passed it around. Everyone in there took turns holding the gun, admiring the gun, talking about the gun, goofing off a bit. Eventually the gun landed in David's hands.

Now, let's remember the gun had no clip. David held up the gun, examined it, and pulled the trigger.

The bullet fired across the room and struck another seventeen-year-old kid sitting in the chair opposite David. Just like David, Mike was there that day getting his hair cut for his prom. The bullet struck Mike in the head and killed him instantly.

David dropped the gun and yelled, "You didn't tell me there was one in the chamber!"

He panicked and tried to help the kid bleeding on the floor. David screamed for help even though it was clear there was nothing that could be done.

The other guys in the shop must have panicked too because they started getting aggressive with David, telling him he needed to get the hell out of there. They forced him out of the door and David ran home. He told his older sister what had happened. She packed him a bag and told him to get the hell out of town. His sister instructed him to head to Chicago and lie low.

Somewhere between his sister's house and Chicago, David's conscience and good sense must have kicked in because instead he walked to the nearest police station. He told the police what he'd done, and like any officer would in that situation they sat him down and asked him to write down a full confession.

But then David did something very interesting.

Instead of writing a confession, he wrote a letter. The letter was addressed to the mother of the boy who he had just shot hours before. It was contrite, full of remorse and sorrow for what had happened. In it, he explained that it had been a terrible accident and that he was sorry for the pain that he had caused.

The police officers promised to share David's letter with the victim's family (which they never did). Ultimately, he was charged for murdering Mike.

A couple of days after he'd been released on bail, David came to my office. He walked in wearing his high school letterman jacket, eyes scanning nervously around the room. It was obvious that this was the first time he'd been in any kind of trouble. Just as he'd been at the hearing, he was polite and humble, but his fear was palpable. Being a public defender, you get used to seeing a lot of people who commit crimes and you get used to their swagger, the way they conduct themselves, the way they look at you, talk to you. But right away, as I measured up this teenage boy standing in front of me, I thought, "You ain't supposed to be here."

I felt strongly that we had a case to bring to trial. Though what David had done was ill-advised, there was no intent; it had been an accident and so there was a chance to win if we went in front of a jury. But David was firm. He felt so bad about what he'd done that he simply wanted to plead guilty and take his punishment.

"I deserve to go to prison for the rest of my life," he kept saying over and over.

He seemed genuinely remorseful, like all he wanted was for everything to stop and for the pain and guilt to go away. I wasn't sure volunteering for prison was the best way to achieve that. I tried to talk him through his options, but his mind was set. He wasn't listening. All he said was, "I should never have picked up that gun."

So David began to go through the exact details of what had happened that day. I was surprised when he told me that he had confessed at the police station. I was particularly interested in how the police had extracted that confession from him. I wondered if they coerced him or put words in his mouth. That's when he told me about the letter he'd written to the kid's mother.

"Didn't she get it?" he asked me. I doubted it, but I decided I'd ask for a copy.

Two weeks later, David and I met again. This time back in the courtroom. David pleaded guilty and a court date was set for his sentencing.

In court, the prosecution agreed with David: that he should never have touched the gun. They called the victim's parents up to the stand and they impressed upon everyone what a good person Mike had been. I couldn't argue with any of this. When it came my time to present David's case, I was determined to show what a good kid he was, too.

But when I stood up I froze.

I had spent the last month working hard to put together strong arguments to justify a light sentence for David. By pleading guilty, we already knew that he was going to prison, so all I could do was try to get his sentence reduced as much as possible. I had compiled character references from the school, his boss, people who'd known him his whole life. They all stood by him. He *was* a good kid. This wasn't some gang-related assassination but a terrible accident that had robbed two promising young black men of their lives because we live in a country where guns get passed around at the barber shop. After countless hours discussing the case with David, I could only admire his maturity and willingness to accept responsibility. I speak from experience when I say how rare that is.

But in that moment, as I stood in front of the court, I changed my mind about how to present my arguments. I'd given sentencing arguments and presented character references a hundred times before; the court had heard millions of them. And I'd defended gang members and murderers; the results were nearly always the same. I knew I had to do something different for David.

David's family sat on one side, while Mike's family were seated on the other. I stood up and glanced at the boy sitting next to me, swimming in the oversized suit his father had lent him, head down, crying. I looked at the notes that I had spent hours writing with all the positive letters in support of David.

Judge Donald urged, "Ms Motley, please proceed."

Putting aside my notes, I looked again at my client and decided to shuffle my playlist. I reached for another document at the back of David's file—the letter he had written to Mike's mother hours after the shooting.

"Ms Motley . . ." Judge Donald repeated impatiently.

"*Dear Ma'am.*" I began, clearing my throat. "*I'm sorry. I am so sorry for what I have done . . .*"

I have always believed that the law needs to be practised with humanity. A lot of my colleagues disagree and prefer to rely on the rules to guide their every step through the legal process. We're trained to learn the book so that we can follow it, but I think sometimes you have to throw the book away and do what feels right. As I read through David's letter, I knew it said more than any character reference ever could.

"*I think about all of the times I've seen your son at this barber shop before,*" he'd written. "*I've never spoken to him, but he seemed like a very nice person. My father always taught me not to touch guns, that guns are not toys, and I should have known better. I'm so sorry that I killed him and I wish I was dead instead.*"

I've always wondered how David must have felt walking to the police station, the thoughts going through his mind, the weight on his young shoulders. How he must have felt as a seventeen-year-old kid who had just killed somebody after he'd been told to run away, to hide, to avoid recrimination. What strength David showed to instead make the decision to say, "No, I'm going to handle this." What did that take? I can't imagine what that walk felt like on his young legs.

Reading David's letter was so emotional and raw that it was difficult for me to even get through it. When I'd finished, I sat down and the court was silent. The judge took a minute before he addressed us.

"This is one of the most difficult sentencings I've ever had to make as a judge," he said. "I recognise that you're a good kid. Mike was also a good kid, too. But still there was a life that was taken . . ."

Then he sentenced David to three years in prison.

It was the best result that we could have hoped for. I hugged David before they took him down. Then I experienced the most powerful thing as I left the courtroom and walked down the hall. I saw the two mothers, David's and Mike's, talking to each other in the corridor. Two women whose lives had been destroyed, consoling each other for their loss.

There were no winners in the courtroom that day. I used David's own words to defend him, to protect him. I didn't know it at the time, but I was exploring something new, something outside of what I'd been taught in law school. I didn't realise it then, but it would become a cornerstone of a legal style that would come to define my career.

In the meantime, I saw that this was another example of the reality of Milwaukee. It's a town where even good kids get shot dead and other good kids end up in prison. Watching the two mothers mourning their sons must have flicked a switch somewhere inside of me because suddenly I felt a profound sense of sadness as well as urgency. I knew I needed to get away from that place. I needed my children to grow up somewhere else because otherwise, one day, I might end up like one of those women.

2

THE MANCHURIAN CANDIDATE

Shortly after representing David, I began to send out my résumé and started hitting up friends for leads on other job opportunities. Friends like Megan.

Megan was a colleague and every couple of months we'd have lunch and catch up. She wasn't surprised to hear me admit that I thought the time had come to leave the Public Defender's Office.

"Well . . . I've got this friend who is doing some cool work," she said.

"Really?" I replied. "I'm keeping an open mind right now. Just as long as it's not in Milwaukee."

"It's certainly not in Milwaukee," she laughed. "He's working in Afghanistan training and mentoring Afghan lawyers."

I still remember my reply: "That sounds cool. Can you connect us?"

At that point I had never left the United States. I was as green as apples. If you'd shown me a world map, I'd have struggled to find Afghanistan on it, let alone tell you anything about the place. All I knew was I needed to get my family out of Milwaukee and to do that I needed another job. So I sent an email.

"Hi. I just had lunch with our mutual friend Megan, who told me about what you do. It sounds really cool and just in case you ever need somebody, attached is my CV."

I didn't think about it again. I'd sent out so many résumés that week that this was just another on a long list. But it turned out to be the email that changed my life.

It was the end of a long day and I'd only gone to the office to collect files for the following morning. My desk is usually a sea of chaos, which means I'm usually stressed that I can't find what I need. Added to that, after a full day in court my sense of humour has usually knocked off long before I have.

I'd finally found everything I needed, packed it all away in my backpack and was heading out of the door when my phone rang. I had one of those "Do I really have time for this?" moments before I finally picked it up.

"Hello. Is that Kimberley Motley?" The voice on the other end sounded like it was on speaker phone. The line was so terrible I could hardly make out what he was saying.

"Who is this?" I really needed to pick up the kids.

"I'm Tim and this is George," said the voice. "I'm calling from JSSP in Afghanistan. Do you have a couple of minutes?"

The JSSP or Justice Sector Support Program is what Megan had been telling me about over lunch. George was the country director of JSSP and he began to fill me in on their background. JSSP was set up in 2005 and, according to the US Department of State, was the largest rule-of-law program of its kind anywhere in the world. It was set up to support the Afghan government in the development of a justice sector capable of managing, equipping, enabling and sustaining its own criminal justice system.[1] In other words, it was part of the US "Nation Building" strategy. Due to Afghanistan's embryonic legal system, Team America had been tasked to help them build a better one.

I hadn't even looked up the job. I didn't know what a JSSP was or what the job involved. I'd simply sent a speculative email and not thought about it again. Now it seemed like I was in the middle of some kind of impromptu interview with two guys on the other side of the world.

The whole time I was thinking, "Who just calls you out of the blue for a job in Afghanistan?" It didn't seem real.

After about half an hour, George and his sidekick explained that they wanted to move me forward to the next stage, which meant I would be invited to a ten-day training course in Virginia. At that point, I had to say, "Whoa!" Ten days? I didn't just have ten days to take off to go to Virginia.

"You'll be paid $10,000 for your time," George said.

Okay, ten days. I could make that work.

Money was tight. Money's still tight. I guess everyone always says that, but back then, believe me, it was *really* tight. On top of our college loans, Claude and I had three kids (my youngest, Cherish, had come along after three years of my working in the Public Defender's Office, in 2006), a mortgage, unpaid bills and all the usual headaches a young family has. Three nights a week, after I left the Public Defender's Office, I would cross town to work my second job lecturing at the local community college. Ten grand was pretty much what five months of Cherish's child care bill came to, so there was no way we were going to miss out on that kind of money.

A month later, I boarded a plane to Arlington, Virginia.

I was picked up at the airport by bus and driven to a hotel on the edge of town with around twenty other people, mostly lawyers, almost all men. I was one of three women. Since the small talk revolved around what everyone's experiences had been working internationally I kept pretty quiet, listening and taking everything in.

The trainers running the course came to meet us off the bus, four guys in khaki pants, Oxford shirts, military boots and Oakley sunglasses. I'd never seen people dressed like that before. I felt like I'd stepped into a quasi-military exercise.

You've probably seen the movie *Private Benjamin*, and though I'm not saying we were scrambling under camouflage nets or anything like that, it's still a useful frame of reference for how ridiculous those next ten days of my life were to become.

The focus seemed to be to make us as terrified of Afghanistan as possible. We were billeted in a pseudo-military base and treated like new recruits. Like Manchurian candidates, three days in we spent a whole morning watching nothing but videos of things and people who had presumably been blown up in Afghanistan. We spent a day doing covert convoy driver training where we learned how to avoid kidnap and capture. Then one afternoon they drove us into the woods and taught us how to shoot. It was the first time I had ever held a gun.

They were trying to toughen up the soft lawyers. It seemed like they wanted us to believe that when we walked off the plane in Afghanistan suicide bombers would come running up to give us a hug.

This was clearly not my world. There'd been some kind of mistake. I decided early on that I would just keep my head down, collect my ten grand, get back to Milwaukee and find a real job.

Meanwhile, the white male American contractors in their Oakley sunglasses tried to teach us about cultural sensitivity. Mostly that involved encouraging the women to be submissive; don't look a man in the eye, never *ever* shake hands with a man, always wear a headscarf. A lot of it was just a bunch of bullshit about what *they* thought Afghans wanted. And you know there wasn't a single Afghan in that training. Not one.

But they did get my interest when they told us what the salary would be. Now, bear in mind that at that time I was making $51,000 a year at the Public Defender's Office, plus another $5,000 from my teaching job. The JSSP job in Afghanistan would more than triple that. Suddenly, I really wanted that job.

I got home from Virginia tired and a little deflated. Even if I didn't want it to work, I now desperately wanted a job that paid that well and could catapult us out of Milwaukee.

Before I could even offload to Claude, he told me his good news: he'd been accepted into law school in North Carolina. I was so pleased and proud of him, but I was also thinking, "How much is that going to cost?"

Claude's news meant I needed the Afghanistan job even more. Moving to North Carolina made sense. It was exactly the kind of place we'd been looking to escape to. It was safe, clean and there's no snow. Plus, there are really good Big Ten colleges in North Carolina: Duke, UNC and Chapel Hill are all nearby. Suddenly, I was thinking about a long-term future out of Milwaukee. All we needed was the means to make it happen.

Shortly thereafter, I received my formal offer to join the JSSP. I was excited about the opportunity but sad that I would have to leave my family to pursue it. I would leave for Afghanistan in September 2008 on a twelve-month contract.

Claude accepted his place at law school and we moved the family across the country to a new house and a new life in August 2008. I immediately felt the pressures of Milwaukee and the safety of my family had been lifted off my shoulders—only to be replaced with the new pressure of navigating uncharted territory. The better this new life felt, the more I was terrified it wouldn't work out.

I was also concerned with how my kids were going to get on in a new place without me. They were all starting new schools. Cherish, now two years old, would be starting at a new child care centre; Seoul was going into the second grade and Deiva into the sixth grade. We wouldn't have the extended family support we had relied on in Milwaukee and Claude would also be a full-time student in law school. He's a great dad, but he had never really been left on his own with the kids for any length of time before.

The challenge of a new job was also playing on my mind. I was fixated with the others I'd met in Arlington. They'd all worked overseas before so I feared they would know exactly what they were doing while I wouldn't know anyhing. I was scared I'd look stupid in front of them.

The night before I left, I stayed awake thinking, "What if something happens to me? How are they going to cope?"

I knew I'd be back in two months for my first leave. Until then, I had to say goodbye and get on with it. The sound of Seoul crying when I left for the airport will always stick with me. At least Cherish and Deiva were sleeping when I kissed them goodbye. I hoped that one day they'd be able to understand that this was not the number-one choice for me or Claude.

Two days later, after a short stopover in Dubai, I was stepping off the plane, brand-new passport in hand, on to Afghan soil for the first time. This wasn't like going to the Bahamas. I was acutely aware of all that I'd heard and read during my training, and as I blinked in the bright sunlight to focus on the huge mountain peaks in the distance, I realised I was terrified.

What the hell have I gotten myself into? I wondered.

I was clutching a red headscarf; I had decided not to wear it in order to have an unobstructed view of this new place. I stared out across the tarmac into the desert, stunned by the natural beauty of the desolate landscape and the mountains in the distance. A bus arrived with bullet-sized holes in the window, and as it ferried us across the runway towards the terminal I became aware that my two new American male colleagues were eyeing me nervously. I was still clutching the red scarf. I glanced across the bus to another woman on board who had already covered her head. We exchanged smiles, a non-verbal understanding that we were both entering a world where we were about to unwillingly become second-class citizens.

The two male colleagues were still eyeing me nervously as I stepped off the bus. I tried to remember some of the things we were told by the American men who trained us in Virginia about how a woman "should" conduct herself in Afghanistan. Don't initiate a conversation with a man, he is to speak to you first; wear your headscarf (Golden Rule number one already broken); don't ever touch a man; no public dancing; and, last but not least, keep your head on a swivel.

Inside the airport we were swarmed by men looking to help with our luggage. The noise, the new smells, the signs in what looked like Arabic script—it was all overwhelming. I avoided engaging with anyone, instead looking around, clocking the armed men patrolling the baggage area. Eventually my bag arrived on the carousel and I gave in and let one of the baggage guys take it. I followed behind him as our group made its way outside into the hot, dusty streets of Kabul.

Our local contacts were waiting for us at an armoured SUV in the car park. Before we got in, we were each handed a bullet-proof vest and hard hat. I had to slide an AK-47 along the back seat to sit myself down. The car sped along the bleached, dirty streets while I struggled to take it all in. The horns of the oncoming traffic screamed as vehicles whizzed past us on both sides, we braked for a man leading a small flock of goats across the road, boys played with kites up on the roofs, while down below the sidewalks were packed with women in cornflower-blue burqas, men in shalwar kameez, amputees begging, people selling fruit and vegetables. There were people everywhere. It was like nothing I had ever seen or imagined. Still so true.

We drove to what would become our new home: a type of makeshift office compound in the centre of Kabul. Our four-car armoured convoy stopped and the drivers signalled to the gatekeepers to open the huge metal gates. We drove inside a compound that housed three huge buildings surrounded by high, concrete reinforced walls topped with razor wire.

I was acutely aware for the first time that I was in a war zone. Far, far away from my comfort zone.

That night, my first night in Kabul, I couldn't sleep. I was filled with anticipation, fear, sadness, loneliness and frustration. As the sound of helicopters overhead came rumbling through the walls, I ran over and over in my mind what the kids and Claude might be doing.

I got out of bed and locked my door. Somehow that made me feel better.

3

I'M NOT A TERRORIST, I'M A TAXI DRIVER

After the initial shock of finding myself living in a war zone, I started to enjoy my new work at JSSP. I was full of optimism about how we could make a difference in a place that clearly needed help establishing rule of law.

I came to Kabul to work, but right away I could see how green I was compared to the other new JSSP recruits. It seemed like everyone else was well travelled, had worked on other international programs and had a wealth of experiences that I'd never had. So my motivation from day one was to make up that ground.

I was assigned to work on establishing training programs for defence lawyers. The aim was to enhance the skills of the Afghan lawyers by showing them the American way of doing things, which seemed logical as that was the legal system we were used to. At first, I fell into the trap of believing things would be that simple.

One of the key points for me when practising law is understanding the environment. It's something that I constantly consider when I'm in a courtroom. I need to think about which court I'm in, which judge I'm facing, what the mood in the room is. There's no such thing as a solution that works everywhere for everyone. One of the biggest mistakes that America made when we came to Afghanistan was to employ a "this is the right way" mindset that everyone was expected to blindly follow.

A good example of how we got things wrong was when the US sent American police officers to train and mentor Afghan police. The Americans began by equipping the Afghans with their "kit", which consisted of the kind of uniforms a US police officer would wear. Of course a uniform is important for the police because having the same clothes makes everyone feel like they're part of the same team. Sounds good in theory, but the police trainers failed to factor in something crucial about the environment they were working in.

Before they could even get into the substantive part of the training concerning how to conduct arrests, interrogate, take statements and all the important stuff, they discovered something else important: most Afghan men wear sandals. The wiping of the feet is part of the ritual of purification in Islamic faith. So when the Afghans received their US standard-issue boots, they didn't know how to tie them.

The first days of the course were spent training the new recruits how to tie their shoelaces. Like Charlie Brown expecting the football to be there when it wasn't, it was a miscalculation that I saw repeated by the Americans time and again. It was the same at JSSP and indeed everywhere else in Afghanistan. Too often it was "our way or the highway" and it didn't make sense.

After a couple of months at JSSP, I began to question why there weren't any Afghans involved in the development of the training materials. Our "capacity-building" mission was led almost exclusively by Americans, and for the most part we only used the Afghan lawyers on staff as translators rather than as subject matter experts. The Afghans we worked with at JSSP had virtually no voice in how we trained them in the legal structure we were ostensibly building for their country.

Even though the mission was funded with American dollars, it didn't explain why everything had to be completely monopolised by us. For example, training on anything that had to do with Islamic law was forbidden. I'm not saying it was our place to teach the Holy Quran, but it was the sort of thing that we should have included in the training. Legally speaking, in the Islamic Republic of Afghanistan there is no separation of church and state.[1,2]

Instead the Afghans were kept at arm's length. No matter how hard our local counterparts tried to help, they were always met with a superior, dismissive attitude from the senior management at JSSP. This attitude extended to all aspects of our relationship with the Afghans. They weren't allowed into certain meetings. They worked in the basement while the Americans worked on the main floor. There were two separate kitchens, one for Afghans and one for us. Meal times were completely segregated, the Afghans dined in another room to that of the Americans. It was like we were there working near the Afghans, but we weren't working with them.

One afternoon, I decided to ask some of the Afghans in

my team if I could join them for lunch. They didn't hesitate. Of course they said yes and made a space for me. I didn't know until later, but it was the first time any American had ever asked.

I learned a lot at that lunch. I sat with Mustafa, Angela and Idress. Mustafa told me about how the Taliban would snatch women off the streets, beat them and sometimes even kill them. He told me about how the once-popular swimming pool was drained only to be used as a place where people were hanged from the diving board. He told me how the Taliban had destroyed some of Afghanistan's oldest and most sacred religious landmarks, like the Bamiyan Buddhas, because they represented religions other than Islam.

I learned, too, that every day many of the Afghans at JSSP either shared their food or did not eat at all so that they could take the leftovers home to their families.

After that meal, I thought it would be a great idea for everyone to have lunch together. I asked the American lawyers why they thought the Afghans didn't eat with us. My colleagues shrugged and John, my boss, told me it was because they didn't want to.

"But there's a lot we could learn from them," I said.

"They've all passed security checks," someone chimed in as though that was the issue.

"Good to know," I replied, winking and swallowing my sarcasm. "Do you think maybe it might be worthwhile then—for security reasons and all—if we could get to know them a bit better?"

"What do you propose?" John asked.

"What if we just invited everyone to lunch," I replied. "Maybe the Rose Garden would be nice."

Somewhat reluctantly, John agreed, and a few days later in the beautiful flowered garden East met West for lunch.

The entire Afghan staff came to lunch: eight Afghan Legal Counsels (ALCs), ten interpreters, and even some of the off-duty guards showed up. Like lawyers often do, we got chatting about where we'd been to school. They were an impressively qualified bunch. All had college degrees and one of the translators had even been to medical school. He explained that jobs were so scarce in Kabul that the competition for a translator's salary was fierce.

I would like to say that after that lunch the Americans and Afghans regularly had lunch together. However the next day both sides went back to their familiar corners and remained there for the many lunches that came after.

But the more I got to know the Afghans I was training, the more I wanted to make the training more useful for them. I didn't want to train Afghan lawyers on what the Afghan constitution said or what the Afghan penal code said— they'd already learned that in law school. What was missing from their training was any kind of analytical thinking. The typical trainings at JSSP just involved reciting laws but did not include how to apply laws in different legal scenarios that they would be representing clients for. That's the kind of training I wanted to do. I wanted to train them on how to use the law to effectively represent their clients, how to interrogate a person, how to write a defence statement, how to help build their case for their clients—the kind of substantive training that lawyers and, more importantly, their clients really need.

But I got backlash from JSSP and the US Embassy for not training the way they wanted us to, for not sticking to the way it was laid out in our binders. Pretty soon my

JSSP superiors stopped giving me enough money to pay the Afghan lawyers I had been inviting to my conferences. I started to get the feeling that I was being set up to fail. Many of my colleagues running other JSSP training sessions were approved with budgets of tens of thousands of dollars. I was given $841 for the whole year.

Privately I was hurt, silently outraged, but publicly I was defiant. I stuck to my guns, arguing that I didn't need to pay lawyers to come to my trainings. The US Embassy and JSSP bosses tried to undermine me, insisting that no one would come if I didn't pay them. I stood my ground and told my bosses that I didn't want any Afghan lawyers just coming for a pay cheque. I only wanted people who were passionate about the training. I would only train lawyers who really wanted to be lawyers.

And guess what? My training conferences were packed. Hundreds of Afghan lawyers came on their own buck. The money clearly wasn't the motivating factor that everyone at JSSP thought it would be. There were many Afghan lawyers who simply wanted to be better at their jobs.

My success made me even more determined to tailor our training to the environment, but my attitude became a threat to many within the embassy and JSSP. Every time I got Afghans to come to a training session without being paid for it, I was undermining the view that the Afghans weren't worthy of our cooperation. If I was right, and the Afghans really were there to work hard, then the Americans would also have to work hard, and some of my colleagues did not like that.

While I was losing friends within JSSP, I was building up trust with the locals. I knew that they'd start to trust me more if I talked to them like a colleague rather than a boss. During one of my training sessions, I tried to impress upon them that you have to really advocate on behalf of your clients. I was on my high horse lecturing them that if the judge tells you to stop talking, you talk even louder. One of the lawyers, looking frustrated, held up his hand to speak.

"With respect, Kim, you don't know what you're talking about because you've never been to court here," he said.

It was embarrassing because he was right. I didn't know what the fuck I was talking about. I was pitching myself as an expert about trials and courtrooms and I hadn't even been in one. That cold glass of shade thrown in my face was the wake-up call I needed to get out and see what was going on outside the walls of JSSP.

I approached Mustafa one afternoon and asked him if he could help me set up a meeting with one of the local judges. I wanted to go to an Afghan court and observe how it worked.

"Of course, that's no big deal," he said.

But in fact it was a very big deal. The JSSP capacity-building program had been running for over three years and yet this was the first time anyone had ever asked to attend an Afghan court hearing. I had to apply for permission from my section leader. I was expecting to be refused, but, to be honest, I think he said yes just to get rid of me.

A few days later, I was excitedly climbing into an armoured vehicle carrying my backpack, while wearing a helmet and bulletproof vest, headed in a convoy to the National Security Court with four British armed guards in tow. As we pulled up to the courthouse, I was taken aback by how dilapidated the concrete building looked. With Mustafa by my side, I struggled to walk straight from the extra 30 pounds of weight on my back as we made our way through a sea of Afghans, who stared, curious as to who we all were or why we were there.

We walked up the concrete steps into a hallway filled with more Afghan men waiting for their day in court, the lights were dim and we were surrounded by dust in the air as we made our way through. Walking up the stairs to the concrete courthouse the grounds inside and out of the building were surrounded by a lot of rubble, bulletholes were indiscriminately scattered outside the walls, and women with small children were begging for food and money on the street outside the courthouse. It looked more like a crack house than a courthouse. Despite the fact that there was no heat, after three flights of stairs, I was sweating under my helmet, but I only took it off once I was safely inside the courtroom.

The courtroom itself appeared more like a living room than a court of law. Couches lined either wall, rugs on the floor, and one huge empty desk on the far side of the room. Behind that desk sat a middle-aged bearded Afghan man who eyed me as I walked towards him.

"Good morning. I am Judge Ibrahim Sediqi," he said politely, holding out his hand.

"Hello, thank you so much for letting us visit your court today," I said.

Judge Sediqi smiled and motioned for me to take a seat on the couches. I was smiling profusely and was so excited that I could barely contain myself.

"It will just be a few minutes," he said.

Five more men with long beards dressed in suits walked into the room and took their seats.

"If you have any questions, please ask," the judge encouraged.

Then there was a knock on the door and a police officer poked his head inside.

"Ready?"

"Yes," the judge replied.

And with that, court was in session.

First up that morning was a case involving a local taxi driver. The prison guards walked him into the court. He was chained from his wrists to his ankles, wearing a blue striped outfit, like an Afghan version of the Monopoly "Get out of jail free" card character, except for the dirty cloth bag over his head. He looked more like a hostage than a defendant.

When the police officers snatched the bag off his head, the guy just stood there trying to get his bearings. He looked utterly dazed and confused. Judging from his body language, I'm pretty sure he couldn't read or write because he didn't even glance down at the statement being read out by the prosecutor, which described his alleged offences.

Mustafa translated for me, whispering in my ear, as the prosecutor read aloud to the court. The taxi driver was being charged with terrorism. According to the indictment, he had been driving a car containing two women and two men. When the police stopped the car, they found mobile phones and guns. No names, no descriptions of the witnesses and no information on where to find these people was supplied. According to the indictment, the taxi driver had been the only one charged.

The prosecutor stood to address the court.

"When questioned," he said, looking intensely at the judge, "the police said the driver appeared 'suspicious'." With that, he stopped speaking and sat back down.

That was it. That was the extent of the case against him. There were no witnesses called, no police officers in attendance, no evidence presented, nothing. The judge looked at the defendant who did not have a lawyer.

"You can speak," the judge said.

The elderly man nervously stood up, visibly shaking. He was clearly scared and seemed out of his depth.

"I'm not a terrorist, I'm a taxi driver," he said. "So whoever said I am a terrorist, bring them here before me." I'm sure he didn't know it, but he was invoking his presumption of innocence and right to confrontation, two basic legal rights of anyone accused of a crime—even in Afghanistan.[3, 4]

Clumsily, the taxi driver showed the court the bruises on his arms and legs where he said he had been beaten and electrocuted by the police in order to extract a confession. I felt pretty bad for this guy, terrorist or not, as I'm sure he had another ass kicking waiting for him when he got back to his cell after telling the judge that the police beat him.

The man continued to deny the accusations, and even uttered the unimaginable: that he "swore to Allah that he was not a terrorist". To say this is a *very* big deal, and some were aghast at this proclamation.

The judge eyed me nervously. With every passing minute, he seemed more and more anxious about the foreigner in the room. He asked the driver why he didn't ask to see a doctor. The driver looked up and then over to me for the first time. He managed to give me an ironic smile despite the helplessness in his eyes. He didn't speak English and I didn't speak Dari, but we both understood bullshit. He didn't stand a chance; he was toast the second he'd walked into court. As time slowly lumbered on, the judge's patience was waning. He pounded his hand on his desk and said, "Enough! Don't disrupt me!" At least that is how it was translated to me. And with that, anything that the taxi driver had to say was over.

The judge's deliberation took less than five minutes and the defendant was sentenced to eight years. He was going to prison and would be labelled a terrorist for the rest of his life.

I didn't interfere. I just watched, running through in my mind the defence he should have received.

If you're a taxi driver in Kabul, you usually have at least six people in the car because everyone shares cabs. The whole city basically runs like an UberPool. The more likely scenario was that the taxi driver was the only person without enough money to pay off the cops when they got pulled over. And so what if the cops found mobile phones and guns in his car? In Afghanistan, everyone has mobile phones and guns.

After court, I began asking the judge a lot of questions about the due process violations that had been ignored.

"Wasn't this guy supposed to have a lawyer according to the law?" I said, asking and answering my own question.

"Oh no, he doesn't need a lawyer," the judge said.

"Umm . . . I think he kinda does." I was fighting the urge to get into full argumentative-lawyer mode.

"No, he doesn't, because he's guilty."

Conversation over.

I'd soon learn that Afghanistan's National Security Court was mostly a sham.[5] It was a US- and UK-funded court that the Americans promoted simply to show that Afghanistan had become tough on terrorism. But when the Afghans ran out of so-called terrorists to prosecute, they started churning innocent people through the system to justify the expense. It was all an elaborate scam to keep the money flowing. I was starting to see the forest *and* the trees.

But whatever the politics of the situation, it was clear to me that something was fundamentally rotten in a system that allowed men to be sent to prison without any evidence or legal representation.

Back in the office, my court visit caught the attention of the bosses. What was meant to be an exercise to help improve what we were doing was instead interpreted as trouble-making and I felt the attitude towards me grow increasingly frosty. Every time I would go to meetings, I was told by some of my colleagues of how I was putting my life at risk and I should just stay on campus as I would get paid either way. I was surrounded by many colleagues who seemed to despise Afghanistan, and, as a result, many of them were drinking heavily to pass the time. I believe the fear was that if I continued to work too hard, that they in turn would be expected to engage with the Afghan legal community and work harder too.

It wasn't long before I started to feel uncomfortable even being in the office, so I decided to grab any opportunity I could to get out into the community. I went back to the courts and I even started paying visits to defence lawyers' offices. I decided that I wanted to make relationships with Afghans at all levels because I felt that they were telling me more than they might tell other foreigners—and because they clearly respected me more than my own colleagues did.

I felt like I'd been lured to Afghanistan under false pretences. Yes, I was there as a trainer and not for real cases, but that didn't mean that we couldn't or shouldn't get involved in the legal system. We were supposed to help strengthen the rule of law, but we weren't doing that at all.

By the time I reached the halfway point of my contract, I was operating more and more independently of JSSP. I was frustrated, unhappy and locked in to working for an organisation on the other side of the world that I'd started to despise. But I couldn't walk away. Everyone at home was still relying on me.

4

PLEASE HELP US

In the Islamic world, Friday is a day of rest and worship. It's the day when Muslims spend time with their families and go to the mosque. Everything shuts down on Friday until the new week begins again on Saturday. In Kabul, that means Thursday night was when we got to let our hair down.

My security team dropped me off along a dusty street in the diplomatic quarter next to a line of black SUVs. From there it was a short walk beside heavily fortified Poppy Palaces, vast mansions built from opium profits post-2003 that still house not only many of the country's corrupt drug warlords and politicians but also various embassies and international companies. I was dressed in my usual evening wear: jeans and heels. Nothing fancy. Of course I wanted to look nice, but that night I was DJ'ing—something I had done casually in high school and picked up again in Afghanistan—so I wanted to keep it casual. I had my laptop in my backpack with a playlist ready to go.

I gave the security guys on the door a nod as I passed into the courtyard. Already I could hear the beats booming from inside and I smiled at the guys in khaki pants, work boots and Marlboro Man tans drinking beers at the front door. It's the nature of this place that parties were a bit heavy on the male side of the gender ratio, which meant that women tended to get a little too much attention. The flip side is that you also get an international crowd like you'd never find back home. I liked that. I scanned the room for familiar faces. I could see French, Americans, Canadians, Brits, and even a few Afghans I knew and who I suspected wouldn't be at morning prayers tomorrow.

I'm not much of a drinker, but I do drink. Every foreigner I've ever met in Afghanistan does too. It's our commonality. We're all stressed. I don't care why you're in Afghanistan, even if you're sitting at the US Embassy all day, it's stressful. Everything here is a compromise. But when it came to the Thursday-night parties, there was no compromise. We all needed them, and they brought us closer together.

I looked around, taking it all in. Already the room was jumping, the drink was free-flowing, some people were dancing, others were making out. It looked like a party in the Thunderdome. A rave.

I thought for a second about what the outside world would make of all this if they could see us. Alcohol, drugs, people making out—so much hedonism that was *haram* (forbidden) under Islamic law. I was pretty sure that the sight of all these Westerners being bad together wouldn't play well.

But I didn't care about that. For me, the two main benefits of the Thursday-night parties were that I got to play my music and I got to meet people. I'd begun to feel so isolated in Afghanistan that these parties were more than my release, they were my saving grace. I'd get up there and spin records for people and gradually they would get to know who I was. To them, I was only Kim, the lawyer, and it turned out everyone in Afghanistan needed a lawyer for one reason or another.

My contract with JSSP was coming to an end and I was happy to be getting the hell out. However, it would mean that I couldn't rely on that State Department salary anymore, so I'd started to hustle by making connections with a couple of foreign NGOs that I was hoping to get consultancy work for. I still didn't have a long-term plan and the idea of setting up a practice hadn't even crossed my mind. As far as I was concerned, I just didn't know the country well enough let alone its legal system to practise law in Afghanistan. Added to that, there were zero foreign lawyers going to court there.

But that didn't stop foreigners asking me for legal advice. People would approach me at the parties and ask me what they should do about the stupid shit they'd done. Maybe they'd overstayed their visa or been caught with smuggled artefacts or they were up on minor drug offences. These would be the kind of problems that slowly became projects that gradually became cases that started to form the basis of a business.

But before any of that happened, a conversation that Thursday night led to a meeting that changed everything for me in Afghanistan.

I had finished playing one of my songs and headed to the bar. There was a group of guys standing around drinking beers, trading stories. The usual drill. One of them introduced himself as a Correctional Sector Support Program (CSSP) Advisor. They were the correctional counterpart to JSSP who also worked under the umbrella of the State Department. CSSP was an American-funded prison training program meant to build the capacity of the Afghans working within the prison system. It was like the prison-training version of the JSSP, so not exactly the most riveting conversational topic as far as I was concerned. I was already zoning out, thinking about how to make my escape, when the advisor said something that made my ears prick.

"Come with us." He said it so casually, like he was inviting me for coffee.

"Sorry, *where*?" I wasn't sure I'd heard him right. I'd been distracted by some of the Afghan staffers stealing a few sips of an abandoned drink.

"Pul-e-Charkhi prison." He said it again slowly so I could make out every syllable. "It's the biggest prison in Afghanistan. I heard you like to go outside the wire."

"Yes," I answered eagerly. "Let's make that happen."

A few days later, I was bumping along in one of five white armoured Ford Explorers, speeding down the dirt and rubble Jalalabad Road leading out of Kabul. My body swayed as the vehicle swerved around potholes, leaving a cloud of dust in our wake. I couldn't help but feel it also made our convoy as conspicuous as a herd of elephants along this danger-prone route. But discretion, I was discovering, was not part of the American M.O. in Afghanistan.

As we zipped along, men with dishevelled beards and boys in dirty salwar kameezes spat in our direction.

Two paunchy middle-aged correctional officers, Randy and Chris, flanked me in the back seat of the Explorer. They had started working in prisons in the US before reincarnating their careers overseas by training Afghan prison officers on how to run penitentiaries the American way. I tried to listen without rolling my eyes behind my Oakley sunglasses as these men talked over and at me about the stupid shit that had happened when they got drunk the night before.

"Did you see Tim?" Randy howled. "What a moron! I've never seen him dance before. What a mess!"

Yes . . . Tim is a moron, I smiled to myself.

The men's bulging chests and round bellies rolled with laughter under their bulletproof vests. The conversation then turned to the usual boring expat listing of all the places they had visited. Each story traded in a lame attempt to impress each other and probably me—Iraq, Venezuela, Syria, blah blah blah.

I turned my attention to what was outside the car. The sky was dark and heavy. Perhaps the first snowfall? I wondered. At 1800 metres (6000 feet) above sea level, the air was thin and sharp, and even in our heated truck I could sense the cold outside.

I had a queasy feeling in my stomach as the vehicle sped up as we passed makeshift towns built close to the prison by the families of incarcerated Taliban and Al Qaeda members. Soon I could see it out of the front window—Pul-e-Charkhi, a dirty-grey, severe-looking concrete structure, substantial and monolithic, dwarfing the nearby mud and clay houses. Nicknamed the Prison of Death, it was built by the Russians in the 1970s and was notorious for its torture of prisoners and indiscriminate executions.

I climbed out of the vehicle. There were fifteen in our party: fourteen men and me. An Afghan correctional officer escorted us up a walkway of broken marbled stone. Randy leaned over to explain. "We have to meet General Balki before we can take you in."

General Balki was a large man with a moustache who sat behind a huge wooden desk in an office surrounded by pictures of President Karzai and Afghanistan's national flag. Brisk and formal, he wasted no time gesturing for us to take a seat on one of his vinyl couches before offering us jasmine-scented green tea and a bowl of fresh almonds.

There are formalities to doing business in Afghanistan. Americans tend to want to get right to it, but Afghans circle around a conversation first, with long hellos, welcomes and questions about family, health and happiness. I've come to believe they do this because the various tribal and cultural groups that comprise Afghan society are all very closed; maybe 40 years of war has made them distrustful of each other. War has also made the people of this country feel extremely isolated from the rest of the world. The Afghans I meet are just as curious about me as I am about them.

"Where are you from?" the general asked, zeroing in on me.

"From Milwaukee, Wisconsin, in America."

I couldn't help but think that middle America must have been as foreign to him as Afghanistan was to me. The general looked puzzled.

"It's about an hour-and-a-half drive from Chicago, where Barack Obama is from," I added.

Afghans *love* Obama so I hoped the reference would earn me some cool points.

"I see." He nodded, as though this had brought the clarity he needed. "And what's your name?"

"Kimberley Motley."

"Kim-bro . . . *What* is it?"

"Kim."

"Ohhhhh, *Kim.*" He untied his tongue as he said it.

"Yes, Kim." I smiled, thinking how my mother, who insisted that I be addressed as Kimberley, would be appalled at me.

"What do you do in my country?" he asked, genuine curiosity hanging in his voice.

My colleagues had warned me that few women ever come to the prison apart from the occasional Burqa-clad wives visiting their jailed husbands. I knew I was an oddity to him.

"I am a lawyer with JSSP. I'm here to train and mentor Afghan lawyers."

He looked at me with a slight smile, like he might have more questions for me, but instead he turned to my colleague who was impatiently tapping his finger against his leg. It was time to move.

I finished my tea, stood up and tossed my backpack over my shoulder, catching the general looking at me. We smiled at each other and an acceptance seemed to form in that moment between us. Even though I had been in the country for a short time, I already had the feeling that the Afghans were a lot more inviting than some of my American colleagues would have had me believe.

While I waited for my colleagues outside the general's office, I was surprised to hear birdsong. It was beautiful. Long before the civil war, the Mujahideen or the Taliban, Afghanistan was a bastion of liberal values, with co-ed schools and top universities, decent healthcare, nightclubs, exquisite gardens, artistic and intellectual scenes, and museums boasting some of the finest collections anywhere in the world. For a moment there, with my eyes closed, the birdsong seemed to evoke the days of old.

Pul-e-Charkhi is divided into around twenty buildings. Each has its own layout and character. I've been inside a lot of prisons in the US, but the cells here were unlike any I'd seen before.

The Afghan guards opened the door to the first block and led us inside. We walked down a dimly lit staircase. With every step, the sound of shouting grew louder from down the hall. It was rhythmical and coordinated, men chanting in unison.

We pushed through one more door and filed into a large, open-plan room where the first prisoners that I would see in Afghanistan were standing. There were no windows as we were below ground; at first my eyes had to adjust to the darkness, but I could feel the dirt beneath my feet. The floor was covered with discarded food wrappers and other trash. The smell of bitter, acrid sweat filled the air and by the time we were inside the sound of the men yelling grew deafening. Gradually my eyes adjusted and I could see who exactly was making all the noise. Lined up in front of us were fifty shirtless, sweaty men, performing some kind of martial arts exercise. I still don't know if they were Taliban or just common criminals, but each was lean and ripped like a professional athlete. They looked more like an army in training.

"Should they be doing this?" I asked Randy.

"The commander knows," he replied stiffly. "He feels it keeps the prisoners active."

"But these prisoners are learning how to hurt guards," I said. "To hurt you."

"If you have concerns, speak to the general," he said, abruptly ending the conversation.

We moved on, from building to building. Some rooms were like the first, open and filthy, while others were overcrowded, with prisoners separated into cells and hidden behind large metal doors with small slits through which to pass food. For each door we passed I'd glimpse a set of eyes watching me. I'm not sure those men had seen a woman in a long time.

Some of the prisoners turned their backs on us in a "fuck you" gesture. Dari and Pashto words were menacingly flung in our direction; I didn't need to know the language to understand that these were fighting words, angry words, words of hate. The Afghan prisoners didn't want us there. Their hatred was palpable.

I couldn't get over the depravity of the conditions. Emaciated bodies with sunken cheeks and glazed eyes stared out at me from behind those bars. The odour caught in my nose was a suffocating mix of men's perspiration, fear and anger. The cells had no heating despite the subzero temperature outside and the only light came from small, barred windows.

I tried to take it all in as we toured more buildings, each one bleaker, colder, darker than the one before, until finally they began blurring into each other. It chilled me. If the inmates downstairs were any gauge, I was observing less of a jail and more of an insurgent training camp. I made a mental note to bring this up with the US Embassy when I finished the tour. I was done. I wanted to go home. Like *home* home. I wanted to fly back to America.

I began thinking about my kids. They wouldn't want me to be in a place like this. I missed them desperately and I felt overwhelmingly homesick. But then, just as we were making our way out of the last block—Block 15—I heard it. *English*. Someone was speaking English from behind the bars. Accented English, but not with a Dari or Pashto accent. This was a Western voice.

I turned and pushed my face to the door of a cell. Again, it took a while for my eyes to adjust to the poor light, but gradually I could make out two figures standing in the gloom. Two Westerners. Filthy skeletons not like their Afghan counterparts, with thin arms stretching out as they moved towards me like ghouls. Until that moment, it had never occurred to me that foreigners were also locked up in Afghanistan.

Seeing that I had stopped, my party doubled back and began uncomfortably exchanging pleasantries with the men locked up inside the cell. It was bland small talk, like nobody wanted to make eye contact or delve too deep into a conversation. What I could make out were their names: Anthony Malone and Bevan Campbell.

My American correctional colleagues began to encourage me to move on. The group shuffled further down the corridor towards the exit, but I wanted to know more. I headed back to the cell.

"Bevan?" I asked. "Is that your name?"

He spoke with an Afrikaans accent, sharp and rough as uncut diamonds. He started to explain to me who he was in hushed, garbled sentences, and I tried to take it in. Both men were ex-military officers who'd been locked up and forgotten about for years. Before long, both were talking at me, their sentences running over each other's. It was clear that they had been waiting for someone like me to pass for a long, long time.

"I have been here for years," Bevan said. "Our embassies have abandoned us."

He looked me dead in the eye. His sunken eyes are still burned into my memory today. Then his shaking hand pushed something through the bars. He had prepared a letter explaining who they were and why they thought they had been locked up.

Now finally someone had passed that might show an interest.

But I shook my head. I couldn't take the papers. I wasn't his lawyer. I didn't know anything about his case. And I certainly didn't want that responsibility or burden.

"I can't help you," I stammered. "I have to go." I spied my party already moving through the far door to leave. "I'm American. I am not from your country," I added. "I'm sorry."

Despite the tears in his eyes, Bevan never once looked away. He nodded, like he had sympathy for me, when it should have been the other way around. And then, slowly, he said in a voice of calm, reasonable desperation, "Please help us. No one is helping us."

Shit.

I couldn't walk away from that.

5

MY NAME IS IRENE

During my final days at JSSP, I realised that everyone was very happy for me to do pretty much nothing, take my pay cheque and sit out my last days in Kabul until it was time to go home. Many of my more illustrious colleagues had been doing just that for months. By then, everyone felt that the JSSP project was a sham; we weren't really here to help the Afghans to build a legal system, so why not see out your remaining days in the safety of the compound playing *Guitar Hero*?

We were all still living together in the compound and our communal area had a pool table, ping-pong and all the R&R facilities that you'd find in a school dorm. Security demanded that each day we share our travel plans in a group email, so it felt like we lived in one another's pockets. I could tell my colleagues still didn't understand why I was visiting the prison. Fifteen American lawyers, in close quarters, operating on a 9 p.m. curfew with limited access to the outside world, we were ready to kill each other.

Confined in this toxic environment for six months, I was hearing things like, "Why are you putting our security at risk by going in the prisons? It's just not worth it" and "Why are you wasting your time? Just chill out and take your pay cheque."

But I couldn't let the negativity get to me. Mainly because I felt too damn guilty. If I was leaving my kids at home for this, then I was going to make it count. I had to keep busy and feel like I was trying to achieve something.

When we first arrived, the other lawyers had shared stories about the time they swam with dolphins in Antarctica or climbed some mountain in Switzerland. Now I felt like visiting the Afghan prisons was *my* mountain. Suddenly it was my turn to say where I'd been. During their time in-country, these lawyers had sat in meetings about what happened in court or what was happening in the prison, but I was the only one who went out and actually saw it for myself. They could tell me all about dolphins, but I would tell them what was going on out there in the real world.

I think that's part of the reason why I hadn't shaken the feeling that I needed to help Bevan and Anthony in Pul-e-Charkhi prison. Here were real-life people who genuinely needed help and I had the expertise, time and energy to give it to them.

I decided to take Bevan's case to the diplomat in charge of the JSSP program at the US Embassy, Sarah. I'd put together a plan for how we could use Bevan as a case study to train up an Afghan lawyer. I would lead the lawyer through the steps

I would take if I were representing Bevan and together we would build a defence. I figured that if done right, this could be a great way to train a new professional and maybe even form a useful template for future cases. We were very short of actual cases with which to engage our Afghan trainees; I believed that the people in charge of the JSSP would see the merit in the idea.

I'd been invited to a pool party at the US Embassy along with the Global Security guys whom Sarah referred to as "the beef cakes". She was an older career diplomat who seemed to know more about the party scene than she did about the JSSP. I always felt that all she really cared about was making sure the daily, weekly, monthly, quarterly and yearly reports made it to DC in time. I suspected her reason for inviting us to the party was to drool over the security guys; we were merely an alibi for her security fetish.

"Sarah, are you familiar with the foreigners who are locked up at Pul-e-Charkhi?" I asked.

"I am sure their embassies are engaged," she replied.

"I wondered if we could use one of the men as a case study for JSSP to mentor the Afghan lawyers? It could show how the program is capacity-building and meeting its deliverables to DC," I said in contractor speak.

The mention of DC certainly seemed to get her attention.

"Why is he in Pul-e-Charkhi?"

"Drugs I think," I said, knowing full well that he was in for possessing heroin.

"We're not here to help drug dealers."

End of discussion.

I was frustrated. I fundamentally believe that every individual deserves representation. That's why I became a litigator. I have always, perhaps naively, assumed that's the way all litigators must feel too; that it doesn't matter if you're innocent or guilty, black or white, a political prisoner or a drug dealer, you have a right to a fair trial and due process. I didn't think I could go any lower in my opinion of JSSP, but when Sarah shut down any discussion on Bevan's case on the grounds of the accusation, I realised I could.

It had become impossible for me to play by the JSSP rules any longer. I simply couldn't square their attitude with my need to do something worthwhile in Afghanistan. Back home Claude and the kids were adjusting to their new life in North Carolina. Deiva and Seoul were thriving in school while Cherish had settled in to her new day care, Claude was also focusing most of his attention on law school. So while I still had three months left on my contract I began to use my JSSP access to quietly work on Bevan's case and also look around for other people I could help.

After I'd pitched Bevan's case, my bosses at the JSSP weren't keen on my revisiting Pul-e-Charkhi again, so the prison was put off limits to me. But despite these new restrictions, they were relaxed about my visiting the women's prison. "Women's issues" were "on message" and so I arranged a visit.

The women's prison, Badam Bagh, is to the west of Kabul and on the opposite side of town to Pul-e-Charkhi. It's a newer building than the men's; when I pulled up outside I thought it looked more like a women's shelter than a prison. Once inside, I began to get a feel for the place. Arranged around a single open space were individual cells with the doors left open so the women were free to move around. Certainly nobody was lined up practising karate.

There was no classification of prisoners, either, meaning murderers and drug dealers were mixed in with the adulterers and thieves. Despite that, I was still surprised to see foreign women in there.

Several women came right up to me and shook my hand. Some even gave me kisses on my cheeks. Nobody blabbed out their stories right away because I was standing next to the guards, but I was keen to hear more about how and why they'd ended up here.

It quickly became obvious that as well as the presence of the guards, there were other barriers for me to overcome. The main one was language: very few spoke any English and it became a bit overwhelming as I met one desperate woman after another speaking in languages I couldn't understand. Then one woman stood out among the crowd. Tall, striking and speaking fluent English.

"Hi, how are you?" She said it clearly, but with a heavy West African accent. She held out her hand to shake mine.

I told her my name and asked where she was from.

"My name is Irene and I am from the Ivory Coast," she said. "This is my daughter, Aisha." She pushed a shy three-year-old my way.

Often in Afghanistan, if a woman goes to prison her daughters go with her, while in many cases sons are allowed to go home with their fathers. Aisha wasn't alone. There were babies and kids everywhere.

I asked Irene if we could go into her cell to talk more privately. I took a seat on the edge of her bed and she began to translate for the other women in the cell, a Thai woman and an Afghan, after I explained that I was interested in hearing their stories.

The women appeared to have even less idea than the men about how things worked in the legal system. Many were used to being confined in their homes for nearly twenty-fours hours every day prior to their detention in prison. In court, women were treated like children. They were ignored, even more so than the men, and they were often chastised when they dared to speak. In some instances when women would try to defend themselves in court it appeared as if they were given an even harsher sentence. Most of the women had never heard of and didn't even know what a defence lawyer was. The only lawyers they were familiar with were the prosecutors who were bringing cases against them. Not one had had any legal defence in court, and instead of being presumed innocent they were treated as though they were guilty from the start.[1]

There's no programming in Afghan prisons, either. There's nothing to do, no classes, so most of the time these women are sitting in their cells all day getting on each other's nerves. I was the new entertainment and for hours Irene translated for me so I could hear the women's stories.

With children running along the halls, the place had an eerie sense of normality, and yet nearly every woman I met communicated how horrendously battered she had been at some point in her life. The vast majority had been charged with what are called "moral crimes" in Afghanistan, usually running away and/or adultery.

Finally it was Irene's turn to tell me her story. She explained that she was in prison because she'd been found guilty of operating as a drug mule. She began to fiddle nervously with her hands and struggled to maintain eye contact. Eventually she reached the part where she detailed how exactly she'd landed herself in jail.

Three years prior, Irene had been arrested in a hotel room in Kabul with a group of other Africans. Like many of the foreign women at the prison she told me that she thought that she had come to Afghanistan for a legitimate job, in her case as a cleaner, but instead found herself working as a low-level drug mule. As I understood, she was hired by a construction company run by an Australian man. Once she came to Afghanistan she decribed how he took her and her daughter's passports, forcing her to travel the country to traffic heroin until eventually she made her way to Kabul where someone else would then fly out with it. One afternoon, she and her roommates had been busted by the Afghan cops. Without legal representation, she had been tried and sentenced to the maximum sentence: twenty years with no hope of reprieve.

I wonder how Irene must have felt as she told that story to me. How high the stakes were for her as she sought even the remotest possibility of help from a stranger. And yet she spoke in such a quiet, calm, soft and humble voice as she described how her life had gone so terribly wrong.

I hope she felt like some kind of weight had been lifted. Finally, someone was there to listen to her story. Someone who might even be able to help. I could sense a hopefulness in her, albeit a checked one, because she had to keep things measured. No matter how tempting, people like Irene can't afford to get over-excited and let their imaginations run wild. I'd seen it before representing defendants in US prisons; hope can be your best friend or your worst enemy.

For a lawyer, this is tricky, too, because everyone wants you to make promises. Inmates will try to put assurances in your mouth.

"Okay, so you'll come back next week and tell me about my case?"

As she said it, we both knew Irene was seeking something I couldn't give. I know as a lawyer, I can't be led down that route. So I had to make myself clear.

"No, I didn't say that."

I'll admit that Irene had piqued my curiosity. Of course there was some empathy mixed in with it, too, but at that stage it was more about my curiosity. People often ask me how I feel when I meet women like Irene or how I handle the responsibility for a client who has a child behind bars. But I'm not a social worker, I'm a lawyer. I'm not sitting there trying to give you a hug; feeling sorry for you isn't going to help, and chances are I've seen cases like yours a million times before. I've been to prisons my whole career as a defence lawyer and I guess I have a bit of empathy overload. After a while, you know what the main goal is: to get that person out of prison. Feeling sorry for him or her is often a useless endeavour. Whether they realise it or not, feeling sorry for them isn't what they want from me.

I'm constantly having to correct and manage expectations. I promise nothing, which isn't always an easy thing to do. I couldn't even promise Irene and the other women that I was coming back to see them. JSSP hadn't allowed me to go back to Pul-e-Charkhi, so what if they took a similar line with the women's prison? All I could do was promise Irene that I'd do my best to see what I could find out.

One thing I knew for sure was that my boss at JSSP, Sarah, wouldn't allow me to have an official client, especially another "drug dealer". So I decided to sneak in and quietly see what I could do to help Irene. Nobody ever noticed as I began to put together a defence for her.

I got off to a good start because the prison gave me access to her file, which isn't always the case for a lawyer in

Afghanistan. From Irene's court notes, I could see that she had been handed a twenty-year sentence by the court, the absolute maximum for drug trafficking. That detail helped me to make up my mind. I could do my best to help this woman, safe in the knowledge that, even if I screwed it up, I couldn't make her situation any worse.

I wanted to run what I hoped to do by Claude, but I knew he was already stressed with my being away, law school and raising the kids. He was trying to settle our family into the new place and their new lives. Added to that, he had exams coming up. I was feeling a huge responsibility to keep providing for all of them financially. We could only afford this great new life because I was making three times the money I'd made before. Now Seoul and Deiva were in soccer, baseball and other extracurricular activities, Cherish was in full-time child care. With Claude as a law student, all the finances were on me.

Money aside, I couldn't go back to being a public defender. I was a different person. Afghanistan wasn't as bad or scary as everyone had made it out to be. In fact, I was growing to like it. But I knew I couldn't renew my contract with the JSSP without going crazy. What I didn't know at the time was that I was planning what I could do to keep the gravy train running outside of JSSP.

And Irene was going to play a big part in that.

6

FALSE PRETENCES

In September 2009, my contract with JSSP ended. I'd managed to find a freelance consulting job from contacts I'd made in Kabul. The role involved working part time for the Italian corporation that was an arm of the Italian Embassy, who wanted research done specifically on incarcerated juveniles. I found that most of the kids were locked up for petty crimes that adults would have never been jailed for.

I was also being approached by clients who needed legal work done around town, so overall I was earning enough money to stay and explore potential opportunities. It was difficult to be away from my family but we had become accustomed to the income, which meant leaving Afghanistan was not an option. Claude was happy, too, for me to stay a little while longer to see how things worked out. I'd taken a bit of a pay cut, but I was still sending home more money than I would be working back at the Public Defender's Office.

Crucially, with JSSP behind me, I now had time to revisit some of the other cases I'd come across, the first being Irene. She'd become my point of contact in the women's prison over the previous few months. Every visit I'd made, Irene would follow me, queuing up pressing cases for me, and translating for the other women. Because she'd never asked for anything in return, in a strange way I felt like we had developed a real connection.

I went back to see her at the prison as an independent lawyer. Irene had known little about her original case, but she knew enough that reducing her sentence wasn't going to be easy. In Afghanistan, drugs are considered so bad that dealers are often given harsher sentences than murderers. And her being from the Ivory Coast didn't offer us any international leverage; other than the Egyptian Embassy, there isn't any other African nation's embassy in Afghanistan.

Another problem was that Irene had already been to all three courts, without a lawyer, which meant that she had already had her case heard at the Primary, Appellate and Supreme Courts. This seriously limited the chances of getting anyone to look at her situation again.

Though I was at a loss as to whether there were any legal remedies available for Irene, I started looking for another option. I found one. According to Article 81 of the Interim Criminal Procedure Code for Courts, there were certain circumstances when a defendant could have their court sentences reviewed by the Supreme Court twice.[1] The "circumstances" we might be able to rely on in Irene's case were the due process violations that had been ignored during her previous trials.

During our conversations, Irene had described to me how she had gone to court with six other male co-defendants. She didn't have a lawyer, wasn't provided with a translator and was not allowed to speak during her trial. Further to that, there was neither evidence nor any witnesses who testified in court. It was six months later, when Irene finally managed to get her hands on the sentencing documents, that she understood she had been sentenced to twenty years in prison. Never once did the court question who had sponsored her visa.

In addition to this, where were the drugs? The indictment claimed that police found over five kilograms of heroin, which was what had justified the twenty-year sentence.[2] However the drugs were now nowhere to be seen, so we had no way to confirm their quantity. Any discrepancy of the amount of heroin found could be the difference between six months to life in prison.

I got to work writing the revision petition to the Supreme Court, which I had to file in person. I wanted to see if any exceptions were ever made to reopen a criminal case for a woman on drugs charges. The secretary at the court didn't know of any cases where a revision petition had been submitted for a woman on any matter, let alone a drugs case. In all my time at JSSP, I'd never come across this situation before, but the law was there: Article 81, in black and white.[3]

The secretary took the petition and asked that I come back to his office in a couple of days.

"Sit down, please," he instructed me when I returned a few days later.

Then he left the room. Ten minutes later, he was back.

"Come with me, please," he said.

I was confused, but I followed him anyway.

He took me to the office of Chief Justice Azimi, the head of the Supreme Court.[4]

The Supreme Court sounds rather grand when in fact the courtroom was like any other office. There was a big desk and two couches. On the walls were the obligatory pictures of President Karzai, two big Afghan flags and a picture of Mecca so everyone knew in which direction to pray. That afternoon, the judge's desk was particularly clean. Except for his name plate, there was nothing on it. No computer, no files, no pencils, no signs of work.

I stood, waiting patiently for the judge to finish what he was doing. Like most of the judges I'd met in Kabul, he was an older man with white hair and a moustache and beard. He was dressed in a Western-style suit. He sat, giving me a cool once-over, as I made to present him with Irene's file. He shook his head and held up a finger.

"Wait."

I stood in silence for a moment while a man scuttled in carrying a tray of cups. The judge waved a hand and implored me to sit. Even though we were in the Supreme Court, there was still time for tea before we got down to business.

Judge Azimi talked first. "Thank you for coming. And how may I help you?"

Weeks prior I had told his office why I wanted to meet with him so I was sure he was toying with me.

"Thank you for taking the time to meet with me today," I said.

As we talked, I began to realise that the only reason the judge had agreed to see me was because he thought I was still in the employ of JSSP. I decided not to go into too much detail about my relationship (or lack thereof) with JSSP and instead focus my attention on Irene.

"What is she charged with?" he asked.

"Drug trafficking," I said. "In the prior court Irene was never given the opportunity to present a defence," I added. "She came to Afghanistan sponsored under the false pretence that she would be employed as a cleaner by an international company."

After I showed the judge her work contract, I explained that I was requesting the court to take another look at her case. I cited the Afghan laws that were relevant. I talked about Irene's good character, explaining she was the only child in her family, the mother of a three-year-old daughter imprisoned with her and that she had been tricked into coming to Afghanistan by an Australian man. I told him how Irene was the main breadwinner in her family.

I was excited, and nervous because I didn't know how any of this was supposed to go. The whole experience felt unpredictable and the opposite to how court was back in the US, where I knew the system like the back of my hand. I hadn't put any Islamic law in the petition because I still wasn't comfortable with my grasp of it, but I was also hyper-conscious that here I was, an American lawyer in an Islamic country, meeting with the Chief Justice of the Supreme Court to discuss a case for the first time in my career.

As I started outlining more details about the case, I sensed the judge was listening. He was being very polite, but the longer I spoke I could feel him becoming more defensive as I highlighted the problems with Irene's conviction. Afghanistan is a huge drug exporter, producing over 85 per cent of the opium consumed around the world, and yet they get so offended about the reality of drug use in their own country. Especially when it involves a foreigner. Being from the Ivory

Coast wasn't helping Irene either, because there was no embassy in Afghanistan.

"This woman was dealing drugs," Judge Azimi said with a slow, sad shake of his head.

"She was *involved* with people dealing drugs," I replied. "That's true. And my client freely understands that now."

"Oh, she understands that *now*?"

"She made a horrible mistake, but it was under false pretences."

Knowing that Azimi was an astute legal academic I reverted to the law.

"No witnesses, no evidence, no lawyer, no translator, no right to speak. Essentially, she has never really been to court in Afghanistan and yet she has been locked up for three years."

"Why should she get forgiveness when she came to our country to ruin it?"

"But she didn't come here for that. She was tricked into coming here by an Australian man who promised her a real job. But when she got here he took away hers and her daughter's passports. She was living and working as a slave, forced to be a drug mule."

Silence. But his body language said it all: "Heard it all before. No sympathy."

"She's willing to tell you the Australian man's name. You know, I think that's who you really want."

Now he was interested. As with so much in Afghanistan, if you want something then you have to give something. The judge wasn't going to lose face by going back on his prior decision. Not without something new to trade.

"Let's see what information she can provide," he said.

And that was it. The terms of the deal were set. If I could get Irene to cooperate, then there was a chance we could get her case reviewed. Up until that point, I thought that the judge and I had just been having an informal conversation. I didn't realise it at that time, but that was court. I'd just completed my first trial.

The next day I went to see Collie Brown, a friend working at the United Nations Office on Drugs and Crime (UNODC). Collie is a Jamaican American and I figured might have some sympathy with what Irene had been through. I gave him the pitch I'd prepared.

"Listen," I said. "You guys are supposedly here to lead the war on drugs. Here's an opportunity where you have this lady in prison who can tell you about a pretty big Western drug guy."

I had his attention. Collie and his team seemed interested in what information Irene might be able to provide and he was happy to schedule a meeting with her.

I was thinking outside of the box. We had to build up enough goodwill to convince the judge that Irene had not only reformed but had also become an asset to the government. I figured Irene had enough insight into the inner workings of Afghanistan's drug trade to be useful.

In my own way, I was trying to get a plea negotiation together for Irene. With a little encouragement, she began to share what she knew with Collie and his UNODC team, and in return Collie agreed to prepare a report to say Irene was helping them to track down the people she had worked for. And because it was the UN, I could go back to the Supreme Court and say this important new information needed to be considered.

A week later, I got a call from Collie.

"Kim, they're going to release your girl," he said in his slow Jamaican drawl.

"*What?*"

"Yup. So you better start thinking about how you're going to get your girl back to the Ivory Coast because it isn't safe for her here now."

Collie filled me in on more of the details. In light of the information Irene had provided, along with the revision petition, the judge had reduced Irene's sentence to time served and she was going to be released. She was free to go home.

I'd won my first case.

7

GIVE ME YOUR WATCH

Word began to spread around Kabul about the American woman lawyer who had successfully navigated the Afghan legal system. It made me smile to think what my old boss from months prior at JSSP must have thought when he heard about it. It felt like I'd well and truly left those days behind me and now Irene's case had fuelled me with a renewed confidence.

The work I'd done for the Italian NGO had led to a similar gig for Terre des Hommes, a Swiss NGO, who'd hired me to conduct another assessment of juvenile justice in Afghanistan. I travelled the country talking to hundreds of kids locked up in detention centres and published a fresh report that was eventually used as the basis for some of the UN's recommendations on reforming the youth justice system in Afghanistan.[1]

Between the two contracts, I was making good money again, so Claude was still happy for me to stay and explore how things could play out. To be honest, we didn't have much of a choice; we'd each become too used to the lifestyle we were living now. I'd also allowed myself to finally dare to dream about whether I could make a go of it alone as a lawyer in Afghanistan.

Soon after that, at one of the Thursday night parties, I met Tom Rosenstock. Tom is an American lawyer focused solely on contract law. It was a pleasant surprise to meet another foreign lawyer working in-country and we traded war stories. When I told Tom about Irene, he was curious to hear that I was handling criminal work. I found out why when a few days later I got a call from him.

"Hey, there's some British security guy that's been arrested. You hear about that?" he asked.

I hadn't.

"Anyway, I told this guy he works for that maybe you could help them out. Okay if I give him your number?"

Damn straight it was.

Later that night I got a call from an Irishman who introduced himself as Kevin, a friend and colleague of Bill Shaw, the guy who'd landed himself in jail. Kevin explained that he and Bill worked for G4S. I knew the name. G4S is a very well known security contractor in Afghanistan. It's one of the big guys, and right away I guessed this was a potentially high-profile situation.

Kevin asked if we could meet later that night. I suggested we head to the offices of the Italian corporation I was working at, just around the corner, where we could talk privately. An hour or so later, he arrived to download me on Bill's case.

Kev's a big guy, in his mid-forties, blond hair and one of those security types who has an immediate presence the second he walks into a room. Despite that, he comes across as kind, gentle, almost sweet. As he shook my hand, I could see his eyes were all red, like he'd just finished crying. This, I came to realise, was because he felt an enormous sense of guilt for what had happened to his friend.

We sat down and the giant Irishman began to explain exactly what had happened.

In the autumn of 2010, Bill Shaw was leading a G4S convoy to the British Embassy building in Kabul, one of their more high profile clients. En route, the Afghan police stopped the convoy and asked Bill to see the vehicle licence documentation. Despite the police probably being illiterate, they said that they weren't satisfied with the documents and asked Bill and his colleagues to exit the vehicle. At the time, the government was aggressively cracking down on private security companies operating in Afghanistan.

Once Bill and his colleagues were out of the vehicles, the Afghan police confiscated everything: the two armoured cars, weapons and radios were all taken. A few days later, Bill was tasked by his boss with reclaiming the vehicles. For the next few weeks, he went back and forth with the police until finally they told him that once the fine was paid in full he could get the vehicles back.

Bill made an appointment to pay the $25,000 fine. He showed up on the agreed day to hand over the cash. Not unreasonably, he explained that he would need a receipt in order to prove the payment to his employers and their client, the British Embassy. The police agreed, took the payment and released the vehicles from their compound. As they released the vehicles, however, they told Bill that they would be unable to provide him with a receipt that day.

Over the next few weeks, under pressure from the G4S accountants, Bill continued to try to get a receipt until, finally, he went to meet with the police chief in person. When Bill explained the situation, he was told that the proper procedures had not been followed in releasing the cars. The chief then accused Bill of paying a bribe and he and his Afghan colleague, Maiwand, were promptly arrested. The final ignominy was that the Afghans kept the cash as they threw the book at the man who'd paid it to them.

"Can you handle this case?" Kevin asked.

"Of course," I replied without hesitation.

Despite never handling a case like this in Afghanistan, I knew it was time for me to get in the boxing ring and show them what I was capable of. To be honest, I never hesitated or doubted that I would find a way to make it work. I told Kevin that I'd been to court before, which was only half true because what had happened with Irene was a quirky situation. Although her case had been heard in the Supreme Court, I felt the judge had let me off easy and had let my foreign-ness slide. Also, since Irene was a woman, her case was considered to be of no real consequence.

This was different: Bill was a British man and that's a whole different story in Afghanistan. With Bill, there was going to be a big and very public court hearing.

The other issue I faced was that of a foreigner representing a foreigner in an Afghan trial court which was still unprecedented. People in Kabul had already been telling me that because there was no legal precedent for a foreign lawyer to stand in an Afghan court it would never be acceptable for me to take on more cases like Irene's.

But, despite all that, this still felt right.

"I've handled cases like this before," I found myself saying to Kevin, leaving out the important detail that those cases were in Wisconsin. "So, yeah, I think I can help."

Kevin looked relieved. These were the words he'd so desperately needed to hear. I asked him to give me a couple of days to look over the case and then we'd talk again. He shook my hand, and as he left I realised that I'd probably just bought myself two days to find a way to make this work.

The next morning, I went straight to the Afghan Bar Association, where I still had good relationships since my time at JSSP. With a letter and my bar card in hand, I met with Rohullah Qarizada, the president of the bar. I wanted to discuss the Advocates Law with him.

The Advocates Law was passed in 2007, meaning it was still relatively new; parts of it, in fact, had still never been used in the courtroom. During my time at JSSP, I'd downloaded all the Afghan laws and statutes to my laptop so I could refer to them later. Within the Advocates Law I had found Article 6(3), which specifically states that:

> a foreigner shall be entitled to defend and represent the rights of his/her client in cases related to foreign natural or legal persons before a court of law and other authoritative tribunals of the Islamic Republic of Afghanistan.

This was exactly what I needed because it meant that because I was licensed in the US, I could represent another foreigner in Afghanistan, too. Article 6 effectively meant that I could represent Bill in court.

A few days later, I called G4S to arrange a meeting at their offices. Even that was a departure from my comfort zone. For starters, I hadn't had a driver since I'd left JSSP, and neither of the consultancy jobs I had included a car, so I had to organise my own transport. To make matters worse, G4S was on the far side of the city. Of course, G4S offered to come and collect me, but I'd just said, "No, no, no, I'll get there, don't worry about it, it's fine, just give me the address."

I was hustling, trying to look like I was running my own law firm, and yes this might have been my first proper case, but I definitely didn't want them to know that. So I took a taxi, which is something you never do in Kabul. People are always saying how dangerous taxis are because, well, taxis *are* dangerous. But what choice did I have? I rocked up outside G4S's shiny corporate offices in a beat-up yellow and white Toyota Corolla, looking every inch like a suicide bomber.

As I stepped out of the car, I found big Kevin waiting to show me inside. He didn't say anything, but I could tell he was concerned about my choice of transport.

I hadn't been in a corporate office since I'd been in-country. All the offices I'd seen up until then were either government- or NGO-run, but this was another league. Kevin led me into a meeting room where he introduced me to the rest of the G4S senior management team. I was thrilled because I'd never had a British client before—and I really like the accent.

Right away, I could tell everyone wanted to be in charge, which made me realise that they were panicking. They needed help. G4S knew Bill was a potential liability because not only was he now a reputational risk to their brand but there was a chance he could sue them.

I started to ask the questions I thought they needed to hear.

"Have you contacted the British Embassy? What about the UN?"

Of course they hadn't. There was no need to contact the UN, but it made them think there might be.

"Don't worry, I can let them know," I said, immediately giving them one less thing to worry about.

I was freestyling. This could be my first real case, but only if they decided to appoint me. I asked more questions about Bill's situation inside the prison. I was keen to get in to see him as soon as possible.

"This really is about getting him out," Kevin said, though I sensed from the higher ups it was more about getting the company out of this situation as fast as possible.

I could tell that I knew a lot more than them about the Afghan legal system. And I didn't know much. And to make matters worse, they'd already started to go the wrong way about things.

If you were a foreign company doing business in Afghanistan, and let's say you wanted to pay a bribe to make a problem go away, then the usual route would be to hire an Afghan lawyer to act as a fixer for you. It has long been a part of the system in Afghanistan for fixers to use cash to grease the wheel, and this is exactly what G4S had done in the hopes of "solving" Bill's case. Unfortunately, shortly after he was paid, G4S's fixer had disappeared, leaving Bill still in jail.

I told them I could help. But I had certain conditions. First of all, I wasn't going to pay any bribes or engage in corruption; and second, I wasn't going to deal with anyone who did. If they wanted my help then from now on they had to let me work my own way. They would have to trust me and the law. Everyone in the room agreed and we shook hands on my appointment as Bill Shaw's lawyer.

The next day, I rocked up to Tolkeef detention centre with five G4S guys to visit Bill. I'd been to Tolkeef a couple of times before while I was still at JSSP so I knew it was worse than Pul-e-Charkhi. Tolkeef was like an open sewer and stank of all things rotten. All prisoners were forced to live in one big underground room. It was supposed to be a temporary holding facility, but it had ended up as something more permanent. Visitors were forced to talk to their loved ones through a huge mesh cage, shouting their conversations to be heard over all the other inmates and their visitors.

That day there were dozens of visitors, with hundreds more waiting in line. It felt chaotic and dangerous. I asked the commander if it would be possible for me to talk to Bill in one of the guards' offices and, to my surprise, he agreed. The G4S guys were impressed that I'd managed to wrangle a private room. I was off to a good start.

I walked into the guards' room and waited. After a few minutes, the door opened and Bill Shaw walked inside. I was expecting to see the usual security contractor type: burly and tattooed. A lot of people I've met and defended in Afghanistan had hardened strong personalities that would have suited them well in prison; personalities that would help them to survive. But Bill was different. He looked younger than I'd expected, even though I knew he was in his fifties. His grey hair was dishevelled, he was unshaven and his eyes were kind of pinkish like he'd been crying. As he rubbed his eyes, I noticed he was wearing an expensive watch.

From that second, I was concerned for Bill's safety.

"Give me your watch," I said.

"Excuse me?"

"You should not be wearing that watch in this prison." I was pointing at his watch. "So, I need you to give it to me."

Bill took off his watch and handed it to me.

"Kevin will get you another one. Don't worry, you'll get this back."

And that's how our relationship started—with Bill thinking that I was trying to jack him for his watch.

When I first agreed to represent Bill, I made it clear that I was representing him and not the company. I was still brand new to practising in Afghanistan and uncertain of how exposed I wanted to be to G4S. I had decided to keep things simple: to ensure the company wasn't influencing my strategy, I would represent him pro bono.

Despite that, the G4S guys had insisted on coming to the prison with me, and there were now six of us in the room. Before Bill and I could get down to business the conflicts began, and what was supposed to be a private lawyer–client introductory meeting turned into a two-hour free-for-all discussion. Just like at the G4S office, everyone thought they had a solution. Someone suggested breaking him out of prison, someone else strongly implied paying bribes; I had to shut down ludicrous plans at every turn. It seemed like no one wanted to listen to anyone else's ideas, especially mine.

After we said goodbye to Bill, I met with Kevin and the others outside the jail.

"Thanks for coming, guys. That was really helpful," I lied. "But next time I think I'll meet him alone."

Nervous glances were shared until finally Kevin spoke up.

"That's fine, Kim. Just keep us updated on developments."

The next day I returned to meet Bill in jail and slowly we began to cover some ground and build up some trust. But it wasn't long before I found out that G4S had already been speaking to the judges about Bill's case without my knowledge.

G4S approached my translator, Mustafa, too. They had tried to bribe him to spy on me and report back on how I was progressing the case. As a result of all the interference I significantly reduced my communication with G4S because Bill was my client, not them. When I left JSSP, Mustafa had also made an exit and I had hired him part time as my main translator in court. We were tight; there was no way he could ever be bribed to betray me.

Meanwhile, while all this cloak-and-dagger bullshit was going on, Bill was getting more and more emotional and scared. I tried to shield him as much as possible from the conflicts outside of the jail. Unfortunately, I couldn't stop his company paying him visits and, to my chagrin, I discovered they were also grilling Bill for details of our planned defence. To add to the chaos, the British Embassy had also got involved and seemed to be operating on the side of G4S. It was maddening that I had to fight my own team, as well as the Afghans.

G4S wanted to know whether I was going to claim that it was their fault that Bill had ended up on the wrong side of the law. From my point of view, it was vital that the details of my client's defence remained confidential. It was in his best interests that we maintain that secrecy. But his best interests weren't necessarily everyone else's best interests.

One afternoon, I was summoned by the British Embassy to update them. When I got to the embassy, the consul, Simon, and Mark, the head of G4S, were waiting for me. It felt like I was walking into the principal's office.

"We are all concerned about Bill's safety at Tolkeef and want him to be moved," Mark began.

"Bill's safety is a concern no matter where he is detained," I replied. "But Tolkeef is his best option."

"It is our job as consuls to make sure that his safety is not at risk," Simon interjected.

"Yes, and protecting him is my job too, but Tolkeef is his best option," I repeated.

"We want him to move to the counter-narcotics prison, which is safer," Simon continued.

Mark looked on.

"Look," I continued, "at Tolkeef we can visit Bill and they give him phone access. We can take in food and give him money. The counter-narcotics prison is on the other side of town, access to him will be more problematic and his freedom will be even more restricted."

I felt that my arguments were logical and based on experience, and we ended the meeting with what I thought was an agreement not to move Bill.

The next day I went home on leave. At that time, I was going home every three months and it was becoming more difficult to parent from afar. In addition to this, Claude and the kids needed to see me and I needed a break. But while I was in the US, the British Embassy moved Bill to the other prison. I was furious.

Now, instead of unfettered access to Bill, he would be locked down for 23 hours a day. My visits would only be allowed twice a week and conducted through plexiglass. I wouldn't be able to pass him money, phones or any of the other things he'd need on the inside to stay sane and safe.

The final insult came when the prison guards shaved Bill's head against his will and took away all his books and papers. All of a sudden, I had a very dispirited client on my hands.

Kevin called me in the US.

"Bill is not happy and wants to be moved back."

"Really?" I replied. "Mark and the geniuses at the embassy arranged this. Tell them to fix it."

For the next ten days G4S and the British Embassy tried unsuccessfully to move Bill again.

I knew I had to end my break early and go back for Bill's sake. My family was not happy. I think they felt as though I was picking Afghanistan over them. It came to a point where I knew to not even mention Afghanistan at home as it would upset the kids. I would notice how Seoul would walk out of the room when I would talk about work with Claude. It was excruciating for all of us, but I had to work because that was how we were surviving.

The next day I landed in Kabul and went straight to see Bill.

"They cut my hair off, Kim!" He was livid.

"I'm sorry, I told everyone not to move you."

Two days later, I arranged for him to be moved out of the counter-narcotics prison. The British Embassy and G4S seemed impressed, but I just hoped that they now finally understood that I knew what I was doing.

Everyone seemed to have an opinion about Bill's case; it seemed the subject had become a favourite dinner conversation on the Kabul social circuit. I had friends telling me I shouldn't be involved. Their logic went that because I was a woman and American I was being disrespectful of the Afghan culture. There were people I knew from the UN, Human Rights Watch and even the British Embassy expressing their disapproval. It felt like everyone was lining up against me.

It was discouraging and overwhelming, and I had second thoughts every day, but I kept reminding myself that Bill was relying on me. He wasn't in a good place. Essentially

I was his only hope. In my job you get to the bare-bone emotions of people, and it gets really personal really quickly. I felt it would be a disservice to him to say, "Well, this is too hard. I'm sorry. I know I said I'd do this thing, but I've changed my mind."

The Italian corporation had offered me a place to live in their secure compound, but it came with unreasonable curfews and endless security rules that I didn't want any part of anymore. I wanted to be free. But I also felt isolated. Added to that, my public profile in Afghanistan was rising as Bill's trial approached.

8

THE MINIMUM IS
NOT GUILTY

Flower Street, Chicken Street, Butcher Street . . . These are
the street names you get in Kabul if you're lucky.

Most streets just have a number, or no name at all, so you
always find yourself describing where you live in reference
to another landmark, like a hotel, a restaurant, or a famous
person's house. My address in Kabul was down the street
from Shirpur Mosque, left, end of the street, yellow door
right before General Dostum's house. It always takes a few
minutes to establish exactly where someone lives when you
first meet. I like it; it's unique to Kabul and it's a good way
to gauge how well a person knows the city.

After leaving JSSP, one of the things I was most excited
about was the idea of getting my own place and exploring. But I was also nervous about it because I wasn't sure

if foreigners lived on their own or even how that might be done. I caught a break when a couple I knew from Canada needed someone to take over their lease. It was a single storey, metal-gated house in a quiet neighbourhood, and I couldn't wait to move in and start finding my own way around.

The problem was I didn't know the streets at all. I had to get cabs all the time. At least, I had to get cabs until the time came to *not* get cabs.

It was one of those crazy-busy days I often have in Kabul where I was bouncing from meeting to meeting well into the evening. My last meeting finished around 11 p.m. and I knew I couldn't go to bed until I dropped off some urgent documents for a case involving an American company I was representing. I jumped in a cab to cross town to meet my contact at the company's compound.

I was sitting in the back of the cab when we were stopped at a makeshift roadblock. One of the cops came to the window, looking into the car while trying to open my door. He tapped on the glass and motioned for me to roll it down.

"Name?" he asked in Dari.

"Why are you stopping us?"

"What is your name?" he asked now in English while trying to open my door again.

I was freaking out because I realised how it must have looked to them. I was a foreign woman sitting in the back of a cab at 11 p.m. and so they had probably assumed I was a prostitute—not something you ever want to be mistaken for in Kabul.

"Kim," I said.

"What is your job?" he asked.

"Consultant."

"*Noooo*." He wagged his finger at me. "Defence lawyer." He stared at me.

"Yeah," I said, staring back.

The driver continued to look straight ahead, fiddling with his phone.

Before I knew it, more cop cars had arrived and dozens of cops started to surround us. A storm was brewing. Another cop approached.

"Please get out of the car," he called, again trying my door.

As they surrounded my car looking at me like a caged animal I became more and more angry. There was no way I was getting out of that car without a fight. I started texting—a few trusted friends I knew. *"If you don't hear from me in an hour, I'm in a cab surrounded by police officers and I am not going with them . . ."*

The fact that they'd worked out who I was didn't exactly make things any easier. I was *that* lawyer who'd been publicly critical of cops, which wasn't a good situation to be in either, but I held my ground and didn't get out of that cab. I was hoping they wouldn't try to pull me out, banking on being a foreign woman in Kabul offering me a little extra protection.

After about an hour, they eventually backed off and told the driver to go. I was rattled and I knew one thing for sure—I could never be in a situation like that again. I hadn't known where I was; I wouldn't have been able to tell people where to look for me. It was stupid. I had to work out this city fast.

Time to get my own car.

One of my Pashtun homeboys, a guy whose friend I had gotten out of jail on a weapons' charge, supplied armoured cars to internationals in town. I asked him if I could get a soft-skinned car. The next day he rocked up at my new place with a shiny silver SUV. From then on, I was going to be the master of my own destiny.

But I was also nervous because people drive like maniacs in Kabul. There is only one rule in driving in Afghanistan: it's your turn. It's always your turn. That can lead to a certain amount of confusion and chaos.

I wasn't sure how a foreign woman driving herself around would go down with people, either. Not that I really cared—the important thing was that it made me more independent and forced me to learn the streets.

At night, when I can't sleep, I like to drive. It's something I did back in Milwaukee and once I had the car it was something I continued to do in Kabul. The city can be gridlocked in the daytime, but in the small hours of the morning the streets are empty. It helps me relax when I get behind the wheel and put on some music.

I moved into a new house which had a space for my car out front. It was a typical Afghan house. No razor wires, no metal bars, no blast-proof windows. Instead I had temporarily adopted a large dog, Martini, from a friend of mine. He became my security.

The week running up to Bill's trial was a typical one. I was putting in 11 p.m. finishes most evenings, coming home, reviewing court papers, maybe Skyping Claude and the kids before treating myself to a well-deserved glass of white wine and listening to some music. But one night I got home to find things were far from usual.

The second I opened the front door I knew something wasn't right. First up, my clothes and things were scattered everywhere, all over the room, the floor—everywhere. My heart skipped a beat and all I could think was, "Is there someone in here?"

I called my friend Brad, one of the ex-security guys from JSSP while I stood outside my house. He went into full-on security mode.

"Just get out of there, Kim. I'll come straight over to make sure the house is clear."

I was about to do exactly that when I remembered the dog.

"Wait a minute," I said. "If there was someone in here, Martini would not be lying on my sofa licking his balls right now."

The intruders had turned the place upside down. Why? Maybe they were looking for evidence relating to Bill's case. They'd left all the taps running, which I couldn't help feeling was some type of cowardly intimidation tactic. I was furious. How dare they? What did they think I was going to do? Pack up and go home? No way. I was a week away from my first real trial in Afghanistan and I had an innocent man relying on me. I wasn't going to be bullied by anyone. I grabbed what stuff I needed and decided to sleep in my car.

Now, before everybody freaks out, I have a really comfortable car. I wasn't prepared to sleep in my house after the intrusion, and with all the work I had to prepare for the trial I simply didn't have time to look for a new place. I figured I could park the car somewhere safe, down a street in a quiet neighbourhood, and that would be home for the time being. I promised myself I'd go house-hunting as soon as Bill's trial was out of the way.

When the big day arrived, I knew I had to look sharp so I took the risk and went home. I showered, put on the black suit I always like to wear to trial, and started the mental preparation for appearing in an Afghan trial court. I was pumped. I was going to court and I was going to shove the law down their throats.

The court set for Bill's hearing was next to the counter-narcotics prison. By now I'd been to a few Afghan courtrooms where the judges would sit behind a desk at one end and the lawyers would sit at the other end. But as I walked into this courtroom for the first time, I was immediately shocked because it looked more like a US court. The kind you'd see on TV. There was a bench for the judges, a witness box, and stands for the defence and prosecution to sit opposite one another.

Okay. I took it all in, thinking, "This is going to be fine." I figured it was just like home. I took a deep breath and decided to take comfort from being on familiar ground.

Bill was already waiting for me. I could tell right away that he was nervous: he was moving erratically and he looked tense and sweaty.

"We're going to be fine, Bill," I said, trying to sound reassuring.

"They're going to give me eight years," he said with stone-cold certainty.

The charge he was facing carried penalties of two to eight years in prison, so it's fair to say his expectations were at the pessimistic end of the scale.

"No, they're not." And I said it because I believed it.

He hadn't committed bribery. I'd defended a lot of guilty and not-guilty people back in the US and, believe me, it's easier to defend people who are guilty. If you defend an innocent person and you lose, it's the worst thing in the world. You really fucked up in that case.

My strategy was to use Bill's personal testimony as a key to the defence. I planned to get him on the stand and ask the court to listen to the evidence and focus on the elements of the accusation. Mustafa and I had prepared a series of charts outlining the exhibits step by step and how the accusations made were inherently flawed. I had a translator, the best in Afghanistan, to make sure the court missed nothing. I was prepared to make the case for a full acquittal and immediate release.

But first I had to wait to hear the prosecutor's case. I was nervous of any new evidence raised that I wasn't prepared for or that the rules of engagement would be different. I needn't have been. My adversary merely stood up and read out the charge sheet. No arguments. No witnesses. No evidence. I had to fight to hide my smile. This was going to be a cakewalk.

I stuck to the game plan. I stood up and made Bill's case. I focused on the material, moral and legal arguments. I pointed out the logical flaws in the accusations made against Bill. I put him on the stand and he relayed the details of the day in question flawlessly. I thought it was obvious to anyone listening that Bill was not guilty of bribing anyone. He was asking for a receipt to cover his own ass. Who wouldn't do the same?

As I sat down, Bill put his hand on my arm.

"Good job, Kim," he said. "But they're still going to give me eight years." I was incredulous.

The judges went out to deliberate. I wish I could remember what was going through my head, but I hardly had any time to reflect because they were back so soon. Fifteen minutes after I'd made my closing arguments I was in my seat again, listening to the head judge deliver his verdict.

"Guilty. The defendant will serve two years."

I was crushed. More than that, I was pissed. And I was sorry for Bill. My head was spinning so fast with all these feelings that I could hardly take it all in. I turned to Bill, expecting him to share my anger and disappointment at this gross injustice.

But he was smiling. He took my hands in his and looked me deep in the eye. "Two years, Kim? That's a great result." He was glowing.

No. No, it wasn't a great result. All Bill had heard was "two years". But all I heard was "guilty".

The clerk of the court came over and presented us with the judgment written out in Dari. There was a space at the bottom for Bill to sign but signing it would be a tacit acceptance of the judgment and therefore his guilt.

I stood back up and asked the judge, "How could you find him guilty? He didn't do this."

He actually looked confused about why I was so mad.

"But we gave him the minimum," he said like that was an explanation.

"No." I was almost screaming. "The minimum is *not guilty*."

Nobody was listening. The clerk pushed the judgment sheet towards Bill.

"Don't sign that!" I shouted.

Bill smiled as he gently shook his head.

"Kim, if I don't sign it now, they'll make me sign it when you leave." He looked me squarely in the eyes. All I could do was throw my hands up.

And with that, Bill took the paper and signed. He would be taken to Pul-e-Charkhi to begin his two-year sentence. The case was lost. I failed.

That night, I sure as hell wasn't going to sleep in my car or my besieged house. I went to the Serena Hotel. In a city where many inhabitants still cook over open fires and sleep next to sewers, the Serena is the only five-star hotel to be found. You can have a perfect slice of cheesecake, work it off at the gym and then relax by the finest heated pool in the country.

The Serena is also the only public place where business can get done in Kabul. Diplomats, business people, warlords, as well as weary international female lawyers gather there to spend a few hours lounging on plush couches in a marble lobby while sipping freshly squeezed orange juice and eating duck salad under shiny chandeliers. Since 2008, when I first arrived in this dusty country, I've always viewed the Serena as my spa, my refuge, an oasis in the desert.

I threw my bags on the bed, ran a bath and turned on the TV. Bill's case was the lead story on the news. The Afghan media was putting a positive spin on the verdict. The insinuation was that Bill *must* have tried to bribe his way out of his situation but the court had risen above temptation and was not biased or corrupt.

"Bullshit," I said to myself as I turned the TV off. I couldn't bear to hear another word of it.

I didn't blame them, I couldn't blame them—not when I was to blame. I sank into the bath and a world of recriminations. Maybe I should have hired a male Afghan lawyer to handle the trial, maybe I could have been better in court, maybe I should have listened to everyone who told me I didn't know what I was doing . . .

I was lying there, going over and over everything that I might have done wrong or could have done differently. I thought about all the evidence we presented, the witness testimony supporting Bill's innocence. I wasn't even thinking of an appeal yet, I was just thinking, "I fucked this up and now an innocent man is in jail."

I knew what I had to do next.

The next morning, I left the Serena and went to see Bill. Our moods couldn't have been more different. He looked like a new man, like the weight of six years in jail had been lifted from him. But I was still really down about the result.

"Listen, Bill," I said, "you have to appeal the judgment. I've been going over everything in my head and it would be remiss of me if I did not take responsibility for losing yesterday."

Bill listened carefully to every word.

"I don't want to quit," I continued, "but I can totally understand if you want to fire me. If you want me to continue, then I'll find an Afghan lawyer—a man—to represent you and I'll help him in any way I can."

I wasn't quitting on him. I'd continue to represent him pro bono until he found someone else, but I needed him to know how sorry I was about the result and that he shouldn't feel like he had to stick with me. He needed to do what was right for him.

Bill was calm. "I told you I would get prison time," he said. The guards had told him as much the whole time he was inside. "Nobody gets a 'not guilty' verdict in that court. You did as well as anyone could."

"No, this is bullshit," I said. "You should appeal. I'm just not sure I'm the right lawyer for you."

He smiled that warm, calm smile of his and simply said, "I don't want any other lawyer."

"Okay. So, do you want to appeal this?"

"Yes."

"Okay then. Let's appeal."

"Okay then. Good."

And just like that we were back on. I had a second shot. Only this time I was going to play by different rules.

9

YOU NEED TO SIT DOWN

One great thing about Afghanistan is that nobody ever seems to mind you hanging out. Especially as a foreign woman: you can just turn up somewhere and if you keep to yourself other people, though curious, rarely care that you're there. In fact, it seems like they're glad you came. Despite all its problems, Afghanistan is one of the most hospitable places I've ever visited.

I knew I only had a few months to prepare for Bill's second trial so I had to learn fast. In terms of evidence, I was confident that I was still well prepared from the first trial and it wasn't likely there'd be anything new to surprise me. I had to change my style as opposed to the substance. For example, judges expected you to speak in absolutes. Instead of saying, for instance, the evidence will show that my client is not guilty of bribery, the courts expect you to say he did not bribe *anyone*. It is a nuanced difference, but an important one. The ambiguity of putting qualifiers into the language was enough to give the judges some doubt.

I had to get my head into the Afghan way of doing things. I needed to know their customs and practices, get a feel for the things that worked in the courtroom—and those that didn't. Crucially, I had to figure out what worked outside the courtroom, too. I became a sponge during that time. I tried not to miss a single opportunity to immerse myself in the Afghan legal system and *jirgas* were a perfect example of that.

Jirgas are a part of Afghanistan's informal legal system. When there's a dispute, the men (and it's almost always men) gather to discuss the issue and find a resolution. It's a form of mediation. I'd first heard about jirgas when I was still at the JSSP, but I'd never met any foreigners who'd been to one.

I got wind that there was a jirga arranged to resolve a property dispute between an Afghan landowner and a guy who'd been living on his land. The landowner now wanted to sell the land and was trying to move the guy on, but the guy was claiming compensation because he and his family were going to lose their home they'd been happily living in for the previous ten years. It is not uncommon for people to live on unclaimed land for decades only to have landowners show up out of nowhere, often with fake deeds, proclaiming the land is theirs and kicking tenants off it. The jirga had been arranged to find a mutually beneficial solution that wouldn't involve the expense of the courts, and I decided to gatecrash to see what I could learn.

Kadar, my driver, drove me to a friend's house in Kabul. Mr Tanin was a former prosecutor and a highly esteemed Afghan elder who I had met at the JSSP training sessions.

He would often pitch in with ideas about how lawyers should practise law, and while I didn't always agree with everything he said I respected his point of view. One day I told Mr Tanin that I felt he was like my Afghan grandfather. "No!" he replied, "I am your Afghan father."

The jirga didn't start until everyone (twenty Afghan men with long beards and one American woman with a curious mind) had arrived and taken their seats on the cushions lining either side of the living room floor. Mr Tanin was there as my sponsor, which meant that I was cool. While I squished up to make room for the last men to file in, I began talking with Mr Tanin. In typical Afghan fashion, he offered me his hospitality, which always means tea in Afghanistan. Never once was I made to feel uncomfortable about being there. Eventually, a few cups of tea later, when there was literally no room for anyone else to fit inside those walls, the drama began.

You might expect Afghanistan to have an adversarial approach to conflict resolution. I mean, they've been fighting invaders, and each other, for decades, one war after another, so that would be a sensible expectation. But the reality is very different. The purpose of the jirga is to avoid having a winner and a loser and instead find compromise through negotiation. Albeit extremely passionate negotiation. I watched as both sides put forth their cases; standing up in front of the other men, screaming, spitting, crying, decrying, anything that put not only the facts across but why it was important to them personally. In the US, I was used to dispassionate testimony where the facts alone were admissible and relevant. But as I watched the jirga, I realised that the rules were completely different here.

Although the ultimate goal is settlement, the style of the participants in the jirga is cordial but combative. It was more like two passionate lovers having a tiff than a trial, full of screaming. It all felt surreal, especially as the wise old men sitting around the room merely listened and nodded like it was totally normal behaviour. In the US, the judge would have adjourned and sent everyone outside to calm the fuck down for fifteen minutes, but in Afghanistan, you could shout away to your heart's content.

I started to think about how I could use this in my own case. If I was going to argue like this, I would need to step outside my comfort zone. I'm used to the exhibits and demonstrative evidence, not standing up in court and yelling at people, or making passionate arguments with little or no supporting evidence. But this was exactly what it was all about in Afghanistan: it's about looking a man in the eye and saying this is how it is. Everyone in the room seemed to appreciate that style. I just didn't know how it would be taken if I adopted the same approach.

I listened to both sides make their pleas until eventually it was time for the elders to deliberate. The landowner's case was largely that he'd never given the tenant permission to live there. The tenant had moved on to what he thought was abandoned property while the owner had been overseas. The landowner never showed any documents to prove in fact that the land or property belonged to him. The tenant's position was that he'd lived there for years with his family during which time he'd been paying rent, so if the landowner didn't like it, why hadn't he said something sooner? It was a classic case of eviction without cause, and I felt like the jirga had some clear options to find a compromise. While they deliberated, everyone else was sent to wait outside.

In the parking area, I talked again to Mr Tanin. He was curious as to why I had come and what I hoped to see.

I explained to him that I knew the Afghan law but I wanted to see better how it operated on the ground.

"Have you read the Holy Quran?" he asked.

"No," I replied.

"Well, if you want to know how our law works, then you'll have to read it."

It's funny because as an American, I was brought up to believe that talking about religion and politics openly is offensive, and that asking people to speak about their religion was somehow taboo. While we waited to be called back inside, my new friend quoted passages from the Holy Quran that related to disputes.

"The Prophet," he recited, "discourages people from having disputes with one another. Maybe someone amongst you can present his case in a more convincing manner than the other, and I give my judgment in his favour according to what I hear."

I wondered which side I thought had made the more convincing case versus who I thought had the law on his side.

"You see?" Mr Tanin said. "We have Afghan laws, but there is no law higher than the law of Allah. We cannot consider one without the other."

Word came that it was time for us to go back inside to hear the verdict. I was suddenly nervous. Was I going to have to study the Holy Quran? Was there an opportunity to use Islamic law as it related to Bill's case? I was ready to get back and get started on that work. I'd already made my mind up what the jirga's verdict was going to be anyway: to ask the landowner to provide an alternative site for the tenant. That seemed like the most just compromise under the circumstances.

But the jirga had other ideas. The room fell silent while everyone listened to the old men delivering their ruling. They decided that the tenant must leave the property immediately. I was shocked. They said if he didn't vacate within the month then they would remove him forcibly. The guy was mad, screaming at the elders about his family and asking them where the hell he was supposed to live now.

I was confused. This ruling seemed at odds with everything I'd been told. There was a clear winner and a clear loser here—and clearly no compromise. On top of that, I was sure no religious man would leave a young family without anywhere to live. I shuffled outside among the throng of men with Mr Tanin.

"What happened?" I asked.

He shook his head and then, pausing briefly to check nobody else was watching us, he rubbed his thumb and forefinger together. In any language that means the same thing: money. I understood. There was another important lesson for me about the Afghan justice system, something that I needed to realise permeates all levels of society: corruption. The jirga found in favour of the landowner because he paid the people who made the decisions and it made a loser out of the man who didn't.

The deeper I got into Afghanistan and its culture, the more and more I was developing a second life. When I went back to the US, I had my life there with Claude and the kids, but I was slowly turning into something else while I was back in-country. The Afghan me was harder, more independent and resilient than the me back home, and it was becoming harder to reconcile the two. I still hadn't told Claude that I had slept in my car, or about break-ins at the house. I didn't want him to worry.

To help keep my sanity, I'd started teaching spin classes at the US military base Camp Eggers. Spinning was a stress reliever for me, and in return, the base let me use the library, take showers, even stay over. It wasn't just Claude; I didn't want to tell anybody what was going on back at my house. So many people were against what I was doing. I didn't want to give them any ammunition, or admit that maybe they were right.

By the time Bill's appeal court date came around that summer, I was physically and mentally in much better shape. I'd attended several more jirgas and put in the time talking with the judges. I'd blocked out my arguments and worked out a different strategy for how I was going to perform in the courtroom.

Ahead of the trial, I found excuses to meet with the Afghan judges who were dealing with Bill's case. I would drop in to see them and they would offer me tea and ask me about America and our criminal justice system. They always wanted to know which I thought was better. I would tell them: it's not about which was better as much as which legal system suits the environment.

During those meetings with the judges, I began to feed them details of the case. I'd seen for myself at the jirgas how people paid more attention to what they heard than what they read. I always tried to be honest with the judges and I think I got their respect in return. The week before Bill's trial, one judge said to me, "I'm so proud of you for being in our system and fighting in our courts." He seemed so genuine that I thought I was going to cry. With all the obstacles that I was having put in front of me, here was someone finally showing me some respect. It was very gratifying.

I also began to foster a relationship with the media. I was learning fast from friends I'd made at CNN and the BBC how the media liked to work and I encouraged Bill's family during interviews to focus on him and not the case. Our strategy was to always talk about what a good guy Bill Shaw was. I learned how the media goes about preparing its stories, constructing a narrative, and I decided to play into that. In many ways, investigative journalism is similar to lawyering.

Understanding the culture of the Afghan press was also vital. I managed to get the Afghan press to report that I hadn't paid any bribes. I wanted everyone to know the judges hadn't been bribed for their decision because I was betting that would free them up to hand down a not guilty verdict without the suggestion of corruption.

By the time the big day came around, the mood at Bill's second hearing was totally different from the first. Even the courtroom was different: we'd been moved from the Western-looking counter-narcotics court to one more like the traditional Afghan courts that I'd seen during my time at JSSP. There was no electricity. The lights were dim and there weren't even enough chairs for everyone to sit on. I was truly practising law in Afghanistan.

That morning I decided to walk to court. I believe that a good walk clears the head like nothing else, but that's not necessarily a view shared by many of my colleagues working in Afghanistan. Even with all the expats living in Kabul over the years, the sight of a woman walking down the street without a headscarf still prompts a reaction. I think every car that passed me honked their horns.

I was ready for a full-on, drag-down fight. Walking down the street, suited and booted, shades on, headscarf off, I was Superlawyer on my way to court to fight for my client. They could honk all they liked, nothing was going to stop me from achieving my goal. Today was the first day of my new life as a lawyer in Afghanistan.

Two months after Bill was found guilty in the first court, I walked into his appellate court trial. The judges sat behind their desks at one end of a large room and everyone else sat in chairs around the room. Bill and I sat together. The prosecutor read the indictment.

This time I had no pretty exhibit boards. I'd printed out my defence statement in English and Dari for the court, but I knew the judges already anticipated what was in it. Over the previous weeks, I'd been dropping into conversation so many elements of Bill's defence with the judges that by the time I was standing in front of them at trial they knew the script better than I did.

The prosecutor must have been worried because as soon as I stood up to speak he tried to interrupt my flow. But I'd learned from the jirgas that you do not concede ground. I had two translators, so that when one got tired the other could sub in. Every time the prosecutor raised an objection, I yelled at him.

"You need to sit down." I raised my voice and moved towards him. "You do not have anything to say." And that's what he did. He sat. The hell. Down.

It was at odds with everything I'd learned as a lawyer in the US, but I had to stick with what I'd learned in Afghanistan. I had to put away all my fears about coming off as rude or emotional and just fight from the heart like the Afghans did.

I had also been studying the Holy Quran. The prosecutor's eyes nearly popped out when he heard me quoting from it.

"Doesn't the Holy Quran say that 'a man has a right to face his accuser'?" I asked the court. All three judges nodded. I had learned that this was a central tenet of Islamic law.

"Well, in that case, where is the person that accuses this man of paying a bribe?"

I didn't know where he was, but I knew there was no way in hell that he was going to be in court saying, "Yeah, I'm the guy who took the bribe . . ."

"So, if the accuser is not here," I continued, "then what charge is it that my client is facing today?"

The judges conferred and asked the prosecutor to produce his witness. He fluffed for a minute until the judges lost their patience. The prosecution had until tomorrow to produce their witness. Until then, the court was adjourned.

I went home that night full of confidence. I'd not only won the battle but I was sure I was going to win the war too.

The following day, we filed back into the courtroom. The witness was still nowhere to be seen. Both sides made their final arguments, but without their witness the prosecution's case now seemed thin. The court took less than an hour to deliberate before Bill and I were back to hear his verdict.

"Not guilty."

Those were the two little words we'd been working all these months to hear. Two words that changed everything for Bill Shaw, and for me.

10

I DON'T HAVE ALL DAY

It's impossible to understand the legal system in Afghanistan and its culture fully without understanding *ibra'*.

Ibra' in Islamic law means to "free from responsibility". It is what the West would probably equate with "restitution". It has also been loosely interpreted to mean blood money, but ibra' is more than that: it is a fundamental part of Islamic law.

Typically, ibra' is successful in the legal sphere when the family members of both the victim and the perpetrator, plus any witnesses, elders and religious leaders, gather together for a jirga. The victim's family asks for compensation for the wrong that has been done, and the perpetrator paying ibra' asks for forgiveness. Everybody involved tries to come to a mutual agreement on how to move forward.

In murder cases, resolving ibra' can be a tricky process, but when done well it represents the fusing of the formal and the informal systems: the sum of money exchanged privately can affect what happens in the court when the trial comes around. That's where the second step to the ibra' process comes in. Once the money is agreed and paid, the victim's family should sign a document for the court to state that they forgive the defendant and request they receive no further punishment from the court. I always take pictures of the victim's family as they write down their forgiveness of my client and that they don't want him punished further. I use these photographs in my presentation to a judge. From a legal defence perspective, the satisfaction of ibra' can be a huge mitigating factor when the judges determine sentences so it's vitally important that you do it right. It can be the difference between freedom and a death sentence.

Every time I've seen the ibra' done wrong it's involved a foreigner, because they misinterpret ibra'. Often foreigners think that simply because you paid the money the charge goes away.

After Bill Shaw was released, pretty much any time a foreigner was arrested in Afghanistan I got a phone call. I'd developed a reputation with the security contractors, in particular, as someone who'd successfully got foreigners out of prison. I was even nicknamed "911" because of it.

One such instance happened a few weeks after Bill's release when, at the end of July 2010, I received a call from Dave, an Australian who'd been one of my security guards during my time at JSSP. Dave had moved on to work for a private security firm called Four Horsemen International (FHI). One of his colleagues had landed himself in prison on a murder charge and Dave wondered if I could help his mate, Robert Langdon.

I'd read about Rob's case in the Afghan and international media. I'd already wondered whether I would be approached, so I wasn't too surprised to get Dave's call. By that time, Rob had already been convicted of murder in the first court and sentenced to death.

The case was rapidly moving to the appellate court, which didn't give me a lot of time. Unfortunately, that was how I would receive a lot of cases back then—appointed long after the arrest and usually after a bunch of their friends and a male Afghan lawyer has fucked it up. But at the time I was still relatively new so I took what I could. Dave needed me to fix things, and I told him I'd pay Rob a visit and see what I could do.

Unlike my earlier foreign clients, Rob had been housed in one of the most vile and dangerous blocks of Pul-e-Charkhi prison. I'd become familiar with the prison from my visits to see Bevan, but this was my first real introduction to that part of the prison; a seedy wing that had been skipped over during my initial tour two years prior.

I followed a guard through a corridor and into a dingy, filthy room that stank of urine. He told me to wait while Rob was brought down. There was nowhere to sit except for a dirty sofa and the room had rats running inside and out. Fifteen minutes later, the guard returned and told me that a defiant Rob had refused to come. Having spent nearly two hours getting to that room, I was enormously irritated by this, so I scrawled a quick note on a scrap of paper and handed it to the guard.

It read, "This is Kim Motley and I don't have all day."

Five minutes later, a haggard but imposing six-foot-two white man came lumbering into the room flanked by four prison guards. His hair was a dishevelled tangle of knots and his beard was scruffy and overgrown. His clothes were grimy and I could smell him the second he came through the door. He looked even more pissed off then, I felt.

I could tell right off the bat that Rob's mental state wasn't great. My anger finally ebbed away and I felt bad for him. I watched in silence as he bent down to plump up the mattress before sitting down next to me.

"What do you want?" he asked, eyes firmly fixed on the floor.

"Your boy, Dave, asked me to come down here," I said. "He said you want me to represent you."

He continued to look down.

"I'm happy to, but you need to understand that I don't pay bribes, I don't get involved in corruption, and if any of your people try to interfere I will cut off communication with them."

More silence.

"And if I think anyone on your team is paying bribes then I can't be your lawyer. Nothing personal, it's just how I do business."

Still nothing.

"So, do you want me to represent you or not?"

Finally, he spoke.

"Do what you want."

Fuck this guy.

"If you want me to represent you, I need for you to say so," I replied.

He looked up finally meeting my gaze for a moment. "Yeah, sure," he said. Then he stood up and stormed back out of the room.

And that was my introduction to Robert Langdon.

Over the next few weeks, I started to piece together Rob's case and what had happened to land him in prison. Rob was a former soldier who grew up in the Australian bush. He had a different type of constitution from most of the other security guys I'd met. He was the real deal. A genuine badass. After several stints with the Australian army in Iraq, East Timor and the Solomon Islands, he had been working in Afghanistan for several years as a security contractor under the tutelage of an American named John Allen, his boss at FHI.

In the winter of 2009, FHI had been engaged to protect a 40-truck convoy carrying much-needed goods to a military base in Kandahar, the most insurgent-heavy province in Afghanistan at the time.

As it was getting dark, the convoy was stopped in Maidan Shahr, a rural town 25 miles south-west of Kabul, which was unusual because security protocol dictates that convoys should be kept moving unless it's an emergency. Rob, who was in Kabul, received calls from two American colleagues in the convoy telling him that Karim, another Afghan FHI colleague, had ordered the stop. It was now late at night and there weren't any street lights. They were sitting ducks with expensive cargo surrounded by terrorist territory.

With no reasonable rationale for stopping the convoy, Rob radioed Karim for an explanation. He got no reply.

Rob jumped in a car and drove over an hour to meet the convoy. When Rob arrived on the scene, the two Americans had locked themselves in their car because Karim was wielding his gun at anyone who questioned his authority. Nobody could explain to Rob why the convoy had stopped. It was now past midnight.

Karim had worked for FHI for a few years; he and Rob knew each other pretty well. But when Rob found him, Karim still refused to explain why he'd ordered the stop. An argument ensued.

Rob suspected that Karim was involved in something untoward. Corruption was rife, and Rob was now worried that something would happen to the men and the convoy if they didn't get moving. The men faced off in the dirt by the side of the road. Rob wanted the convoy to move, Karim did not.

While the two men argued, Karim put his gun in Rob's face. Rob in turn pulled his gun out and shot Karim several times, killing him.

Rob didn't panic. He and a couple of the men took Karim's body and went to store it in the boot of one of the vehicles. When they opened the boot, however, they discovered it was loaded with many kilos of heroin, hidden underneath the mail that was to be delivered to the military base. Again Rob didn't panic. They placed Karim's body in the vehicle, laid on top of the drugs and mail. Rob and the Americans ordered the convoy to continue towards Kandahar immediately.

But before they could resume their journey, a group of armed Afghan men appeared from the desert out of nowhere. The men apparently saw Karim's body being placed in the boot of the car and decided against attacking the convoy. It was clear that Karim had set up the convoy to be robbed and that these men had arrived late.

About five miles out from their final destination, Rob ordered the trucks to stop. Not wanting to show up with kilos of heroin to a military base, he ordered that the drugs be destroyed. What happened in the following moments sealed his fate.

The car with the heroin inside was set ablaze—the same car containing Karim's body. How this had happened, who knows? Perhaps the order was a lost-in-translation situation? Despite this awful turn of events, Rob continued on. When he arrived with the cargo at the base in Kandahar, he advised the American contractors who had been part of the convoy to take the next flight out of Afghanistan. Rob then drove back to Kabul as he was now in charge of the convoy. Once he arrived he called his boss, John Allen, who was in Dubai at the time, and he told Rob that he had bought him an airline ticket to fly out of Kabul that day. After about twelve hours of driving he quickly packed his bags and made his way to Kabul airport. At the airport, he got through customs and was waiting for the bus that would transport him to the plane. Ten minutes before the plane was scheduled to take off, Rob was arrested.

I was fascinated by Rob's case from the start. It was an imperfect self-defence case, but I believed that it was a self-defence case nonetheless. Purely from a litigation standpoint, murder cases are fascinating because the stakes are so high. If you're a litigator and you're not doing murders then, really, what are you doing? Murder is the Super Bowl for criminal defence lawyers. When your client is facing a life sentence or the death penalty, you better be at the top of your game.

Never once did Rob change his story. He said that he had no reason to order the burning of the body. From a logical standpoint, who murders a person in cold blood in front of dozens of witnesses and then tries to destroy the evidence? Nevertheless, fearing how the incident could be portrayed by Afghan officials, Rob had been advised by his boss, John Allen, who he trusted implicitly, to flee the country. He had been arrested at Kabul airport, just minutes from the plane that would have flown him to safety, and was promptly charged with Karim's murder.

I returned to Pul-e-Charkhi several times over the following weeks to visit Bevan and to see Rob. Bevan's case was strolling along at a frustratingly very slow pace as no one knew where his case file was. I wish I could say that my relationship with Rob improved during those early visits, but it didn't. Every time, he would listen to updates in silence, saying very little.

His cell block was ridiculously overcrowded. There were a few Africans and mostly Afghans in the block. There was no electricity and it was difficult for me to take in things because there were more guards there. On the rare occasions when Rob did share what he was thinking, he would talk about his friends and what they were doing on the outside to help get him out. Increasingly, this caused me concern.

First, Rob confirmed that FHI were indiscriminately paying bribes to anyone they thought could help, but when I confronted them about it they maintained that Rob was wrong and they weren't paying anyone. The vibe I was getting from FHI, however, was that they were a bunch of gangsters. But everyone's a gangster until gangster shit happens. Like most of the security guys I knew, they could talk the talk: during one meeting with them, the conversation even turned to how they were going to just bust Rob out of prison as though we were in the Wild West.

"We know the area, we know the coordinates," Dave bragged.

"Yeah, you should do that. It would save me loads of work and time" was all I had to say about that idea.

Despite their plans to get their boy out of prison, the big talk resulted in nothing. Absolutely nothing. What particularly irked me was that they shared these ludicrous plans with Rob. They would hype him up with all the "we're gonna get you out" bullshit, with no thought about how Rob would feel when no audacious escape materialised. Of course Rob, stuck in prison, soon went into a downward spiral of depression.

The second problem I had to deal with was the ibra'. Unfortunately, FHI had already conducted the ibra', but I was still hopeful that they'd conducted it properly. Dave came to my office to discuss it. I nearly fell over when he said that Rob's family in Australia had mortgaged their house to get the money together and the ibra' they'd already paid to Karim's family was US$100,000.

Not to devalue Karim's life, but $100,000 to an Afghan family is like a billion dollars in America. Sure, the ibra' is supposed to compensate a family, and chances are that Karim was the main breadwinner with dependants, so a considerable sum would have been expected. But Karim was far from an innocent victim, and in light of the circumstances a figure around $10,000 would have been more what I expected.

"At the very least, tell me you have something in writing from Karim's family explicitly agreeing that they do not want Rob prosecuted further," I said to Dave.

He did not.

Like so many Westerners, FHI had erroneously believed that once the ibra' had been paid, the perpetrator wouldn't be punished. But they'd made a fundamental mistake: in Afghan legal procedure, this absolution did not have any legal binding. So while Karim's family may have chosen to free Rob from responsibility, without that written down on paper there was little I could do with it.

The following week, I met with the judges on Rob's case. I wanted to see where things were and get my eyes on the court file.

FHI had beaten me to the punch. The judges told me that FHI had been interfering on every level. They had been paying anyone they thought was a judge, they were paying prosecutors, they were even paying people at the prison. They were paying for Rob to stay in the shitty part of Pul-e-Charkhi because they didn't realise he was in the shitty part of Pul-e-Charkhi. I started to realise that I was being played. FHI weren't taking my advice at all; the only reason they wanted me on board was because I had a good reputation and they didn't stop for a second to think why that might be.

At Rob's request, I went to meet with FHI for one last time. At the office, I met with Rob's former colleague, George, an American security contractor.

"Since you all can't stop yourself from fucking up this case, I won't work like this," I said as I walked into his office. "And you guys are doing everything wrong. If he gets killed, it's on you."

George didn't want to listen. He was sure the latest set of bribes they'd paid would free him.

"Listen, we don't want you to quit," he said. Then he opened his desk drawer and took out $75,000 in cash. "So this is a bonus if you don't."

I was livid. He had tried to bribe *me*. That was the final straw. I said, "Fuck you," and walked out of his office.

The next day, I went to see Rob for what I expected to be the last time. I did the one thing I hate doing. I quit on a client. I had visited Rob in prison for weeks and I was still very concerned about his mental state. I worried that he was suicidal and I was concerned about pushing him over the edge. But I had to be straight with him.

"I can't work like this. The strategy you and your guys at FHI are employing is not going to work and it is running in direct contradiction to what I am trying to do."

Suddenly Rob was more talkative than he'd ever been before.

"I understand, but I trust my guys," he said.

He was blinded by loyalty. I tried to tell him that his company was only out to save themselves. That they didn't care about him. He asked me the first question that he ever asked in all those visits.

"Why are you quitting?"

"I am not quitting because of you. It's about your company," I explained. "Your people are hanging you out to dry and I can't be a part of that. They are playing with your freedom."

Rob still refused to hear the reality I had tried to impress upon him for weeks.

"Good luck. I'll continue to keep an eye on you and I wish you well."

We shook hands and I left.

Two weeks later, Rob went to the appellate court and was sentenced to death for the second time.

11

IMMORAL CRIMES

I'm not a traditional human rights lawyer, I'm a litigator. I have a lot of respect for human rights lawyers, and I certainly do not think I'm in any way above them, but the difference between their job and mine is important.

There's a tendency in Afghanistan to label all sorts of legal injustices as "human rights issues", but I think it's a mistake to ride on that description because labelling a case as a human rights one can actually diminish its significance and limit the options available to the client.

For example, the human rights lawyers I've met in Afghanistan don't litigate and don't go to court. They mostly focus on treaties and statements adopted within international human rights conventions, they write reports, march and argue behind the scenes. So, as a private lawyer who does litigate often, and often in cases with a human rights element, in Afghanistan at least I'm keen to avoid being labelled as a "human rights lawyer".

Every female client I've helped in Afghanistan has been affected by much wider issues than their human rights, so while a human rights approach often avoids the nitty-gritty mechanics of a criminal trial, I absolutely focus on specifics as they relate to the local laws. That's the most effective way to represent and protect my clients.

Where possible, I cite from the Holy Quran, I draw from Islamic laws, I quote local Afghan laws, and only then, if I still need to, will I revert to international legal standards from treaties and international conventions. As a litigator in Afghanistan, I'm not arguing my case to the media or to a panel of human rights experts, I'm arguing it to Afghan judges and I must convince those judges that my client is innocent.

There were times when my reluctance to jump on the human rights bandwagon brought me into conflict with NGOs and embassies in Kabul. The human rights label can make a case sound more important, and it can certainly attract media attention, but I sometimes suspected that certain ambitious individuals were keen to use that label because it was good for their résumés without always thinking whether it was helping the client or their case.

A good example was in the autumn of 2011 when I was asked to represent a sixteen-year-old Afghan girl named Gulnaz. Gulnaz had been sentenced to twelve years in prison for "adultery by force". She'd received her sentence shortly after giving birth to her daughter, the product of the adultery, while in prison.

Gulnaz had been raped. She had been visiting her cousin when the cousin's 40-year-old husband attacked and raped her. He grabbed Gulnaz, threw her on the cold, dirty living room floor and raped her while his four-year-old son was in the room.

Weeks later, Gulnaz and her mother went to a doctor because she was feeling sick—it turned out that she had morning sickness. Then, to add insult to injury, and ignoring all standards of doctor–patient confidentiality, the doctor turned her over to the police. The police immediately locked Gulnaz up on a charge of "adultery by force", which they labelled as a moral crime.

To Westerners, Gulnaz's ordeal was unthinkable. It represented the epitome of the oppression of Afghan women: a teenage rape victim, turned in to the police by the doctor who examined her, arrested, convicted and jailed for her "moral crime". In 2011, a UN study revealed that more than half the women locked up in Afghanistan had been convicted of so-called moral crimes.

In Afghan society, a moral crime describes any action by a woman perceived as humiliating to a man within her family. In addition to adultery, the other most commonly punishable moral crime for Afghan women is running away. So, women, often very young women, who have run away from a bad, often life-threatening situation in the home, typically end up in court on charges. It's almost exclusively women who are charged with "moral crimes" and it's usually in the aftermath of some extreme domestic abuse. It is an effective tool for subjugating women.

Gulnaz's case represented much more than just a violation of her human rights. At its core, it represented extreme domestic violence, child abuse and systemic misogyny— exactly the argument the United States had used as justification for going into Afghanistan in the first place. The Bush administration, appealing to women's rights groups in the US, stated one of its top priorities in Afghanistan as the targeting of the country's systemic oppression of women. In November 2001, during the run-up to the war in Afghanistan, Congress passed the *Afghan Women and Child Relief Act* specifically citing the Taliban's extreme repression of women.[1] As I started building Gulnaz's file, I could see she was an example of how little progress had been made since.

Naturally the human rights community in Kabul swarmed over Gulnaz's case. But what was clear from the outset was that these advocates were failing to recognise that Gulnaz had been charged with a very specific crime. Her freedom wasn't going to come from any human rights report; she needed to prove that she was not guilty of the specific charges that had been levelled against her. From a legal standpoint, she would have to demonstrate that the sex was non-consensual and that she had been raped.

She needed a criminal defence lawyer, not a human rights lawyer.

It's worth noting that in Afghanistan women are rarely viewed as victims of rape. This interpretation is simply impossible in such a male-centric culture. The logic goes that the woman must have wanted the sex; she must have induced or seduced the man in some fashion, meaning it couldn't have been the man's fault. Questions are asked, such as, "Why was she there in the first place?", "Why didn't she scream?", "Why didn't she tell anybody?", "Why didn't she do x, y, z to escape?"

Shortly before I got involved in the case, I went to a shopping centre in Kabul to buy a shirt. While I was in the dressing room, half-undressed, three men barged in. Instinctively, I knew not to scream because if I did other men would come, and I felt that I would be interpreted as the problem. So, what did I do? I fought, using my body to ram those bastards into the mirror, knocking them off balance and managing to shock them enough to create a space to push past. I ran for my life, scrambling back out onto the street, covering myself up as I hurried towards my car. It was a scary experience and I was lucky to leave unscathed.

Most Afghan women are not so lucky. Women have no voice, they have no say. Their relationship with men is like a slave's relationship to the master. The degradation of women by Afghan men is especially pervasive in rural areas, which is most of Afghanistan. Contrary to popular belief, the practice did not start with the Taliban, either; it was a cultural norm long before the Taliban took over in 1996.

The widespread abuse of women is one reason why I didn't feel compelled to wear the headscarf. I'm not trying to be disrespectful, but a part of me sees forcing the wearing of the headscarf as a shackle, a representation of misogyny. Whether a woman chooses or chooses not to wear a headscarf, absent any formally legislated laws to the contrary, I believe that is *her* choice to make. Of course, I respect that there is a religious connotation, and I cover my head when I go to the mosque. The headscarf and the veil separate men from women; in Afghanistan I intentionally act to separate myself from ever being judged solely by my sex.

When I came to Afghanistan and decided to start representing people, I wanted it to be me representing people, not some version of me. Sure, I'm culturally sensitive to an extent, even in public. I don't wear shorts and I would never wear a short skirt in public. But to represent my clients effectively, I needed to come from a position of strength, which meant behaving as a man would. I shake men by the hand. I look them in the eye. I'll be in the same room alone with them. When I think back to my initial JSSP training in Arlington and about how I was told how women were not allowed to do any of these things, I cringe. How would anything change for Afghan women if Western women simply bow down and accept these absurd rules they wouldn't dream of adhering to in any other environment.

Gulnaz's case received a considerable amount of international media attention, which meant my uncovered head got a lot of press too, but much of the press stemmed from something that happened long before I was involved.

Prior to my representing Gulnaz, a team of foreign filmmakers had been commissioned by the European Union to make a documentary about three Afghan women jailed for moral crimes. Gulnaz was one of the women. When the film was finished, however, the EU did a U-turn and refused to allow the film to be shown. They argued that releasing it would pose a threat to its three subjects, despite the fact that these women desperately wanted their stories to be told. I wasn't alone in asking whether the real reason had been that the EU was more afraid that the film's release would damage their relationship with the Afghan government.

The decision to suppress the film not only made headlines but also added a political dimension to Gulnaz's case. The hypocrisy was clear: the film commissioned to shine a light on the abysmal treatment of women in Afghanistan was suppressed in order to not upset the very people who were responsible for the oppression.

Men in Afghanistan may have been raised in a culture in which women are subjugated, but as far as I was concerned that's no excuse for the international community to follow their lead. Yet the EU was perpetuating the misogyny by overriding the wishes of these women to have their stories told. It was all maddeningly ironic.

Meanwhile Gulnaz and her daughter were serving an eight-year prison sentence after her last trip to court. The judges offered her a lighter sentence, but only if she would marry the man who raped her. They also called her a whore, stated that she had wanted the sex all along, and one judge even stated in the court that it was physically impossible for a woman to get pregnant the first time she had sex.

Of course, Gulnaz refused to marry her rapist and instead appealed the verdict. By that time, she had become a household name in Afghanistan, which didn't help. The media had reported, long before I got involved, that she had been raped, which is a very dangerous thing to say about an Afghan woman. Many of the women I've represented have been raped but I never bring it up. I focus instead on the non-sexual physical abuse, and only bring up the sexual abuse in closed-court hearings when it is absolutely necessary. In Afghanistan, when you say a woman was raped the result can be that they are sentenced to death.

Stigmatised by the rape, Gulnaz's family had also disowned her. As far as the wider Afghan community was concerned, she was guilty.

The officials from the EU didn't want me to represent Gulnaz, believing that Afghans should represent Afghans. But their opinion did not matter as they weren't my client and they didn't do anything to help her case. Despite all of their criticisms of me representing Gulnaz, the EU, who also were investing millions of Euros in audacious rule of law programs throughout the country, had not even bothered finding an Afghan lawyer to take it on. Supposedly, Gulnaz was deemed such a hot potato by all the Afghan lawyers that no one wanted to even meet with her.

I eventually met with Gulnaz in 2011 in Kabul's Badam Bagh prison. She was in the cell where she had given birth to her daughter, Muska, on the floor almost two years earlier. I knew I'd have my work cut out gaining her trust. She'd been through an awful lot and had no reason to trust some American woman claiming she was there to help. But because I had a good relationship with other inmates at Badam Bagh, the women there vouched for me. Slowly, Gulnaz began to talk.

I really wanted to get an understanding of what had happened that day at her cousin's house. Did she feel comfortable with her attacker being there? What did the room look like? What did the floor feel like? I got very specific. What else was in the room? What kind of day was it? As far as I could tell, no one had ever asked Gulnaz about the specific details.

I made sure during our first meeting that she was aware of how our relationship would work. One of my top priorities is always to educate and empower my clients. I do that by letting them know I work for them. I do what they want me to do and I act as their voice. I also let them know they have the power to fire me at any time for any reason.

I'll walk away with no hard feelings.

"You can fire me," I told her.

She didn't look so sure.

I explain this to all my clients during our first meeting and then leave them with my contract. This is part of the process of them making an informed decision to have me represent them, even if I'm working pro bono.

Gulnaz couldn't write her name and instead made her mark on the contract by rolling her inky fingers over the paper. It was the first document she'd ever signed.

For many of my female clients, this contract will be the first and only time they sign anything in their entire lives. It's a very big deal. I can see the change that washes over them after they sign. That's when they start asking me questions. It's really cool because that's part of the process. It's about empowering.

"I can't go home," Gulnaz said to me sadly. "So what can you do?"

"Well, I'll write a defence statement on your behalf and argue in the Supreme Court for you."

"No," she said.

"No?"

"I don't want to go back to court. The last time my lawyer tried to get me to marry the rapist and the judges said many bad words to me," Gulnaz replied.

"I see." I could understand her reluctance to go through that a third time. "Are you okay if I just go to court to argue your case for you?"

She thought about it for a long while.

"Okay."

Due to the heavy media attention I heard that the Afghan government had begrudgingly arrested the guy who'd raped Gulnaz so I went to speak to him at Pul-e-Charkhi. In many cases of rape of women the men quite often were never questioned let alone arrested. You might assume he wouldn't want to meet me, but like pretty much every person I had ever met in an Afghan prison he was happy to talk. At first, he denied ever having sex with Gulnaz and said the baby was not his. But the court had ordered a paternity test.

That was enough to frighten him into making a confession. Before the results came back, he admitted that he might indeed be the father. (In fact, there are no paternity-testing facilities in Afghanistan so what they actually did was a simple blood test.)

The next time I visited him, the 40-year-old man admitted that he had sex with sixteen-year-old Gulnaz, but claimed that he didn't understand what the big deal was. He was angry that he was in prison and blamed Gulnaz. His anger seemed to be focused on her and how she had selfishly taken him away from his wife and children. I was not surprised at his response as this was the misogyny that I saw Afghan men had against women time and again.

While Gulnaz wanted me to represent her, the courts were going to be a bigger problem. Up until that point, I had only represented Irene and Bill Shaw. I had Bevan and a handful of other expat clients, but no Afghans. There were US diplomats, foreigners working at the UN questioning whether a foreigner could ever represent an Afghan in an Afghan court. It was interesting because not one Afghan questioned my wanting to represent Gulnaz.

But the law can be a wonderful thing. Seek and ye shall find.

Years before, I had found a section of the Advocates Law that said a foreigner could represent other foreigners if the person is duly licensed. That's what allowed me to represent Bill Shaw and Robert Langdon, but I had to dig around to find something that would help me to represent Gulnaz.

Again, I struck gold. Afghanistan's Advocates Law Article 2 specifically states that "Every person has the right from the time of arrest to appoint an advocate of his/her choice to defend and represent his/her rights."[2]

I'd done it again. Or, rather, the law had. Afghan law would permit me to represent Gulnaz, an Afghan, and in the future, I would use that same law to represent other Afghans in court.

After my meeting with Gulnaz, I researched more about adultery in Afghanistan. I found that according to Afghan law there isn't anything related to adultery "by force". It's a significant issue from a criminal point of view that neither "adultery by force" nor "running away" are codified as a crime anywhere in Afghan law. It may be culturally accepted that when a woman is raped she must have committed adultery, or that if she's running away then she must have committed a crime, but it's not written in their law.

The lack of these laws had never been mentioned in the media or in anything written by the human rights activists who claimed to have been involved in Gulnaz's case. Meanwhile, the Afghan lawyer who'd represented Gulnaz during her first two court appearances had only focused on trying to arrange a marriage between her and her rapist.

The question remained: what law was Gulnaz charged with breaking? And how could Gulnaz be guilty of doing anything by force? That's an oxymoron. If she was forced, then she wasn't compliant. That became a key crux of my argument. That's what my defence would be focused on.

We went back to the Supreme Court, where I began by arguing that adultery by force was not a crime. I argued that according to Afghan and Islamic law, Gulnaz had indeed been forced into this situation, as everyone had agreed at first trial, but that this alone was proof that she hadn't been compliant and therefore not guilty of adultery. I argued that the sex not being consensual, her being underage and her being a virgin at the time of the attack were all mitigating circumstances to be considered. I argued that her daughter was also a victim and that the two-year-old baby was being treated like a criminal too. Finally, I argued that it was illegal under Afghan and Islamic law for a judiciary to try to force her into marrying her attacker.

The Supreme Court judges agreed with me and overturned her eight-year sentence, reducing it to three years. They also agreed with our legal arguments that she should not have been forced to marry her attacker. Gulnaz had already served two years and a couple of months when the new sentence was handed down, so she still had time to serve.

I felt she should have been acquitted. Gulnaz now had two options. The first was to re-argue the case to the Supreme Court. Based on our first experience with the court and the urgency with which Gulnaz wanted to be freed, this did not seem like the best choice. The second option was to apply for a pardon from President Karzai.

Strategically speaking, applying for a pardon seemed like a riskier option. A pardon for a moral crime case had never been granted before in Afghanistan. Also, from a political point of view, the case was so high profile that it probably would be perceived as a test of Karzai and where he stood on women's rights.

If we went for the pardon first and failed, we would still have the option to apply for a review via the Supreme Court. On balance, we decided that it was worth putting pressure on Karzai first and see if he was ready to weigh in on the case.

I started writing the presidential pardon petition on Gulnaz's behalf; the first one I'd ever written. I put those same legal arguments on paper, the whole time conscious that I was writing for President Karzai. The *president*.

Family is very important in Islam, which meant it would have been great to include letters from Gulnaz's family, but unfortunately she did not have that support. Her brothers wanted to kill her and her mother refused to speak to her. Instead I decided to post an online petition. I hoped to find people in support of Gulnaz's pardon application and banked on getting a couple of hundred signatures. The documentary filmmakers Leslie, Clem and Sam were very involved in this endeavour and together we put out the word that Gulnaz needed signatures.

Before we knew it, Gulnaz had over 6000 signatures of support from all over the world, and I attached these to the pardon petition. Finally all the international publicity surrounding the case had lent something to Gulnaz's benefit.

Before I submitted the application to Karzai, I went to the prison to visit Gulnaz. It was important for her to agree to everything that was being submitted on her behalf. I read the entire pardon application to her. I showed her the petition with names, and read some of the messages from people all around the world. People had signed from Afghanistan, Denmark, Dubai, France, the United Kingdom, the United States . . . The list went on and on. She got very emotional, shocked that so many people would care about her.

"Gulnaz, a lot of people care about you and think you are very brave. You even have your own Wikipedia page." She looked confused. I don't think she knew what Wikipedia was.

On 11 November 2011, Gulnaz signed the second document in her life, making her mark with her thumb on the pardon application that was going to the president.

From the women's prison, I went straight to the presidential palace, determined and inspired. I'd never been there before, and while I had researched the ins and outs to writing a pardon in Afghanistan I had neglected to research the protocol for submitting one. So I just showed up at the Presidential Palace, all five hundred pages in hand, nicely binder clipped, in triplicate.

"Ah, can we help you?" The two guards at the gate seemed genuinely confused.

"Yes, please. I've got to give these documents to President Karzai, please," I said in my most this-is-not-crazy-I-am-really-supposed-to-be-here voice.

"Do you have an appointment?" one of them asked, lowering his AK-47.

"Thank you for asking," I said sidestepping the question. "But these documents are very urgent and need to get to President Karzai today. It's really important." I held my poker face.

They didn't know what to say. Eventually one of them blinked.

"Who should we call?"

"Call the president," I said. "It's very urgent. I'm sure he will want to read the documents right away."

Of course, I didn't want to tell the guards that this was related to Gulnaz. I was concerned that if they knew that the documents would never reach Karzai. I sat on the kerb while they radioed inside. I knew it would make them uncomfortable having a weird foreign woman sitting on the ground outside the presidential palace.

Finally, Karzai's spokesperson appeared. He took the documents from me, gave me his business card and promised to take them to Karzai.

The next day, I asked every reporter I knew in Kabul to ask Karzai about the pardon. I was concerned that the application would not reach his desk despite the assurances I had received from his spokesperson. I figured that the more people who knew about it, the more likely he was to address it.

The morning of 1 December I received a text message from the spokesperson informing me that the petition was on Karzai's desk. Less than fifteen minutes later, I received another text informing me that Karzai had granted pardon 84, entitled "Bestowing Clemency to Gulnaz". He'd had my application for less than a week.

The pardon fully exonerated Gulnaz, and Karzai also acknowledged that the charge of adultery against her was a "misjudgement".[3] More importantly, it said the cultural norms that led her to be charged in the first place were long overdue for reform.

Shortly thereafter, I received a phone call from Karzai's spokesperson. He wanted me to deliver something to the president.

"We understand that there was a film made of Gulnaz and some other women at the prison," he said. "His Excellency would like to see it."

I contacted the EU. Being worried that if they didn't comply with the president's direct request then they could lose favour, they relinquished all rights to the film.

Even before Gulnaz was released, there were countries offering her and her daughter asylum. Of course, I wanted her to leave Afghanistan, but it was not my choice to make. Gulnaz was a young woman, estranged from her family with a two-year-old daughter. I spent hours outlining the pros and cons of each location, all the while making clear to her that she would need to decide quickly.

But she surprised me. She didn't want to go to another country. She wanted to stay in Afghanistan to try to rebuild her relationship with her family.

I was actually getting a lot of pressure from other foreigners, the EU, the UN, various embassies, all telling me to convince Gulnaz to leave Afghanistan. I understood their point, but I didn't like the pressure. We may not agree with her choice, but it was *her* choice to make. The hypocrisy was amazing; the same people meant to be promoting women's rights were the ones who wanted to stop Gulnaz from exercising her own.

Gulnaz had never seen the inside of a school in her life. If she left the country she'd be completely isolated, on her own, with a new language and culture to learn. There would be no option for family reconciliation, which she desperately wanted. There were so many obstacles. Even though I wanted her to go, I knew that I wasn't really empowering my client if I took those decisions away from her.

Ultimately Gulnaz chose to stay at a women's shelter in Kabul. It was there that I really started to understand how ugly women's rights can be in Afghanistan. The natural assumption was that women would protect other women, but that's not how it was for Gulnaz. When she went to the shelter, the other women told her she had lied. Oppression against women in Afghanistan is so ingrained that even other women raised in that culture believed Gulnaz's persecution was righteous and just. Many Afghan women have been brainwashed all their lives to believe that men are superior so that when they see another woman defying that cultural norm they view it as wrong and have no qualms about expressing it.

Gulnaz was stuck in a shelter that was even more oppressive than prison. At least in prison she could go out in the yard, but as per the shelter's rules, any time she left the shelter she had to wear a burqa. She was stuck in a place with women who hated her, not to mention the tribal issues that were going on between the Pashtuns, the Hazaras and the Tajiks. Gulnaz often complained about these conditions. I would visit her and she would argue with the staff. One worker who insisted on sitting in on our meeting said, "I'm not interested in your conversation, I have to be here for security reasons."

"I need to talk to my lawyer alone," Gulnaz snapped back. Finally, the worker left.

Gulnaz's brothers continued to threaten her and she told me how the Ministry of Women's Affairs was still pressuring her to marry her rapist. They were telling Gulnaz how much the rapist loved her and how sorry he was. I went back to the countries I'd heard from to see if asylum was still on the table, but unfortunately, without the media spotlight, Gulnaz's cachet was not as valuable and not one country was willing to revisit that option.

After more than a year of being imprisoned in the shelter, and feeling like all her options had been exhausted, Gulnaz married her attacker. I was devastated. A big part of me felt like all that work we'd done had just been flushed down the drain.

But I was wrong. Gulnaz's case has had historic implications and an enormous impact on women's rights in Afghanistan. It was the first time that an Afghan president had given a pardon for a moral crime case. Gulnaz's case had gone straight to the heart of Afghan culture and revealed how Afghanistan has structured its legal system to oppress women.

Not long after signing Gulnaz's pardon, President Karzai issued Presidential Decree 107(2)[4], which outlawed running away as a crime. This was followed up by a formal directive by the Attorney-General's office that all prosecutors "should be instructed not to prepare unjustifiable case files regarding running away cases that haven't been criminalised under Afghanistan laws and can't be heard by courts and refrain from conducting baseless investigations".[5]

Because of Gulnaz, more women have been emboldened to report to authorities when they have been victims of violence. There was also a newly created Elimination of Violence Against Women Unit within the Afghan Attorney-General's office for them to report to that women began to take advantage of.

Gulnaz now lives a very difficult life, but in a sense her choice to marry her attacker represents an expression of her own rights. Once she was pardoned, Gulnaz had a choice. She could have accepted asylum and left her country; instead she opted to try to mend the relationship with her family.

All my clients have a right to make their own decisions. And Gulnaz made a choice that many would not. She decided to stay and fight for a life in her own country rather than risk running away for a better life in a foreign one. I might not have liked her choice, but I did respect it.

12

WATCH YOUR BACK

People always ask me if I am scared in Afghanistan. It's the most common question I hear when I go back to the United States and I always say the same thing: "It's fine." Then they wonder why I'm not worried about being attacked, blown up or kidnapped. The truth is that I think I've just become a bit numb to it all. When I hear about a bomb going off, my first thoughts are, "Do I have any meetings over that side of town today? How is that going to affect traffic?"

It's hard to describe how security even works in Afghanistan. Everything is securitised. Every meeting in the city involves a long, laborious security protocol. Every building is surrounded by bombproof concrete walls fifteen-feet high topped with razor wire. The only way in is always through a security barrier, where my driver, Kadar, and I will be

ID-checked before the car is scanned for bombs. Once we get through that, there's almost always another, similar checkpoint. Then we'll usually come to a steel security door, where another vehicle check will take place, and then finally another steel door where we are checked *again* . . . We may at any time be asked to step out of the vehicles to be body-searched and have our bags rooted through. And nearly always, I'll be asked to turn in my laptop and my phone at the door.

Just stop and imagine for a second how many security guys are required to make that happen in one building. Then multiply it by every building in Kabul frequented by foreigners. Not just the embassies and the military compounds but the NGO offices, private companies, all the UN buildings, every single restaurant, bar or house that foreigners might visit or reside in. It adds up to a lot of security.

Which is probably why every second Western guy in Afghanistan is built like a brick wall and carries a gun and more than a whiff of PTSD. Security guys are everywhere. Including inside the prisons.

During Bill's trial, I'd wanted him moved to Pul-e-Charkhi because I'd needed better access. To make that idea work, I got back in touch with Bevan. Bevan had been in the back of my mind since I first met him and I knew that he was still in the same cell in Pul-e-Charkhi.

My plan could work to everyone's advantage. I offered to take on Bevan's case pro bono if in return he looked after Bill. I figured Bill needed protection and there was no one who knew the ins and outs of the prison system better than Bevan. Without hesitation, he agreed to my terms. I arranged for Bill to be moved to the same cell block as Bevan, and just like that I suddenly had three clients in Afghanistan's most notorious prison. But after Bill's release, I felt that Bevan needed a new cellmate and my mind returned to Rob.

The whole time I'd been visiting the other guys, I had been acutely aware that Rob was still on the other side of the prison. It bothered me that he was so isolated; security was getting worse in Afghanistan. The US troops had drawn down, and despite what everyone had said about the Afghan army picking up the slack, there was a real feeling in the city that security was deteriorating. Also, when the troops pulled out, CSSP, the guys responsible for training the Afghan prison guards, stopped making visits to Pul-e-Charkhi. The mood in the prison had changed dramatically and I had first-hand experience of what that meant.

I was making regular visits to Bevan shortly after Bill had been released. It's the same protocol every time: multiple driving checkpoints, searches inside and outside the gates, body and bag searches inside the doors. One day as I went to move past the metal detectors inside the compound, my translator, Khalil, paused and seemed to be unusually distracted by his phone.

"You go ahead, ma'am," he said.

"No, Khalil, I'll wait. You do what you gotta do." We weren't in a rush and I didn't want to be waiting on my own inside for him.

"No ma'am, I'm fine." He didn't look up, but I could tell he was stalling.

"What's going on?"

"Nothing. I have to . . ." He trailed off. He looked nervous. "I have to give my phone."

"Okay. I'll wait," I said it again, firmly this time. I could tell he was uncomfortable. He looked at me again, helpless this time.

"What's going on?" I repeated.

"Outside, ma'am."

I followed him back outside the door we'd just come through.

In the courtyard outside, he began to whisper. "Last time I was here in the prison, ma'am"—he looked around nervously—"somebody approached me."

"Who approached you?" I asked.

"They want to kidnap you, ma'am. They want my help to kidnap you."

Khalil looked to the ground, I could tell he felt ashamed.

I was becoming quite well known in Kabul as my work had been covered in the press many times. I guess from the outside looking in, the impression was that I was running a big law firm, working around the clock with an army of vicious lawyers and had the backing of the US Embassy. However, in truth, I was working alone save for Kadar, my driver, Khalil my translator, and with Claude handling the finances back home.

The bad guys were always looking for a weakness, a way to exploit and take advantage, and they thought they'd found it in Khalil. But they didn't anticipate that he'd have so much integrity. We were a small team, but we were tight: we had each other's backs and our security was always paramount. It sucked, but this meant that Khalil could no longer be my translator in Pul-e-Charkhi, or indeed any prison in Afghanistan. For both our sakes, we simply couldn't afford to be seen together again.

"Okay. I'll go in on my own today, Khalil," I said.

"Ma'am, watch your back."

I collected my stuff and went back through security.

Events like that seemed to be a sign that things were changing in Afghanistan. The good old days were hardly good, but they felt a lot more secure than what was coming around the corner. So even though Rob had been an asshole when I'd tried to help him, and even though his company had well and truly pissed me off, as a human being it disturbed me to think of him alone in the block.

To be clear, there were bad apples in Bevan's block too, but they were the big guys who had a different philosophy. They were a mixture of Taliban and other insurgent groups, but since they were the strategy guys with bigger fish to fry they were less likely to chop anyone's head off in the night. Bevan told me that the Taliban approached him and told him that while he was in Pul-e-Charkhi they were comrades fighting the same enemy.

The block where Rob was housed was a different matter altogether. He was in with the foot soldiers, the uneducated maniacs who would happily slit his throat the second he fell asleep. I had to change that.

The obvious place to start was the Australian Embassy. All the embassies rotate staff every couple of years, so if you don't get on with the current crew, you can sit it out and wait for the next. The old Australian crowd and I didn't have the greatest relationship after they'd been so resistant to a foreigner representing Rob.

When I started to practise in Afghanistan, I would often clash with embassy staff because I'd get frustrated about how their view of the country was so different from my experience. In all my time in Afghanistan, I've never once seen any embassy staff visit a prison. Their security clearances usually prevent them from ever leaving their compounds, which means their impression of what's really happening out there is skewed and sometimes naive. But, over time, I've learned to roll with it and instead of fighting it I use it. I can be a source of news about what's going on outside the walls for many people constrained by their security.

The new Australian Embassy crew, headed by Consul Majell Hind, had a much better attitude and this rotation felt like a breath of fresh air. They were keen to hear about Rob and what conditions were like inside Pul-e-Charkhi. Majell was a formidable woman who took no bullshit and I liked her immediately.

The Australian government had managed to convince the Afghan government to commute Rob's death sentence to a life sentence. I talked to Majell about my plan to move Rob into the cell that Bill Shaw had left when he'd been released. The stars were in alignment for once because she backed me to make it happen. I went back to see General Balki at Pul-e-Charkhi. Seeing no objection, he agreed to move Rob.

The next time I went to the prison to visit Bevan, Rob was there too. He still had no idea that I'd been responsible for moving him and we still hadn't spoken since our falling out two years before, so things were still frosty between us. Truth be told, I still didn't like him. I didn't trust him, I think, because I didn't really know what his deal was.

But Bevan started working on me.

"Kim, just talk to him," Bevan said during one of our visits.

"I'll talk to him, but I'm not representing him," I said.

Bevan nodded towards their building. "He's in there waiting."

I walked into the meeting room. Rob was sitting, silent as usual. Eventually he looked up.

"What do you want?"

Australians can sound so blunt when they want to.

"I thought you wanted to talk to me." I tried to keep my voice level and professional.

"Nope."

"Okay." I began to walk out again. Fuck this guy.

"No, wait." It was the first time I'd heard any vulnerability in his voice.

I stopped and turned to face him. "I don't have time for this shit," I said.

He looked at me with that cold attitude of his.

"So what?" I asked. He had to say it. I had to hear him actually say it out loud.

"I need to talk to you."

I took a step back into the room and looked down at the space next to him. He'd made the move and I didn't want to be a complete jerk. He shuffled over a little and I sat down next to him. And I let it go.

"Okay. What's going on with your case?"

He shrugged, I think because he genuinely didn't know.

"Right. Do you want my help?" I asked.

"Yes." He paused. "But I don't have any money left."

I felt for him. This stone-cold attitude was a survival technique. Underneath it all was a scared man who wanted to go home. I recognised a little of myself in his stubbornness.

"We don't need to worry about that." I held his eye so that he had to look at me. I wanted him to see that this was for real.

This is what you get sometimes. You have to deal with personalities. Rob had been in prison for five years and that changes a person, it toughens a person up. Rob wasn't ever going to hug me and say, "Thank you."

"Listen, if I'm gonna rep you, then I have some rules. And if they are broken, I walk."

I couldn't have a repeat of last time. I wasn't going to stand for any more interference from FHI, his family or his friends.

"They're all gone now," Rob said.

"And that includes your family, too. You gotta trust me. Okay?"

"Okay. My family have abandoned me too. There's no one left."

"If I get any inkling that anyone is fucking with this case, I'm gone. Understand?"

"Understand."

"Okay. Let's get to work."

"How long is this going to take?" he asked.

"I don't know. But I am not leaving Afghanistan without you," I said. And I meant it.

Once again, I was representing two guys inside Pul-e-Charkhi prison.

The more I went to the prison and got to know Bevan, the more I knew we had a unique connection. I had been so impressed by him from the start, despite him being a convicted drug dealer. I can honestly say that if it were not for Bevan I would not be practising law in Afghanistan today. As his case had gone to all three courts, the only way that he could be released early was by a sentence reduction or by getting a pardon. While I would try to work on his case from the outside of the prison and argue to reduce his prison sentence to the government, Bevan would provide legal advice to several of the inmates whom he was imprisoned with.

In the beginning, he would send me letters to help me catch up with where his case was at. I began to appreciate that for well over a year, long before Bill or Rob came along, Bevan had survived as the only Westerner in a prison full of anti-Western Taliban fighters. Not only that, he was a devout Christian who resisted all attempts by his cellmates to convert him to Islam. Instead he had learned to speak their language. By the time I met him, bearded and gaunt, in that dark cell, he was fluent in Dari and Pashto.

I was reading Bevan's letters one night, just imagining what it must have been like for him getting locked up in 2007, a solitary white guy, abandoned, forgotten about by the outside world, and how that compared with the strong, resourceful, honest Christian man that I knew. And it made me realise I was representing someone very special. Bevan wasn't broken by his situation, he hadn't become angry like Rob. He set about how he could get on top of things by learning the language—and the law.

How could anyone be that strong? In many ways, he became the jailhouse lawyer of Pul-e-Charkhi and, initially at least, he knew his way around Afghan law a lot better than I did. I may have been his lawyer but he was my mentor, the best law teacher I ever had.

Bevan and I would talk during our visits about more than just his case. We would share information about the system and how it related to some of my other cases, and then I would advise him on some of the inmates whom I was not morally opposed in giving legal advice to. I was learning too. He would educate me on how the security world worked from the inside out. We were helping each other and everyone around us. It wasn't that I was sending him out to find me new clients, but people were coming up to him and asking him to introduce them to me. I was in demand and I like to think not just because I was still the only lawyer who dared to visit.

There was very little going on inside Pul-e-Charkhi that Bevan missed. We would be in the prison garden and he would point out different groups of men, such as a bunch of parliament members negotiating with the Taliban guys, asking them not to blow up stuff.

Bevan also schooled me in Pul-e-Charkhi's "black" prison. Right across from Block 15, where Bevan and most of my guys were locked up, is another prison. The two areas are separated by a low wall. I've never been in that other prison. It had a helicopter pad on the roof and it's where the US military would drop off prisoners from places like Guantanamo Bay. There was a handful of prisoners who were first taken to that prison and then moved to Block 15, and Bevan would tell me about their experiences. According to him, there was a lot of torture going on, with the US military conducting interrogations seeking intelligence on the different terrorist groups operating in Afghanistan.

It was valuable for me to understand how the drug trade worked in Pul-e-Charkhi because that's also how it works outside the prison. Bevan knew which guards were corrupt and the methods they used to squeeze the prisoners. According to Bevan, he and other foreigners at Pul-e-Charkhi provided help to the US and British military on what the insurgent factions inside the prison were up to. He was told by the military that if he helped the foreign forces that they in turn would lobby to get him out of prison. But that never happened. He was lied to constantly but still fed the military with information. Bevan's ability to speak Dari was especially useful in the prison to gain an understanding of what was going on.

Outside the walls of the prison, on a personal level, things were starting to improve for me. I found another place to live when a friend offered me a room in a shared house owned by CNN. I'd jumped at the offer partly because I was sick

The 2004 Mrs. America pageant in Palm Springs, Florida—I was Mrs. Wisconsin that year.

At Jalalabad Juvenile Detention Centre interviewing kids while on an NGO assessment of juvenile justice in Afghanistan. *(Lorenzo Tugnoli)*

Bill Shaw and Maiwand at their first court hearing in 2010.
(EPA/S. Sabawoon)

Bill Shaw, me and "Big" Kevin on the day of Bill's release, 4 July 2010.

My first meeting with Rob Langdon in Pul-e-Charkhi prison in 2010.
(Travis Beard)

Discussing Gulnaz's case at the women's prison prior to her hearing.
(Atia Powell)

Shopping in Kabul. *(Kiana Hayeri)*

At work in my office in Kabul.

One of my many visits to Pul-e-Charkhi, Afghanistan's most notorious prison. *(Henrik Bohn Ipsen)*

Niloofar Rahmani (second from left), the first female fixed-wing pilot in the Afghan Air Force. I successfully argued her case for asylum in the US.

A visit home in 2013, with Seoul, Deiva, Cherish and Claude in Washington DC for President Obama's second inauguration. *(Kimberley Motley)*

Visiting Darul Aman Palace, Kabul, before renovations began in 2012. *(Henrik Bohn Ipsen)*

Fifteen-year-old Sahar Gul, one of the strongest people I've ever met.

Bevan after his release from Pul-e-Charkhi. *(Henrik Bohn Ipsen)*

With Gul Meena in Sweden after successfully securing her asylum there.
(Stina Rosen)

At Kabul airport escorting the abducted Australian kids home.

At Mazar-i-Sharif airport with the three rescued British boys.

Nikki and her boys being reunited in the UK after nearly two years apart. *(David Loyn)*

Meeting with police while on business in Kampala, Uganda. *(Henrik Bohn Ipsen)*

With Naghma, Taj and Naghma's mother at the hospital waiting for their ride home after Naghma's operation.

Presiding at Naghma's jirga while her fiancé signs documents with his thumbprint, releasing the six-year-old from their marriage agreement. (*Tim Facey*)

Naghma with Flat Black Stanley after the jirga that stopped her marriage going ahead. *(Kimberley Motley)*

Meeting with Richard Branson at the Burj Khalifa in Dubai to discuss Naghma's case.

Signing Rob's final release papers at Pul-e-Charkhi prison.
(Jessica Donati)

Out working in Kabul with Rob after his release. *(Joel van Houdt)*

Working with the former Deputy Prime Minister of Malaysia Anwar Ibrahim's legal team. Left to right: Anwar's daughter MP Nurul Izzah Anwar, barrister Surendran Nagarajan, barrister Latheefa Koya and another member of parliament.

Visiting Afghanistan's only all-woman network, Zan TV. *(Jim Huylebroek)*

Back home with Deiva, Cherish, and Seoul, doing something we love to do: cooking. *(Natan Dvir)*

International Women's Day 2018, with the future of Afghanistan. *(Mina Sharif)*

of the insecurity at my place but mostly because I thought I'd enjoy the company. Plus, it couldn't hurt to learn a little about how journalists in Afghanistan operated, or what they really felt about things.

I began to settle into a life in Kabul. As well as the boys in Pul-e-Charkhi, I'd signed up some corporate clients engaging in tax work, company registrations, contract negotiations—less fun than murder trials but more lucrative. It was important to have a balanced practice if I was going to make a go of it here.

And in the meantime, I was there for all my clients. I saw them at their most vulnerable. I saw them when they were depressed, I saw them when they were suicidal. I was the one who told Bevan that his wife wanted a divorce. I had to give them bad news all the time and often I was the only person they had on the outside to talk to about their lives. Part of my job was sometimes to talk them off the ledge.

It was January 2014 and one night I got a call from Rob.

"Hello," I said into the phone.

Nothing.

"*Hello?*"

"I'm going to do it," he said with a whisper. "I can't . . ." He trailed off and I knew exactly what he meant.

It would have been great to try to reassure Rob with the whole "Don't do it, your family loves you" speech, but that wasn't going to be enough. Rob was severely depressed and had convinced himself his family had abandoned him. That would only add to his feelings of desperation.

"What happened?" I asked.

Rob finally got it out. About once a week, a man would walk around the prison with a creaky wheelbarrow full of cookies and candy that the inmates could buy. It was one of the few luxuries they enjoyed. On this particular day, an execution had been scheduled, but because the guards did not want to waste bullets, and the electricity at the prison was so unpredictable, death by hanging was the preferred choice. Rob heard an inmate kicking and screaming as the guards dragged him from his cell. The man was then tied down and forced onto the wheelbarrow as its creaky wheels shrieked in the night. The inmate was then transported to the prison kitchen where, in the rafters, a pipe had a noose hanging lazily over it. The guards stood him up on the wheelbarrow, placed the noose around his neck then violently kicked it out from under him. Shortly thereafter, Rob heard the creaky wheels of the wheelbarrow being rolled away with the now dead inmate on it.

"*Hmmmm,*" was all I could say after hearing that.

"So, I'm done Kim," he said.

"What? I'm doing all this work and you're going to kill yourself?" I asked.

Silence.

"Really? You're just going to fucking end it?"

"What's the point?" he replied.

"Okay, fine. Just do it. But I swear to God that if you do I will tell everyone that you converted to Islam and I'll insist that they give you a Muslim funeral," I said, knowing that being associated with religion of any kind was one of his triggers. "I'll make everyone call you Rashid at your funeral," I added for good measure.

He giggled. "That ain't right Kim. That's blackmail."

We both laughed.

"Damn right it's blackmail," I said, "and you know I'll do it. Hang in there. You're much stronger than this. I'll see you tomorrow."

"Okay." He hung up.

We met the next day with a newfound trust. It felt like a turning point in our lawyer–client relationship. We were now friends.

Although I was happy that he had not committed suicide, I knew that I needed to get Rob's case moving and part of that was to resolve what happened at the ibra' hearing back in 2009. I knew that his family had put up their house to help raise US$100,000, which they had sent to FHI to help secure Rob's release. But getting hold of the documentation was proving exceedingly difficult. FHI had since disbanded amid rumours they had been involved in running drugs, creating private militias and selling guns, and there was no one left to contact. I tracked down the Afghan lawyer who had initially handled the paperwork, but when I went to his office he was nowhere to be found.

Then I heard that Rob's former boss, John Allen, was still in-country and holed up in the house of a notorious warlord. He made contact with me through Jessica Donati, a talented journalist with the *Wall Street Journal*, and requested that we have a meeting. A week later I was pulling up outside a Kabul poppy palace with Jessica knocking on the heavy metal security door.

John ushered us up to the third floor of the enormous, marbled house. John was a short, middle-aged, clean-shaven white American man with a buzzcut, and as I followed him up the stairs I noticed that he also walked with a limp.

After three flights of stairs, we walked into a dimly lit room where music was playing from a stereo. John sat on a chair behind a desk covered with half a dozen empty whisky bottles and he introduced us to Tim, a thin, weird African guy who was sitting in a corner silently smoking hash.

The room was full of sweet blue smoke. John offered us both a seat and began to explain that he'd been in the house for the last nine months. It was like a scene from *Pulp Fiction*—the Afghanistan reloaded version.

"I haven't been outside," he said, yelling over the music. "It's not safe out there for me."

"Safe?" Jessica asked.

"Yeah, the CIA are after me," John said in all seriousness.

There reaches a point in any expat's time in Afghanistan when they just need to get out. The stress, isolation and prison-like conditions can do funny things to a person. I nodded as John raved about how he knew he was being followed and bugged, all the while thinking, "Yeah, this guy needs to go home."

He'd lost it. Colonel Kurtz style.

Jessica and I just sat there, trying to make sense of the words coming out of his mouth.

"Hey, you girls wanna dance?" He gave us each a drink and hopped out of his seat to change the music. "I haven't danced with a beautiful woman in a real long time."

Jessica and I looked sideways at each other. Neither of us had brought our dancing shoes.

"Come on. 'Mr. Bojangles' is my favourite song." John started dancing and singing along.

Fuck.

Weirdo Tim continued smoking hash in the corner like a crackhead while John was bouncing around the room like a maniac. Things were getting seriously weird.

"Hey, I saw Rob Langdon. You remember Rob?" I practically shouted over the music.

John nodded. "I lost my business over that guy." He sat down again.

"Do you know what happened?"

"You wanna know what really happened with Rob?" John walked over to a safe on the wall. He opened it then handed me a pile of papers from it. "I still have the confessions."

They were documents I'd never seen before detailing statements from some of Rob's colleagues at FHI. I scanned through, noting how each one was so similar to the next that I suspected they'd been dictated by a third party. All the statements had been made by individuals who were either Afghan or third-country nationals. Each statement said verbatim that Rob killed Karim, unprovoked in cold blood for no reason. These were people who needed their jobs and I suspected John had leaned on them, coercing them into making statements that would protect his company. This business was his bread and butter and I could see he was still angry at Rob for jeopardising that.

"I was the one who turned him in, you know?" John said, taking a shot of whisky. "I booked his flights to Dubai and called the police when he was at the airport."

Damn. Rob revered John. I wasn't looking forward to telling him this.

I stopped on one document. It was a copy of Rob's ibra'. The document had been filled out by Rob's Afghan lawyer and it detailed the time and size of the payment. I did a double-take on the amount: 100,000 Afghanis, roughly US$2000. It was clearly written in black and white. Those fuckers. Between FHI and the Afghan lawyers someone had taken $100,000 from Rob's family and somewhere along the way $98,000 had disappeared.

"We need to go," I said.

"Is she always like this?" John asked Jessica.

"Yeah," she said.

I never saw John again.

Now I had the hard evidence of how Rob's ibra' had not only been screwed up but was downright fraudulent, I knew I had to tell him. I took the papers to the prison and showed them to him.

Rob was gutted. At least he was for a second—until that changed to anger. I'd have been angry too in his situation, and anger can lead to revenge, and revenge can be a good motivator for a guy like Rob. Having evidence that he'd been stitched up by FHI helped banish any lingering feelings of loyalty towards them. It helped convince him to see the truth and made him determined to get out.

There was no more suicide talk after that. Things started making sense to him and he started sharing with me what FHI had been saying to him about me. "She asked for more money", "She can't be trusted" and all that kind of bullshit. They'd been playing us against each other the whole time.

My strategies for getting Bevan and Rob out of prison were similar. The plan was to work at chipping away their sentences by exploiting a particular Afghan practice of clemency during Islamic holidays. On most major Islamic holidays, the Afghan president issues decrees allowing prisoners a portion of forgiveness depending on how long they've been locked up. You have to apply for this reduction for your client and prisoners don't even know about it.

It is not easy to get sentence reductions even if you might be entitled to them. The Afghan prison system has a prison board that determines which prisoners are entitled to what decrees, and they have no vested interest in getting it right. If a prisoner applies for it themselves they are often ignored. Having an outside person to argue for you is key. To make matters even harder, the commission has a haphazard schedule, and knowing even when they meet is a job in and of itself. Then, once you get there, it was like court.

I had researched all the presidential decrees that Rob was entitled to while he was locked up and decided that I would argue for them to be applied retroactively. Up until that point, Rob had not been given any sentence reductions so there was a lot of ground to cover. With a little perseverance, we succeeded in shaving down Rob's time to eight remaining years.

Meanwhile, to put together Bevan's defence, I had first to find his court file, a task that proved nearly impossible. Afghanistan has been completely devastated by four decades of war. Everything is being rebuilt practically from scratch. Electronic records don't exist. Everything is still written on paper and those papers frequently get lost. To find Bevan's file I would have to retrace his steps.

Afghan court record rooms are filled with thousands and thousands of files. I spent hours and hours literally combing through them. The files are strapped together with twine in a filing system that only the record-keeper could make sense of. I went through them one by one. When someone gets arrested in Afghanistan, the case is immediately given a file number, which is written down and catalogued. When the person goes to the police station, the case is given another number that is catalogued somewhere else. When it reaches the judges in another building it gets another number.

Sometimes I'd visit a police station or a courthouse and someone working there would tear off a little piece of paper and write the file number on it. That was record-keeping. Then I would have to go look for the file in some other police station, prosecutor's office or courthouse. It was impossible, just insane. I looked in vain everywhere for Bevan's file, but I just couldn't find it.

In the end, I decided that although I'd never find the file, the odd documents I was finding here and there might allow me to build another from scratch. It was a daunting task, but, in the end, one document at a time, I rebuilt Bevan's file for him. We could now explore how to begin reducing his sentence.

Like Rob, Bevan qualified for past presidential decrees issued on Islamic holidays that allowed us to shave time off his sentence. He'd been given sixteen years, but by applying presidential decrees I lobbied on his behalf to get his sentence to less than a year more to serve. There was a snag, however: even after he'd completed his sentence they wouldn't let him go.

On top of his sentence, the courts had levied a US$75,000 fine against him. Bevan was broke. Many people assumed that because he had an American lawyer he must be rich; they didn't know I was representing him pro bono.

I went to the head Attorney-General of Afghanistan, Alako, to discuss Bevan's case. Alako had been the head Attorney-General for years and it was harder to get an appointment with him than it was with many ministers. He wielded a lot of power and people were generally very intimidated by him. I'd read somewhere that he spoke German and liked speaking it when he could, which was hardly ever in Afghanistan.

I had gone to a Catholic school in Milwaukee where the vast majority of my teachers had been German nuns. One teacher, Sister Francis, a particularly strict nun, always insisted that we speak German to her. As a result of this trauma, I still knew a few words.

As I walked into his huge office, I saw Alako for the first time, a heavy-set, looming figure, sitting behind a wooden desk. Like General Balki's office, Alako's office was laden with rugs, Afghan flags and portraits of President Karzai. There were couches on both sides of the room occupied by five large male Afghan prosecutors, who all looked at me with curiosity as I walked into the room.

I extended my hand to Alako and in my best German accent I said:

"*Hallo, guten Morgen. Es ist toll dich zu treffen*" ("Hello, good morning. It is great to meet you").

Alako immediately lit up and started speaking fluent German back at me.

I stared blankly and reverted to my best English.

"I am so sorry, I only know a little German."

"No problem," he replied in English.

The intro certainly lightened the mood, and after talking with him for about ten minutes about the fact that I had successfully argued Bevan's prison time down to where he should be freed, he agreed to write a letter for his release.

"Come back tomorrow at 9 a.m. to pick it up."

"Sure."

"I want to teach you another German phrase," he said.

"Oh yeah?"

"*Ich liebe dich!*" ("I love you"), he said with a big smile as he shook my hand.

True to his word, the letter was ready the next morning. Skipping into Pul-e-Charkhi, I finally held the golden ticket to Bevan's release. I went straight to General Balki's office. I couldn't wait to show him the letter. We really developed a great working relationship over the years and I was practically beaming with pride.

"Here you go," I said confidently. "A letter from Alako approving Bevan's release."

Balki slowly read it.

"Good. Very good."

"So am I just going to take this to Block 15 to start the process after you sign it?" I asked.

"No problem," he replied. "I will just radio the commander to come here."

A few minutes later the block commander came in and Balki handed him the letter. The commander read it then he and Balki began arguing in Dari. Obviously I couldn't follow, but I could sense from the body language that the commander was getting the upper hand.

Finally, Balki turned to me and said, "Bevan still has to pay his fine so he should not be released."

"Oh no. Since Alako signed for his release the fine is waived, and it's illegal to hold anyone based on a fine."[1] I was trying to style it out.

The commander, Balki and I went back and forth again. But neither man would budge. Both insisted the fine had to be paid. Bevan had no money so that wasn't going to work. Eventually Balki held up a hand.

"There is another way, Kim," he said.

"What?"

"He can be released without paying the fine, but President Karzai has to approve it."

Jesus Christ. "The president?" I wanted to be sure I'd heard right.

The commander nodded his agreement. Balki nodded, too.

The goalposts had suddenly just been shifted to the other side of the pitch, but I had learned long before that once

government officials get something in their head it's impossible to change their minds. I knew there was nothing I could
say to move them. I stood up, shook General Balki's hand
and, trying to keep my cool, walked to Block 15 to give
Bevan the news. It felt like someone had kicked me in the
stomach.

The prison would only release Bevan if President Karzai
signed off. I kept repeating it over and over in my head.
The government would not release Bevan Campbell until the
president said it was okay.

It never fucking ends.

13

LOCK YOUR DOORS AND HIDE

By the first half of 2014, I had been in Afghanistan for nearly six years. I felt that my legal practice in Afghanistan had really taken off. Everything had changed since the early days and I was now comfortable taking on new clients. In fact, there were very few clients I was turning away.

But it could be lonely work. Several times I tried to hire other lawyers to share the growing caseload, but it just never worked out. It wasn't that I had problems recruiting people; I think foreign lawyers, in particular, were often attracted to what they saw as the intrigue of the job. Despite my best efforts to start them off on the corporate cases and slowly bring them over to the more involved work, they always wanted to hit the criminal and human rights cases right off the bat. I used to say to them, "That's fine, but if I'm going to trust you with those cases, you've first got to prove to me that you can handle them."

My test was to take new recruits on a trip to the prisons. I'd have them come with me to meet a client because that's a basic requirement when taking on criminal cases in Afghanistan: you must be able to visit clients in the jailhouse because they can't come and visit you.

Now, I'm not trying to sound like a badass or anything, but when I go to the prison it's just me and my notebook. Once you clear the gates, you're in the pit, surrounded by prisoners. Male prisoners, many of them on serious charges like murder, rape or terrorism. There could be Al Qaeda or Taliban fighters in the same block as your client and there are no guards with guns protecting you. If something happens, it just happens.

So, from a security standpoint, I have to present a different persona when I'm inside the walls of the jail. I have to appear strong or those guys are going to treat me like I'm weak. They don't care what you are or who you are; they work only on *how* you are, so if I go in there with someone acting weak, it's going to negatively impact me. That's going to put me in danger.

But every time I would take these foreign lawyers in with me, I would see it in their eyes: fear. They were scared. The longest any of them lasted was seven days.

Eventually I figured I'd try hiring Afghan lawyers because they might at least know the system better. But that proved more of a problem than a solution.

I took on one local lawyer around the time I had a case involving three foreign teachers. These guys had bought visas extensions in-country, but when they tried to leave the country months later they found out their visas were forgeries. Unsurprisingly, when the first teacher was trying to fly out of Kabul for vacation he was immediately arrested at the airport.

This was the perfect case for my new Afghan recruit to jump in. So I had him shadow me through the process of making a forged visa valid. Visa extension and correction cases are straightforward, the kind of bread-and-butter work that I'd been using to bring in money since the early days, so I knew the process well and we got the first American guy out of jail no problem. One down, two to go: an Italian and another American. We started with the American, and my Afghan recruit and I worked together on the case. I made him follow the blueprint while I supervised, and together we got the American teacher out of detention and home to his family.

So far, so good.

For the third guy, I said, "Okay, since you know the blueprint now, you handle the Italian on your own."

And he did handle it. He made the third client's visa valid and on to a flight back to Rome. I was super proud of him. But that feeling didn't last long. Two days later, I was on my way to a meeting when I heard banging on my front door. I went downstairs to find a whole bunch of police officers standing there, armed to the teeth demanding "their money".

"Um. What money?"

At my office, I slowly uncovered what had happened. Instead of following the blueprint, my new recruit had taken it upon himself to bribe the police and pay money to get the visa fixed.

Of course, I didn't pay. I would never pay, so I had no choice but to fire him. I'm sorry he did it, but that kind of thing puts my life and my reputation on the line. Time and again, when I hired Afghan lawyers, I'd find that they couldn't get the corruption out of their system. And that didn't work for me. I'd worked too hard to develop a good reputation in Afghanistan and it is vital to everything that I maintain it.

I'm hopeful that things can change in time, but until then I decided that it was better to work alone.

Which is exactly what I was doing in my office on a cold March evening in 2014.

I had a lot of stuff going on that month. I was working on Gul Meena's case. She was a young Afghan girl who was forced to marry her husband when she was twelve years old—he was 60. Due to the constant abuse the husband imposed upon her, Gul Meena ran away from home. When her husband found her months later, he along with Gul Meena's brother, visciously attacked her with an axe, striking her more than fifteen times to the point that her brain was exposed. She somehow survived but had unspeakable medical and mental health issues which could not be properly addressed in Afghanistan. Gul Meena needed to get out and I was trying to build her file to convince a country to take her in.

Thankfully, Bevan had finally been released, which had required me to build a file to write a petition requesting a pardon from Karzai. I had to compile good-character references for Bevan from Balki and the other guards at the prison. I also included a letter from Alako. What made it harder was that there was no South African embassy to support Bevan and every step required that sit-down with Karzai's people to advocate for his release. In the end, I was happy with what we had and sent it to Karzai. It wasn't easy—it was over three years of work—but it was worth it when Karzai finally granted the pardon for Bevan's release in which he also waived the $75,000 fine.

Bevan might have been back home, but Rob's case was slowly rumbling on, though mostly I was working through corporate cases. A couple of embassy jobs, a hospital being investigated for malpractice, a few tax cases, contract work. Standard fare, steady work, and I anticipated 2014 would carry on in the same vein. Until that night when I got a call.

The voice at the other end of the line introduced herself as Zoe, a barrister based in London. Zoe said she'd happened to read a piece about me in the British press. She explained that she was representing a British client whose three children had been kidnapped and she suspected they might have ended up in Afghanistan or Iran. The kids had last been seen in the UK with their father over a year prior, and now he was back there in prison on other charges and refusing to cooperate in the search. The parents were estranged from one another and the trail for the kids had gone cold. Zoe was calling to ask for my help.

Sometimes being in Afghanistan can be painful. I often feel like this when I find myself taking on a fresh case. I know it's going to take time and I know it's going to mean me rolling up my sleeves and getting stuck into something new. I think this case was like a certain kind of self-punishment for me. This kind of self-flagellation was becoming a part of my life.

Zoe was still talking, telling me details about the case. The kids were young: two months, three and five years old when they were kidnapped. I understand what being a mother away from her kids is like. I can identify with that. I knew as I listened to their story that I was going to try to find them because I didn't like it: I didn't want another mother forced to be away from her kids like I was.

People have said, "Yeah, but you're different, you've got the choice, you could go back to your kids any time." This pisses me off because they'd never say it if I was a man. The truth is, I can't just leave. Who's going to pay the bills if I go home? Real talk. Who's going to support my kids if I don't work? Claude was studying part-time in law school while looking after our family. In my family, I was the breadwinner and I'd worked hard to get to a place where I was making good money in Afghanistan. Sure, this case wasn't going to be the most lucrative, but I figured it was going to keep me interested while I did the stuff that was.

I'll admit I do get bored sometimes. I needed cases like this to keep me sane while I did all the other less exciting stuff that sent money back home. So I didn't even think about not taking the case of the British kids. I said to Zoe, "Yes, I'll take it. I will help as best I can." Right away, I knew I was going to find those kids.

I told Zoe I needed a couple of days to work out how it should or could be done. I was already starting to formulate a strategy about where I might start, but this was completely new ground for me. Added to that, it was almost Afghan New Year, 20 March, when everything in Kabul shuts down, and many expats take advantage of the break to head home and see their families.

A good friend of mine, Duncan, who worked with the UN, offered me his room at the Serena Hotel while he was away. I never need to be asked twice to stay at the Serena so I gladly took Duncan up on his offer.

I gave Kadar the day off and drove myself through the crowded streets of Kabul, looking forward to a break, but also wondering where I was going to start looking for three British kids. My friends used to warn me about driving myself around in Afghanistan: it's not safe for women, they'd say. But as I mentioned earlier I'd been in-country nearly six years by then and I found it relaxed me to make my own way around the city. Besides, everything in Kabul is monitored with the cabbies reporting everyone's movements, so when I drive myself I actually feel *less* conspicuous, more in control, and safer.

I called Claude, to check up on how things were at home. He was stressed because of his impending mid-term exams and Cherish's latest proposal: a dog instead of money for her lost tooth, which we both laughed about because it sounded suspiciously like the kind of plot her older brother, Seoul, would come up with. After years of working in Afghanistan, my relationship with Claude was at times contentious. We were still very supportive of each other when it came to work and the kids, but being away from the US for so many years had also created an inevitable divide between us.

I rushed Claude off the phone when I arrived at the first security checkpoint about 200 feet from the hotel. The New Year's revellers were already out in full force, celebrating in the streets, dancing, singing and preparing for the countdown. I drove straight through the checkpoint without being checked. I remember thinking it seemed lax, which was unusual at the Serena, where security was probably the best in the country, but I figured the cops and security guards usually stationed there were probably off-duty preparing for the New Year. In hindsight, the absence of security at the checkpoint was doubly strange because Afghanistan also had a presidential election a few weeks later and the run-up had left Kabul especially volatile. Violence in the city had escalated in recent weeks.

But I was more concerned with getting into the Serena and switching my mind to rest and relaxation mode before an important conference call at 9.30 p.m. It's hard to fully relax anywhere in Afghanistan—even at the Serena with its high walls and throngs of guards strapped with AK-47s everywhere, but it's still the safest place in Kabul, so if you can't relax there then you can't relax anywhere.

I parked my car and walked across the courtyard, running through my mental to-do list. My first stop: a steaming-hot bubble bath while relaxing to music, then a conference call to Los Angeles to attend to some business in the US, followed by a drink with some friends at the Gandamack, a restaurant nearby. As the water filled the bathtub, I checked my emails and read the draft contract from the US in preparation for my 9.30 p.m. call.

A little after 9 p.m., I poured a glass of wine and got into the tub, allowing the lavender suds to attack my body. I could hear gunshots outside but didn't give them a second thought; just part of the holiday revelry, I thought. I cranked up my music so that Jay-Z was blasting out of my speakers. The bubbles spilled over the edge of the tub and onto the white marble floor. I closed my eyes and listened to Jay-Z preach through my speakers. My thoughts drifted away to my kids back home. I missed them so much.

My phone rang and I reached over to answer it, irritated that the caller had disrupted a special and rare moment of solitude. It was Brian, the head of INSO, a security NGO that's been operating in Kabul for almost a decade. He was one of the people I was meeting that night for drinks.

"I have to cancel tonight," Brian said. "There's some shit going down at the Serena."

"*What?!?*" I lurched up, water splashing out of the tub. "What's happening at the Serena? I'm at the Serena."

"Why are you at the Serena?"

Then I heard it: more gunshots. I told Brian I'd call him back and jumped out of the tub, still dripping, and went into the bedroom to call the front desk. Busy line. Then more gunshots, this time louder and more frequent.

I called my friend Matthew Rosenberg, a seasoned reporter for the *New York Times* based in Kabul, to ask him if he'd heard about anything going on at the hotel.

"Hey Matt," I said, trying my best to sound calm. "Is there something going on at the Serena because I'm at the Serena."

"Turn off your lights, lock your doors and hide," he said.

I stood frozen in the middle of the hotel room.

I'd faced death threats and had my home broken into and searched. I'd been repeatedly hassled by men with guns. I'd grown up in a bad neighbourhood so the soundtrack of my childhood was occasionally punctuated by ambulance sirens and gunshots at night. But the shots I could hear were close and more threatening than anything I'd experienced before.

I forced myself to ask the one question I already knew the answer to.

"Are they in the hotel?" I whispered. More gunshots.

"Calm down, Kim. They're shooting outside." He lied. "Just stay quiet, hide and I'll call you back." He hung up.

There was no place to hide in that hotel room. Under the bed? In the wardrobe? It was too obvious. I began carefully placing my things in the closet, thinking that if the room looked untouched then it may trick anyone kicking down the door into believing it was empty. Trying to be as quiet as possible, I crept on the floor behind a sofa chair in the corner, my makeshift fort, and hid. All my senses were heightened. I could hear running, doors opening and closing, furniture being dragged about, more gunshots.

The shadows in the room made everything feel even more threatening. Then my Skype started ringing over my computer like a bull horn. *Shit.* I scrambled across the room to slam my laptop shut. But then my mobile phone rang. Double shit. Who the hell was calling?

I answered in a whisper: "Hello?"

"Hey, Kim, we're all waiting for you to conference-in." Nina in Los Angeles said outwardly polite, but clearly annoyed.

"I can't talk." I could barely get the words out. "I'm at the Serena Hotel and it's under attack."

"Oh my God," Nina said. I hung up mid-sentence. This wasn't the time for chitchat.

I was shaking, sirens ringing in my head. I called Matt back determined to get more information.

"Okay, Kim, don't panic. They think there are four gunmen in the Serena."

"What! Where?"

I looked back outside to the courtyard. People were running and hiding, diving behind bushes as gunshots rang out from everywhere. When the gunfire started popping outside my door, my head began pounding and my body started shaking. I pinched myself hard on my bare thigh. "Get it together." I needed to focus. I was getting angry with myself for being weak, for panicking.

It's not like me to panic. In fact, people who let their emotions get the better of them in difficult situations have always irritated me. I've always seen it as a sign of weakness and my mother was very good at instilling that view in me. "This is how people get killed during a crisis," I told myself, "by reacting to their fear instead of trusting their instincts." I closed my eyes and tried to breathe.

Then the footsteps in the hallway grew louder. I jumped at the sound of heavy furniture moving outside my door. Then more gunshots, rapid like firecrackers. I pushed my back hard into the corner, feeling like I could press right through the concrete wall. "I can't die. I can't die," I began to repeat in my head.

Then suddenly I was gripped by something even more paralysing than fear: guilt and . . . *regret*. My thoughts turned to my kids—Deiva, Seoul and Cherish. I thought about all the gifts I'd given them over the years. I thought about how the kids always loved the bedtime stories I made up describing the fantasy worlds we'd travel to. My heart ached and I banged my head against the wall in rage and frustration. I thought of all the mistakes I'd made. Maybe I was wrong to have stayed in Afghanistan.

"I won't die. I won't die," I repeated.

With gunshots ringing in the courtyard below, I suddenly realised I was still dressed in only a bath towel. I was shivering, as much from fear as the cold. My skin was covered in goosebumps. I swallowed hard, my throat dry from the stress. "Goddammit," I cried, pinching myself again on the leg. I wasn't going to be a victim to these bastards. I owed it to my kids, Claude, my clients and, most of all, to myself.

I picked myself up, opened my laptop and called Los Angeles back.

"Are you alright, Kim?"

"No, we're still under attack," I replied. "But, frankly, I need to get this off my mind, so I would like to have the conference call now if everyone is available." Nina gets everyone on the phone and we take care of business.

An hour later, conference call over, sitting in a chair, staring out into the courtyard, my phone rang again.

"The attackers are all dead, but they have murdered nine people," Matt said. "It's over."

But it wasn't over. I still had three British kids to find.

14

OKAY, BABY. BREATHE. SLOW DOWN.

I sat in my office looking at the big map of the country hanging on the wall. Afghanistan isn't a huge country—roughly the same size as Texas—but still plenty big enough to hide three kidnapped kids. Where do I even start? I needed a clue, a lead, to begin the search with purpose. I decided to call Zoe in London.

"I need to talk to their mom," I said.

The following day, Zoe organised for me to talk on the phone with the kids' mother, Nikki. I could tell right away that this was a genuine British woman who had endured an abusive relationship. She shared her story with me: from her falling for a good-looking younger man, to their marriage and them having three beautiful boys together. Once the wedding was over, however, the abuse started.

I'd seen this before. It happens sometimes when you get men from Afghanistan coming to Western countries. There's a marriage and then the abuse starts. Now, of course, I'm not saying that all Afghan men beat their wives, but due to the nature of my work I've come across many who have. The problem is that you can't get away with beating your wife in London like you can in Afghanistan. There are criminal consequences to behaving like that in the West that aren't there in Afghanistan. The wife's usually going to call the police, the police will come, and then the man gets pissed off.

And then what do they do?

In bad situations, the husbands often want to find another way to punish their wives. They sometimes do the most abusive and cowardly thing, which is either ostracise the kids or take the kids away altogether. Nikki's husband did the latter.

I told Nikki that if I was going to find her kids, I was going to need her help.

We had already found the boys' travel records. The flight logs showed that they had been flown to Tehran from the UK. But I had to find somewhere more specific to start the search, whether it was an address, or a name of a place, or a relative. It could be something as simple as which tribal region her husband was from, but I needed something that could help me work out which part of the country the kids might be. Nikki had no idea where her boys were.

"Do you have any recent pictures of your husband?" I asked her.

"No. Sorry. No pictures of him in either Afghanistan or Iran," she replied.

Not a single photo. Nothing. I began to have second thoughts. I started to wonder if maybe I had bitten off more than I could chew on this one. I'd just assumed we'd be able to identify something in Afghanistan, find somewhere to start looking, but by the time I hung up the phone I was wondering if I should have taken this case at all.

Something else was bugging me. What would I do if I found the kids? Would I go get them? No. I wasn't going to kick down a door to get anybody's kids. Especially in a foreign country. I would need to follow a process that would allow for me to get these kids legally and extract them safely. Neither Iran nor Afghanistan are signatories to the Hague Convention on the Civil Aspects of International Child Abduction, which meant that were no legal obligations for either country to get involved in this case. That added another layer to an already complicated situation. I was going to have to come up with something new.

I called Zoe again. My plan was that she would argue in the UK courts that I be awarded guardianship of the kids. Because Nikki was in the UK and the father was in jail, we believed that Zoe could make a strong case for me to be made the legal guardian. Nikki had never travelled to Afghanistan before so it was not wise for her to travel here to try to find her children. Getting legal guardianship of the kids was especially important because when the kids were found this would provide me with the legal authority to take custody of them and travel with them. The UK courts agreed.

Now all I had to do was convince the Iranian and Afghan governments that the order should be applicable in their jurisdictions too. That, and work out where they were, of course.

I have a lot of favours stored up in Afghanistan from different people I've helped over the years. I don't have private investigators working for me, but I've done tons of pro bono work for a lot of different people. I met with some of my most trusted Pashtun homeboys who I knew had a better ear to the ground in rural areas than I did. I also hit up some of my trusted contacts in Iran. Together they started to put out the word and before long I had Afghans and Iranians all over the place casually checking for any evidence of three British kids.

Meanwhile, I visited Nikki in London and collected the guardianship papers as well as more pictures of her sons. Meeting Nikki in person, a sweet, motherly woman who desperately missed her boys, made me even more determined to comb the earth for them.

When I arrived back in Kabul and set about getting the documents legalised in the Afghan Ministry of Foreign Affairs, I started thinking that to find the kids I would require the cooperation of the Afghan police, an institution that I generally tried to avoid. So before engaging them, I decided that I would meet with the British Ambassador, Sir Richard Stagg. Because of the work that I had done for the embassy over the years, I had been appointed in 2010 as Her Majesty's Legal Representative to the United Kingdom's Ambassador and Embassy in Afghanistan, a position that I still hold. It gave me a bit of sway with the Brits.

Ambassador Stagg, or Dickie as he liked to be called, was a very social and knowledgeable leader for the British government in Afghanistan. Unlike many diplomats, he's extremely down to earth. He also has five kids of his own, so when I shared the details about the case he was immediately engaged and keen to help.

Soon after I got another call from Nikki. She was sobbing down the line and trying to tell me about a letter she'd received. Eventually she calmed down enough to get the words out.

After Nikki's husband kidnapped the kids he went back to London—without the boys—and was arrested on unrelated criminal charges. Nikki's husband was in prison in London serving time on the other criminal matters, but he still refused to offer any information on the boys' whereabouts. Despite this, I had encouraged Nikki to maintain communication with him on the off-chance he might reveal something.

She had received a letter in the post.

Happy birthday, Mommy, it began. *We all love you but we love our daddy much more.*

It got worse.

Mommy, why are you such a whore?, it continued and was signed, *Love, your son Randy, who you hate.*

I can only imagine how damaging it was for her to receive a letter like that. Of course it wasn't actually from her little boy. It was yet another form of abuse that Nikki's husband had concocted to get at her. And even though she knew that, she couldn't help but feel provoked. I tried to calm her down and explain that the best thing she could do was continue to engage with her husband. No matter how much of an asshole he was, it was important that she maintain that relationship: we needed to continue to keep the door open in case he made a mistake.

Then something occurred to me. I asked Nikki, "Does he ever call you?"

Looking back, I think that was the question that changed the case. Nikki explained that not only did her husband still call her up routinely from the jail to abuse her, but she was still paying his phone bills. We had something.

"I want to see those bills."

Nikki sent me the bills for the past year and it didn't take long to find what I was looking for. Right there, in black and white, were calls to an Afghanistan phone number. Finally, I had a lead.

I'd represented a telecommunications company in Afghanistan so I planned to ask them for help. The problem was that everyone in Afghanistan was on a burner phone because people there don't often register their phones with their addresses. You know a house by the colour of the door or how far it is from the store. There aren't street names like there are in the US, which meant that all we could get from the phone records was a name. But it was a familiar-looking name. The number Nikki's husband was calling from jail belonged to his brother.

By now, the summer had arrived in Kabul and the mood was still tense from what had happened at the Serena Hotel and a Taliban car bomb that exploded outside the US Eggers base. Another attack felt imminent. As it turned out, it didn't hit until September, but it came hard. Six NATO soldiers were killed outside the US Embassy.

The British police had taken statements from Nikki, but if the kids really were in Afghanistan, the case fell outside their jurisdiction. I was still hesitant to go to the Afghan police, but my homeboys' enquiries had thrown up no results so we were running out of options. I went back to Dickie and he suggested that I meet with the British National Crime Agency (NCA) who were delegated to train Afghan police within the National Directorate in Security (NDS). The NDS was the primary law enforcement intelligence agency of Afghanistan, I guess the equivalent of the CIA.[1, 2] Dickie directed me to Mark, the head of the NCA in-country.

Culturally and legally, fathers in Afghanistan have more rights than mothers. Afghanistan's Civil Code Article 218 specifically states that "any child born as a result of marriage belongs to the husband".[3] In addition to this law, Article 249 states that "the care period of a mother to a male child shall be ended when he attains the age of seven".[4] I was worried that the Afghan police officers wouldn't be on our side.

But with Mark helping me, I wondered if we would exert a little pressure. Mark set up a meeting with the NDS so I could do my best to appeal to their sensibilities as human beings. The NDS surprised me. They couldn't have been more receptive and they were immediately happy to get involved.

I shared with Mark and the NDS the name and number of Nikki's brother-in-law. The NDS came up with a plan to trick him into meeting them so that once we had him in custody we could find out what he knew about the location of his nephews.

It was all coming together. If I had been Indiana Jones, then I would have been approaching the Temple of Doom. I could finally see traces of a shiny light, perhaps the treasure, at the end of the tunnel. Unfortunately, like in those movies, there was another obstacle heading my way.

Saturday, 21 June, I'd had a long day of running around meeting with clients, conducting investigations—it was like the bad old days when I had the caseload of a public defender. It was a stifling-hot day and I wanted to end it with takeout and an ice-cold glass of wine. I like to eat while I grind through paperwork in the evening at home. It should be a quiet time, but it's always the time everyone in the US decides to call me.

Because they're half a day behind and they never care what time it is in Kabul, they call at any time of night. So as I was turning in for the night at around 2 a.m., my phone kept buzzing. First Claude's sister and then another call from my sister, Jade. I ignored them because I was tired and I needed to sleep. I'd call them back the following day. Then the phone buzzed again, only this time it was my daughter Deiva. The whole family was back in Milwaukee on vacation so that was unusual.

I picked up the call to hear Deiva crying. She was trying to tell me something, but she was so upset that she couldn't speak.

"Okay, baby. Breathe. Slow down," I said.

She eventually managed to stop crying long enough to tell me. "Daddy's been shot in the head . . ."

Time stopped.

That was all the information she had. She'd been staying with relatives while Claude was out at a high school reunion. Now he was in a hospital having taken a bullet to the head in a botched carjacking. What kind of state he was in now was anybody's guess. I tried to calm Deiva as best as I could and got off the phone.

I immediately got up and got dressed. Since the electricity at my office was sketchy at best after someone had cut the supply a couple of months earlier, I called my friend Nathan Hodge at the *Wall Street Journal* to ask if I could go there. I drove across Kabul running scenarios through my head. I was pissed. I was mad at myself for not being there, for letting this happen. I couldn't even think about the guy who'd shot Claude, I had too little information. All I knew was that he had been shot in the head; I couldn't process that another person had even done that. The thing I could process was that he's going to die and the only place I could focus my anger was on myself.

Around 4 a.m. Kabul time, I got some good news: Claude wasn't dead. The bullet had gone in through one side of his cheek and out the other side without hitting his brain on the way. He wasn't good, but he was alive.

In the *WSJ* office, I was able to Skype to Deiva's phone. She handed it over to Claude. He was in his hospital bed, heavily bandaged, slightly medicated, and could barely talk. Even still, he found some words for me.

"Did you do this?" he joked.

At least I hoped he was joking.

Claude and I had separated. We were headed for divorce in the new year. We had told the kids, and although we were still living together while we worked out the details, the relationship was over and we both knew it.

Still, seeing him there in that hospital bed, knowing that he'd been shot, what was I to do? We'd have to put the divorce on pause. I had to go and make sure he was alright. I had to make sure my family was okay. I needed to make sure my kids were okay. There was no doubt in my mind that it was my responsibility to help Claude get back on his feet. That was priority number one and everything else would have to wait.

A few days later I was back in Milwaukee, ready for war.

15

IRON DOE

Claude had been back in Milwaukee that summer for his high school reunion. It was the first summer in a long time that we had decided to visit Milwaukee. Claude was staying with friends, while Deiva, Seoul and Cherish would stay with their cousins. The plan had been that I would fly in to join the kids the following week, and then Claude would take a trip overseas.

The evening of the shooting, Claude had dropped one of his friends at their house around 1 a.m. He was still parked outside the house when he heard someone tap on the car window and when he turned around he saw a gun pointing at him. Immediately he hit the accelerator. That's when the guy fired the gun.

The bullet shattered the glass on the driver's side, then ricocheted off the door frame back into the car and ping-ponged through the car, slowing down enough not to blow

Claude's head right off. Instead, the bullet hit his left cheek, went straight through the other side of his face, cracking some of his jawbone and a couple of his teeth on the way, and exited through his right cheek.

In the moments that followed, Claude didn't even realise he'd been shot. He drove away as fast as he could, making sure he wasn't being followed, checking for the guy in the mirror—and then he noticed the blood. That's when he thought, "Oh, shit. Where's the nearest hospital?" Some old memory must have kicked in right about then because he somehow got himself to the hospital at around 2 a.m. He parked the car out the front, walked himself in the door and passed out right there in the lobby.

Claude was losing blood and consciousness fast. While he was lying on the ground, he said that he remembers motioning for the doctors to push him over on his side as he was afraid that he was going to choke on his own blood. In the midst of all that, one of them was trying to cut off his jeans. When they pulled out the scissors, Claude started swatting the guy away.

"Don't cut my Trues! [True Religion Jeans]," Claude managed to say. With his remaining strength, he helped the doctors take off his jeans. His beloved Trues had been saved. Then he passed out again.

Milwaukee is fucked up. We moved away because it's fucked up. When Claude finally woke up the next day, he was in a different hospital and both of his hands were secured to the bed. The doctors obviously assumed that a black guy with a bullet hole couldn't possibly be a victim. They didn't even bother looking in his wallet for his driver's licence, and on his charts the doctors renamed Claude "Iron Doe". I would like to say that this was all a misunderstanding; that the hospital did not racially profile Claude. However, when he asked to use a telephone, the nurses refused to give him one. By then it was 5 p.m. the following day, which meant that for over fifteen hours no one had heard from him or knew where he was.

It was only when Claude, barely able to talk, asked a passing visitor if he could use their phone that he was finally able to inform anyone who knew him where he was. The only number Claude knew by heart was his sister's. She worked out it was Claude as he mumbled: "Shot in the face. Froedtert [hospital]."

They operated on him that night while I was still in Afghanistan. I was working out how to get back as soon as I could at the same time as calling the hospital to check when he was getting out of theatre. I was angry and went into lawyer mode, making Claude tell me everything that had happened. I basically started deposing him while he was still lying in his hospital bed covered in bandages. I needed all the information. When I realised he wasn't going to die, I started to think that we needed to find out who did this. So I called the local police department.

The police knew nothing. I had basic questions for them about the crime scene, witnesses, standard procedural kind of things, but they hadn't done anything to find out that stuff. They had dismissed it as just another black-on-black shooting and only gave me the "it's under investigation" response. They even refused to give me the name of the person in charge of the case. They were acting as though Claude was just another black guy who'd been shot.

So I called Claude's best friend, Scott, who he'd dropped off the night he was shot and asked him to visit the crime scene. He called me from the exact spot where Claude had taken the bullet.

"What do you see?"

Scott walked up and down the street describing the scene to me in detail. He described the shattered glass on the ground and the car bumper lying in the middle of the road. I realised that Claude must have hit the other guy's car and knocked it off as he drove away.

"Take photos," I said to Scott.

Step by step, Scott and I did the police work that should have been done by the real police. Him in Milwaukee, me in Afghanistan. This was all vital evidence that had been ignored by the cops and it made me even more pissed that they hadn't visited the scene to investigate. It was time to make some noise.

I called the police again to share the evidence that my "investigator" had found at the scene. I asked them why I was able to find more evidence than they could when I was in Afghanistan. They became slightly more interested after that and finally gave me the name of the detective in charge. I called the mayor's office, the senator's office and even the governor's office. I called every media outlet I knew. I was going nuts.

Making noise works. It's part of my strategy in Afghanistan when I need it. I don't always use the media, and sometimes it's better to operate under the radar, but when I do need it I use it. And it's no different in the US. I was on the plane home when I started to see a change. In-flight wi-fi is a great thing. I was asked to write an op-ed piece comparing crime in Milwaukee to Kabul. I had a perfect public platform to express my rage. And I went nuclear. The piece ended: "Milwaukee, you need to do better." By the time I landed, the police were calling me with updates.

I called Deiva, who was still very upset, and she gave the phone to twelve-year-old Seoul.

"Hey, baby, how are you doing?" I asked.

"I'm fine, Mommy. How are you?"

"I'm good, thank you. Listen, how are your sisters doing?"

"I think we need to stick together, so we're all going to stay at Uncle Jay-sun's house," Seoul said, clearly taking charge of the situation.

"That sounds like a really good plan, Seoul. Protect your sisters. Love you," I said.

"Love you, too," Seoul replied, ending the conversation. It made me sick to my stomach. Seoul sounded like me.

Back in the United States, I think I'd started to transfer a little of the anger I felt at myself on to the police force in Milwaukee. Milwaukee has a lot of shootings. The US has a lot of shootings. But this was Claude. Don't stereotype him. This wasn't just another black-on-black shooting. I was angry that they'd tied him to the bed, not given him a phone, not checked his documents to see who he was, and then I'd come up against this "I don't give a fuck" attitude in my home town. I get enough of that in Afghanistan. I certainly was not going to take it in the US.

It was a strange reunion when I got home. Claude was already out of the hospital because they don't like to keep you in longer than they have to in the US. Shot in the face? You're out in a few days. And Claude is tough. Really tough. My kids are tough, too. They seemed to all be taking it in their stride; it was just another thing that the Motleys had to deal with. We weren't tripping about it, but Claude and I were supposed to be separating. We weren't supposed to be seeing each other during this period.

We'd come up with this whole plan for how our separation would work. Claude was a few months away from graduating from law school, which meant he could focus on getting a job. That would take some of the pressure off me so I could spend less time in Afghanistan and more time with the kids. The end goal was a 50/50 share, which would give the kids some stability and allow us both to build our new lives apart.

But I guess life had other plans for us. It wasn't that Claude needed me to nurse him. He was up on his feet in days and walking around, as if to say, "I'm fine. Let's just find the dude." So that's what we set our minds on doing.

The op-ed I'd written had led to lots more press. With the governor, senators, mayor and the media involved, the detectives started calling me. They came to the house a week after the shooting to ask Claude to identify some pictures of potential perpetrators. At first, Claude was worried he hadn't seen enough of the shooter to identify him, but soon his memory started coming back. When the police turned over the picture of fifteen-year-old Nathan King, Claude knew right away. That was the kid who shot him. The police didn't look surprised. They knew Nathan King. They knew him because he was in hospital nursing a gunshot wound.

Victoria Davison is a Milwaukee woman. She worked in a hospital and often worked late shifts. The night after Claude was shot, Victoria left work and pulled up in her driveway outside her house. As she got out of her car, she looked up and saw two guys approaching her. They attacked Victoria and wrestled her to the ground. Victoria, armed with a gun, managed to pull her firearm out in the melee and shot one of them. The other guy jumped in a car and drove away, abandoning his wounded friend on Victoria's lawn. It was Nathan King. Victoria called the police and an ambulance whisked him away to the same hospital Claude was in.

Nathan King confessed to the police that he and his friends were behind hundreds of carjackings in Milwaukee. He also confessed to having shot Claude and attacked Victoria. He was the youngest in the group and the only one without a prior record. The bullet from Victoria had left him paralysed from the waist down: he would spend the rest of his life in a wheelchair.

The final insult was that while Claude lay in his hospital bed, hands tied, refused a phone and treated like a criminal, a few hallways down King had been allowed to keep his phone and was posting pictures of himself and his friends on Facebook. The pictures showed him holding a gun, which his friends had brought into the hospital.

King turned sixteen and his trial was scheduled for the juvenile court because he was still underage. Under Wisconsin law, a minor tried in that court could expect a sentence that held them until they were eighteen. Two years for what he did to Claude.

When Claude saw me going after King, I think a part of him was angry at me for taking over as I sometimes do. But I just didn't want Claude to be a victim. I was fine with him being mad at me, but at the same time I knew he was angry at the kid too and he wanted justice. I wanted to empower him, like I do my clients. I wanted him not to be a victim but a survivor.

A month after the shooting, we were in our car driving through a neighbourhood in New York City and we were both super jumpy. I realised then that we were in the same boat. I still had a little PTSD from what had happened at the Serena and Claude was showing signs of it from his shooting. We were like two crazy people. For me, the best way to let that go was to focus on his case. Not just for Claude but for our kids too. Because everyone in our family was shot that day. We didn't all have the physical injuries, but we were all hurt.

By now I'd been away from Afghanistan for the longest time since 2008. I knew that King's sentencing was going to take months. In the meantime, I had a family to support and Claude's medical bills were running into the hundreds of thousands of dollars. There was no getting around the fact that I had to go back. We needed the money and Afghanistan was the only place I knew where to find it.

My clients in Afghanistan were starting to ask me when I was coming back, too. Rob was becoming more impatient by the day. Added to that, the British kids were still missing, and I wasn't going to forget that I'd made a promise to their mother that I'd find them. Now more than ever, I could feel how Nikki must be feeling. My family had nearly lost one of our own but she'd lost three of hers. I couldn't just abandon her.

Then I got a call from Kabul. The NDS had found the boys' uncle.

The NDS explained that they had "persuaded" the uncle to reveal what he knew about the boys' location. That's when I realised that these guys were involved in this case emotionally just like I was.

I flew back into Kabul to find a lot of people acting as though I was never coming back. Some of my competitors had even started approaching my clients telling them that I'd decided to pack up and leave. That's the thing with what I'm doing in Afghanistan: if I'm not there then the business is going to get taken over by the lawyers who are. I was going to have to work even harder to get things back on track again, but first I had to find out what the NDS knew.

I asked them to keep holding the brother until I got in-country. He had lied during his initial detention, which was enough to charge him and justified holding him longer. We were all keen to prevent him from sharing information that could place the boys in danger. Time was running out.

From the brother's interview and the father's phone records, the police had a strong suspicion that the boys were being held somewhere near Kunduz in the north of the country. Along with the British NCA, we began to liaise with the chief of police in Kunduz. It was time to put an extraction strategy in place.

On the night of 11 August, the operation was a go. Mark and I were on standby on the runway in Kabul ready to fly in to Kunduz, while the NDS and the local Kunduz police raided the house where they suspected the kids were being held. It felt collaborative in a way Afghanistan rarely does, I think because for once everyone could agree both legally and morally that what had happened to those kids was wrong. I said to the chief of police, "Imagine if someone did this to your sons. Imagine how that would feel. And this guy who did this is a criminal. He's in jail." I got him pretty hyped up to the point where he was saying, "Yeah, this is bullshit, let's do this." It felt good.

The only person left to tell was Nikki. I'd delayed it because, first, I didn't want her to get excited until we had the kids in custody and, second, I suspected that her reaction would be to fly out, which was a bad idea. It's heartbreaking to say it, but I was sure those kids would have been brainwashed into hating their mother. They'd been living a different life for eighteen months with unscrupulous people. A reconciliation before we had them back with us was out of the question. Of course, I'd eventually need

Nikki to identify the kids, but I made the call to leave that to the last minute. That minute was when I got the call from the chief of police in Kunduz to say he had three boys in his custody—and by his custody, he meant at his own house. He was taking this personally. It was time for the moment of truth. He emailed me pictures of the boys and I forwarded them to Nikki.

"Are these your sons?"

Nikki was hysterical. She was so happy she couldn't control her emotions. Who could in that situation? As I predicted, she wanted to fly straight out to Afghanistan to collect them, but I counselled her against that. Better to let me take them to her. I'd fly them to the UK as soon as I could get everything in order.

We took off for Kunduz. I had been working this case for five months. It was a rare moment of happiness in what had been the craziest year of my life. I couldn't believe this had actually happened. I felt great. Against the background of everything at home, I realised I needed this. I really needed it.

Now, you might expect those kids would be super happy and smiling because they'd been released and were heading home to their mom. But you'd be wrong. Very wrong. They were pissed. Three dirty, hungry, angry little boys were who greeted me. They had been held captive for over eighteen months. The police chief brought them to meet us, and I walked right up to give them a hug, some sign of kindness, a smile to let them know that I was someone trustworthy, but right away they started lashing out at me. It was like I was kidnapping them. They weren't the same kids who had left the United Kingdom. They weren't even speaking English. They had to be physically carried onto the plane, one by one. By the time I finally got them all on the plane I had scratches all over my face from the boys fighting against going with me.

Back in Kabul, there were no social services to greet us. Instead we drove from the airport back to my place in my car. On the way, the eldest, now seven years old, actually lowered his window and started yelling, "Help! Help!"

It was going to be a long night.

First up, I needed to feed the boys so I put out an array of food for them to eat. They just looked at it and, in an act of extreme defiance, walked out of the room without taking a bite. After I finished eating, I showed them their rooms. I lived on my own and had two spare rooms, all furnished. But they all climbed into the one bed. They didn't speak to me. They didn't acknowledge anything I said. They just went to sleep.

I lay in bed that night wondering what I was doing. I'd left my own three kids back in the US again and now here I was with three kids in my care who belonged to someone else. Never mind that I somehow had to get them onto a commercial flight back to the UK. As things stood, they were still a million miles from being ready for that.

The next morning, I came downstairs to find them all sitting up at the table devouring the food I'd left out the night before. I didn't make a big deal of it. Just poured three glasses of milk, set them on the table and quietly left the room. I figured I'd let them come to me in their own time.

Later that day, I went shopping and bought them all toothbrushes, which they got excited about. I've never seen kids so enthusiastically brush their teeth. I ran a bubble bath and the boys, with toothbrushes still in hand and fully clothed, all jumped in. It was hilarious. Finally we'd made a breakthrough. They were beginning to trust me. Soon I hoped they'd trust me enough that we would be able to leave Afghanistan.

I finally won them over the next day. I had been invited by David Loyn to the house the BBC runs in Kabul. David, a father of two boys himself, was interested in meeting the kidnapped boys. David was the chief correspondent for the BBC in Afghanistan and this house had a pool. At the end of the day, David persuaded me to stay over. It didn't take much persuasion: I was exhausted. The boys were exhausted, too. So that night we all just passed out in bed. And in the morning I heard them calling me, "Kim. Kim." That was another breakthrough. But then, "Food. Food." The eldest boy was speaking English again. Okay. Now I knew we were really making progress.

Over the next few days we all really bonded. The boys began speaking more and more English as I prepared the paperwork for their return to the UK. I was feeling more confident now that they'd trust me enough to get on a plane together. What was going to happen after that was anyone's guess.

As I was readying myself to make the trip to Britain, and then back home to the US, I got a call from Claude. He was really pissed. King was still posting pictures of himself on his Facebook page holding up a gun. It also seemed that he was still hanging with the same crew and he'd even been involved in another attempted carjack despite being out on bail in a wheelchair.

That's when we both flipped. Claude said to me, "This kid can't go to juvenile court, he's not taking what he did seriously. Even now, he thinks he can just shoot someone and it's all cool." So we decided to push to get him waived to adult court where he could get real time. I was thinking, "You want to be a thug? Well, you're welcome, we're going to let you be a thug in adult court." Once again, it was time for me to get back to Milwaukee.

Usually in Milwaukee you don't have a lawyer represent a victim in a criminal case, but it can be done. In fact when I was still working as a public defender I was surprised it didn't happen more often. But I knew I could represent both Claude and Victoria. That put me in the middle of the action from where I could start to influence what was going on.

From my office in Kabul, I put in a call to the District Attorney in Milwaukee to push for the adult court waiver. She kept insisting that juvenile court was the right path, but I couldn't accept that. It wasn't that Claude wanted him to get twenty years, but he needed King to realise that there were serious consequences for what he had done. We were getting reports on King the whole time, including several violations of his bail conditions. Finally, the DA agreed and King got waived into adult court. I was sure as hell going to be there to make sure it went right.

I packed up the British kids and arranged with Nikki to meet in the UK. Nikki still hadn't even spoken to her sons. During their time in captivity in Kunduz, they had been told that she had abandoned them and had been abusive to them when they were babies. I knew it would be an uphill battle convincing them otherwise so I'd discouraged her from talking to them until they were home. Nikki wasn't happy with that, but that's the thing: I'm not there to make her feel better, I'm there to get her boys back home.

I wish I could say that it was a tender and emotional reunion, and that everybody cried tears of joy, and that

I felt warm and fuzzy on the inside at what happiness I'd brought to this family . . . But it wasn't like that. It was complicated. Of course Nikki was crying and very emotional, but the kids didn't want to go to her. They were holding onto me and saying that they wanted to stay with me, which I think was very hard for Nikki to hear. It made me feel bad, too, because I had to tell them that I was leaving.

Nikki and her boys had their own path to follow to rebuild. I'm happy to report that they've got there. Nikki is a good mom and she updates me about how they're happy and thriving, which makes me feel good. Although what makes me feel really good was what happened next in the story: a call I received days later.

My success with the British kids hit the international press and no sooner had I returned to Afghanistan did I get a call from an Australian solicitor. She wondered if I could help her with a similar situation. She explained to me how she was representing an Australian woman whose kids had been abducted by their father and were missing, presumably somewhere in Afghanistan or Iran. The father was now in jail for an unrelated crime and was being uncooperative. The similarities to the British case were striking.

Part of what I'm trying to do in Afghanistan is establish blueprints that can in time become effective precedents. It's vital that the country establishes a system of case law as it relates to areas where there's never been case law before, and child abduction is a great example of that. I had worked hard to return the British kids and I felt I had a template that I was actually excited to see if we could make work again. If we could, we could show other people how to deal with this issue in the future.

There is no Australian special police force equivalent to the NCA in Afghanistan, but the British NCA were happy to advise the Australians and the local police on what they had to do. The main thing we'd learned from the last time was to aim our searches towards the father's immediate family. Once the police had successfully tracked down the father's brother, I had the Australian Embassy call him. And, just as we expected, he had the kids in his care.

The only complication this time around was that the brother wanted to do a deal; in exchange for returning the kids, he wanted an Australian visa for himself. The official Australian Embassy position was clear; they didn't do deals like that, but I implored them to play along. The agreement they struck was that if the uncle brought the kids to the embassy then an official would be there to discuss his visa application. In fact, there were a lot more people there to welcome him.

Two days later, the Afghan police, Afghan NDS, embassy staff and I were parked in vehicles surrounding the Australian Embassy. We each took up positions in cars parked strategically around the barriers and waited until the uncle's car pulled up. Then we swooped, officers racing towards the car from every angle.

It ran like clockwork, every step identical to what we'd done before. Two hours later, I had the children in my custody, the uncle was threatened with kidnapping charges unless he dropped his claim (which of course he did), and two weeks after that I was on another flight, this time to Perth, with another set of children in tow.

The whole process felt a lot less stressful. That's significant. It felt easier because we'd done it before, and if we have to do it again, which we will, it'll feel easier still. What's more, another lawyer could now follow the path that we've made for this type of situation. Everyone involved now knows how to play their part to perfection, and I hope that the result is that the next Afghan man who wants to kidnap his children away from their mother will think twice before he does. But if he doesn't, we have a much better chance of getting them back.

I rarely shared details of the existential problems that I face with my cases with Claude and the kids because I never wanted them to worry. I knew the more I told them, the more they'd want to know, and I wasn't comfortable with them finding out about the threats I'd received and dangerous situations I'd been in. So, for at least the first five or six years (until Deiva worked out how to Google me), I always tried to hide my work from them and refused to take Afghanistan back home.

I'd never really told them what was going on with the British kids, or the Australian kids either. I guess I also didn't want them to feel jealous. I'm not sure if that was the right thing to do, but it's what I did, and since I was also feeling so guilty about everything that had happened back home, it felt easier to keep it quiet.

16

A MAN OR A MONSTER?

I was sitting quietly outside the Milwaukee courthouse, composing my thoughts, waiting for Claude's case to be called. It was the day of Nathan King's sentencing.

It was the first time I would be practising in a US court since leaving for Afghanistan seven years earlier so I was a little nervous. I always get nervous before a big court hearing, but I find that listening to music calms me down and helps me focus. This hearing, however, was different. It was personal, and there were so many family members present that I didn't even get a chance to put on my headphones.

The media were out in full. Claude's case had generated some press; there were reporters and TV-news crews lined up outside the courtroom. Everybody wanted a comment, but I batted them off. I only engage with the media after court is finished, and even then only if I think it's in the best interests of my client.

If I had talked to those reporters honestly it would not have been pretty. Half an hour earlier, Claude and I had had a heated conversation about what length of sentence he wanted Nathan King to get. Claude told me he wouldn't be happy with anything less than fifteen years, which I disagreed with.

It was remarkable how strong Claude had been up to now. It had been an uphill battle, but he'd tried his best to soldier through it. For the most part, he'd chosen to put a positive spin on the situation. He'd even started organising events to promote rehabilitation for victims of gun violence and help bridge the gap between the community and black youths who'd fallen into criminality. I felt that asking a court to send a sixteen-year-old to prison for fifteen years wasn't consistent with his messaging.

"You have to ask yourself what kind of person do you want to come out of prison," I said to him. "Do you want him to be a man or a monster?"

Claude was my client and I would vigorously argue for whatever punishment he wanted, but it seemed to make more sense to argue for a lesser sentence and suggest significant rehabilitation programming be attached to it. I felt Nathan could benefit from anger-management and General Educational Development courses, and drug rehab. A longer sentence only increased the chance of him ending up the apprentice of some hardened criminal. I understood that Claude wanted justice, but at the same time it's difficult to try to empower the community if you're also trying to punish it. Whether you like it or not, Nathan was a part of the community and that was the bigger picture.

Ultimately, Claude agreed, and we decided to argue for a five-year prison sentence with programming, but the problem was that all the back and forth it had taken to get us there had left me feeling a little edgy.

The clerk came outside to call us in. It was show time. On my way into the courtroom, a woman stopped me.

For months and months we had been approached by various people in Milwaukee wanting to express how sorry they were about what had happened, or to offer us support, so I wasn't surprised to see a pretty middle-aged black lady reaching out to me. I was already anticipating what she was going to say.

She began to offer her sympathy for what had happened. I said thank you and smiled. It's nice when people take the time to make contact. She even reached out to give me a hug, which was when I thought she looked familiar.

"I'm so sorry, Kimberley," she said my name with a real familiarity.

The only people who call me Kimberley are my family.

"I couldn't believe it when I heard what happened to Claude, I was so sad."

I smiled, looking closely at her face, desperately trying to remember this woman.

"I'm Nathan's grandmother," she said.

I stepped back, holding up my hand. "No. Stop." I wasn't ready to engage with Nathan's family.

"Don't you remember me?" she asked, looking for some recognition in my eyes.

Now I was confused. "No," I said defensively.

"I'm Willy's wife."

Boom. Time stopped again. Willy is my uncle.

This woman was married to my uncle, which meant that Nathan King and I were some sort of distant cousins.

I just shook my head. *You've got to be fucking kidding me.*

"Thank you," I said. "But I really have to go."

It felt like this whole thing couldn't get any crazier. It also felt even more like this was a crime against the whole community. Nathan King had acted like a thug, but more than that he was an irresponsible idiot. Right there in front of me was the proof that under all the stupid violence there was a beating heart of a real community. Milwaukee was better than Nathan King thought it was and it made me even more determined to stand up in that courtroom and argue for a fair sentence for him.

It was clear in my mind what I wanted to achieve as I walked into that courtroom. It felt good and bad to be back there—bad, of course, because of the circumstances, but good because somehow it felt like home. The benches, the jury box, the smell of the room all came flooding back to me. I'd spent so many years of my life there. Even the judge presiding over the case was a former prosecutor who I'd stood against when I was working at the Public Defender's Office. We'd had a great working relationship. I stood, taking it all in for a second, when Nathan King's lawyer approached me.

"I just want to say how sorry I am about what happened," she said, shaking my hand.

I was a little stunned. I would never do that before a case. She was nervous: no other lawyer in Milwaukee had wanted to represent Nathan. I think other lawyers had also avoided the case.

When court finally got in session, I asked the judge to sentence Nathan to five years in prison. I argued that rehabilitation could positively impact his life and said that we believed that there were programs that he could benefit from.

I told the court that while Claude felt Nathan should be punished, he firmly believed that punishment should come with an opportunity for rehabilitation.

Every time we had seen Nathan over the previous months, he refused to make eye contact with any of us. He would sit silently in his wheelchair, looking down at the floor. But this time, after I'd finished making my arguments, he turned and looked up at me, nodded and said, "Thank you."

I have wondered what would have happened to Nathan if I had been his lawyer that day. First of all, I would have challenged the confession he made at the hospital to the police. He'd just been shot, he was emotional, on meds, he didn't have a lawyer or his parents present—his confession should have been challenged. The state of mind of a fifteen-year-old kid right after he'd been shot was clearly suspect. I would have tried to work a deal to have him plead guilty to a lesser charge in return for cooperation with the prosecution. I would have compiled reports from teachers and family to show his good character. I would have allowed for more time between his plea and sentencing dates to let the media cool down. I'd have made sure he had a better chance at a future.

But I wasn't there to represent Nathan.

Deiva wanted to say something to the court. Part of the reason I had wanted to move my family away from Milwaukee in the first place was to avoid them ever becoming part of the system—and yet here we were, in the system. It made me sick.

Deiva stood up, full of nerves, and began to speak on behalf of her brother and sister. Suddenly I realised that she'd prepared her statement on her phone. I couldn't believe it. I sat there almost laughing to myself, wondering why she hadn't written it out on paper. It drives some judges crazy if a lawyer dares to pull out a phone in court.

Deiva began by talking about what a good dad Claude was, which was sweet, but as she found her stride, speaking up loud and proud, there was a more serious message.

"I'm seventeen," she said, "and I don't go shooting people. I don't carry a gun. Being seventeen is not a good enough excuse; being young and stupid isn't good enough. I don't do that; my friends don't do that; my brother, my sister, my cousins who are here today—we're all young and we don't do that. Even though you're young, you're still responsible for your actions."

And then she sat down. I was so proud of her: not just because what she said was right, but because she was talking on behalf of our whole family. She nearly lost her dad; her brother and her sister nearly lost their dad, and she wanted to tell everyone how she felt. I could see the budding lawyer in her.

I was still in lawyer mode so I had to keep it together. Everyone else might have been crying, but I never cry in court. I always thought I would probably quit as a lawyer if I ever cried in court. I'm not trying to say that like it's a badge of honour, but it's just not my style. Imagine having a lawyer who cries in court. How ridiculous would that be?

It was Claude's time to speak. He spoke in a very low, slow, measured voice as he tried to keep it together. While the physical scars were healing, there was still a lot of psychological scarring that would take longer to mend. He hadn't prepared a speech so he spoke from the heart about how this had affected him and our family. He told the court how he thought about the kids while he was lying on the ground, wondering if he was taking his last breath.

"I want the court to limit Nathan's sentence to five years in prison because I see a lot of him in myself," he said. "He deserves a chance."

It was a passionate, strong and selfless speech.

The whole experience felt like deja vu. I was transported back to David's case and the barbershop shooting in Milwaukee all those years before. From the lawyer approaching me, to sixteen-year-old Nathan silently crying throughout the hearing, to the courtroom packed full of families for and against the defendant. The similarities were stark and I realised that as much as I had tried to shield my kids from Milwaukee we had still become another of its sad statistics.

After all the arguments and statements had been heard, we waited for the judge's sentence. I could tell right away from his face that it wasn't going to be good. You get a sense of these things when you know someone, and everything was telling me to prepare for the worst.

"What you've done is inexcusable in any community that values people. I'm giving way to protecting the community in what I think is present dangerousness," he said. Not a good start. "I am going to impose twenty years on the two counts. Essentially twelve-and-a-half years in prison and seven-and-a-half extended supervision once you are released from prison. So, if my math is correct, Mr King, you'll be in your late twenties by the time your incarceration is over."

I was disappointed. It was too long.

I couldn't help but feel that if this had happened in Afghanistan, Nathan wouldn't have been sentenced to five years. But it's much harsher sentencing in the US. If this had happened on the streets of Kabul, he might have even walked free that day.

As it was, Nathan said nothing. He sat slumped in his wheelchair as the courtroom filled with the sound of his mother's wails and sobs. She cried out, pleading for the judge not to continue, but he did, raising his voice to be heard over her.

"And I think, by then, you'll be much less of a danger to the community than you are now."

Three correctional officers walked to the front of the court and began to wheel Nathan away.

The rest of the courthouse began to silently file outside. Was that justice? I guess justice of a sort had been served, but it didn't feel right and I could tell Claude agreed. He was genuinely upset.

Outside, in the hallway, emotions continued to get heated as Nathan's mother's wails and sobs grew louder and louder. The media were in full force, pushing microphones in our faces, looking for statements from anyone who'd speak. Added to the drama, Nathan had to be wheeled past us back to jail. It was intense.

Finally, we got out of the courthouse and took the first steps into the next chapter of our lives. I felt relieved that it was all over, but I also felt a nostalgia for the US courtroom. I missed its familiarity and I wondered if I wasn't missing a trick by limiting my operations overseas. Could I be an Afghanistan-based lawyer and still take cases in the US, or anywhere else in the world?

In the meantime, it was time to get back to work.

17

WICKED NINJA

I came back to Afghanistan with a vengeance—energised, focused and ready to fight.

I'm always under pressure. I feel it from my family, I feel it from my clients, I feel it from people who want to be my clients. It never ends. Sometimes it feels like I am in the middle of the Atlantic Ocean being pulled in two different directions. When I'm home, my kids are happy and want me to stay, but at the same time I'm getting calls from my clients asking me when I am coming back. It's like I constantly have two voices in each ear.

People might ask how I could go back to a "normal" life after a big family trauma like we'd been through. Some have asked me whether I felt after Claude's shooting that enough was enough, and it was time to reconsider Afghanistan. But I never really saw things that way.

I still had to work. It's not like people who have tragedies in their lives don't have bills to pay. When something bad happens, you can't just quit your job. Sure, Claude was shot, and, yes, we had to deal with it, but I still had my career and my career is how we live. I'm not a money-hungry person, but I do want my kids to live a nice life. I want them to grow up in a safe neighbourhood and to go to a good school. My career is how those things become possible.

Because of the shooting, I had taken a long hiatus from Afghanistan. As a result, we had lost a lot of money and I needed to make up for it. Our insurance wasn't even nearly going to cover all of Claude's medical bills. All the financial gains we had made during the previous seven years I'd spent in Afghanistan were virtually erased.

On top of that, I had my own sense of pride and responsibility to contend with. For me, being a lawyer is not just a job, it's a vocation. I have a responsibility to my clients. I had worked hard for years to grow the business and my client list. You don't just walk away from that. Even after a tragedy. Of course, the work was hard, but it was much harder for my clients who were still imprisoned in Afghanistan. I couldn't walk away from them. I couldn't just abandon people like Rob.

But there was also another reason I found myself flying back to Kabul two weeks after Claude's court hearing. In the seven years that I'd been there, it had become a second home for me. If you travel a lot then maybe you can understand where I'm coming from. Afghanistan is in my DNA. It was as if something chemical was telling me that I had to go back.

Just before eight in the morning the plane touched down in Kabul, and I woke to my phone beeping. My voicemail was already full of messages. I hadn't told anyone that I was coming back, but it seemed that everyone in town knew.

Rob Langdon was already on my mind.

For a few years Rob's attitude dramatically improved and a large part of that was because of Bevan. Bevan was a naturally positive person and had been the perfect person for Rob to be around in Pul-e-Charkhi. They had become like brothers. Rob wasn't nearly as depressed while he had had Bevan, and Bevan had schooled him on how the legal system worked, which helped him focus.

My plan was to chip away at the twenty-year sentence he'd received after his death sentence had been commuted. I wanted to retroactively shave off time using the presidential sentence reductions. Often the sentence reductions don't apply to violent offences, but sometimes you can successfully argue for them. I'd already set the blueprint with Bevan, I knew what I needed to do for Rob.

I went back over each and every decree that Karzai had made during Rob's time inside and gradually, piece by piece, after three years of working on his case I managed to whittle his sentence down to eight years. The next step would be to formally apply for a pardon.

I disagreed with Rob about putting in a pardon application immediately. I knew you shouldn't just put pardon requests in any time you feel like it because, like everything in Afghanistan, there was a method to it and I thought the timing wasn't right.

Unfortunately, after Bevan's release, Rob had returned to being a bit of a problem child in prison. The US troop drawdown in Afghanistan in 2014 had made Rob's security situation inside the prison more vulnerable. Added to that, Rob was now the last Western prisoner in Pul-e-Charkhi and an easy target for the less savoury prisoners he was sharing space with. It was a powder-keg situation ready to explode.

After Bevan was released, Rob started getting into fights with prisoners again, and sometimes even with guards. He was fighting for his life, which was a good sign because he had energy and a will to live, but every fight was another setback on the road to getting a pardon. I needed him to be a good boy for a little while to put some time between the pardon application and his bad behaviour. In the meantime, I would begin to prepare.

It was time to engage with Rob's family again. I asked them to get as many letters together as they could in support of Rob's release. We particularly needed male references— "he's a good son", "he's a good brother"—because this kind of good character is really important in Afghanistan.

We also needed to get the original ibra' documents, which was a real sore spot for everyone. By now, we knew from my meeting with Rob's boss, John, a few months prior that nearly $98,000 of the ibra' money had been stolen by those he had trusted. Even so, these documents were still vital because I wanted to include them as leverage when I argued for the pardon.

Despite the fact that no one had stated in the ibra' document that the victim's family had forgiven Rob, it was at least a sign that he had remorse. Of course it would have been better if we'd been able to show $100,000 worth of remorse, but I figured $2000 was still better than nothing.

In order to argue the pardon, I also needed the backing of the Australian Embassy. Much to my chagrin, Majell Hind, the Australian diplomat who had been instrumental in obtaining the ibra' document, was no longer working in

Afghanistan, so I had to start over with a new Australian diplomatic crew. It was frustrating, but there was no way around it. Six months later, the Australian ambassador met with the president and Karzai agreed to release Rob. The two men shook hands on a promise that Karzai would write the letter.

Unfortunately, he never did.

In September 2014, Afghanistan had its first free democratic elections and President Ashraf Ghani came into power. Ghani, an intellectual, had a reputation for being far tougher on crime than Karzai.

This was demonstrated within the first few weeks of Ghani taking office. A group of Afghans were picnicking at a popular spot in Paghman province and four women were viciously gang-raped by five men.[1] The women survived and the perpetrators were immediately arrested. Though the men had been sentenced to death, Ghani ignored the fact that the men were still fighting their cases in court, and all five were hanged in Pul-e-Charkhi. There was a new sheriff in town.

I knew that I was not only back to square one but I was now on an even steeper hill to try to secure a pardon for Rob. On the positive side, however, another couple of Islamic holidays had passed so I was able to argue for more time off Rob's sentence. He was soon down to serve less than four years.

I met with Ghani's legal advisor to discuss Rob's situation. I was desperate for us to get the pardon and I hoped that, politically, everyone was at least keen to get the last remaining Westerner out of Pul-e-Charkhi.

"There is no law that would allow for this," the advisor said after reviewing the pardon documents.

"I represented another foreigner on a murder conviction and was able to get a pardon for him based on the fact that the victim's family were in agreement. I have provided for you, as I did for the other foreigner, the ibra' documents."

But what complicated Rob's case was that we were both right.

In February 2014, a new Criminal Procedure Code was signed into law by then president, Karzai, which explicitly forbade pardons for those who had committed murder. It did, however, contain one caveat in so far as it allowed for pardons if the "inheritors of the victim waive the convict's punishment".[2] As politely as I could, I tried to argue that, as a result, the law actually supported a pardon for Rob.

Ghani's man wasn't buying it. But he did have an idea.

"We have to create a new law to make this all legal," he said.

"No, we don't. The law already exists." I wasn't happy with that suggestion at all.

He shook his head. His mind was made up, and so that also became the position of President Ghani. In order for Rob to be released, we would need to create a brand-new law in Afghanistan. There was no way of talking them out of it.

So we began to draft a new law to submit for a vote in parliament. It took months, but it was finally ready for a vote. How a bill becomes a law begins with the National Assembly, which consists of an upper and a lower House and 352 parliamentarian seats. In order for this bill to become a law, it would first have to pass the scrutiny of the presidential palace. Once the president felt that it was appropriate, the House of the People could pass the law with a majority vote among its 250 members. Once this happened, it would then need to be passed by the infamous conservative House of the

Elders on a majority vote among its parliamentarians. Then and only then would it become law.

Up until this point, I had tried to keep my Afghan political manoeuvrings to myself. This would be navigating new terrain by becoming openly involved in legislative drafting.

Early drafts of the bill suggested that Rob could be extradited to a prison in Australia rather than released outright, but the problem with that was that Afghanistan could not legally impose its prison sentence on another country. Especially when there were so many due process violations that should have rendered the court verdict invalid, including Rob's forced confession, the absence of any witness testimony, no translators present . . . There was no way that the Australians would swallow it.

But the Afghans were insistent that they would not move forward on the law unless he was extradited. So we played around with the definition of extradition. Generally, "extradition" means the surrender of a criminal by a foreign state to which he has fled from prosecution by a state within whose jurisdiction a crime was committed in order for the criminal to be dealt with according to their laws. We wanted Rob to be flat-out released.

For months, the Afghans and I argued back and forth on this point. Ultimately, we came to a compromise and redefined extradition so that it came to mean that if there is no treaty or bilateral agreement between two countries, as is the case with Afghanistan and Australia, a prisoner may be handed over to another foreign government or their designee who can choose to do with the prisoner as they see fit. Essentially, under our newly created definition of extradition, Rob could be handed over to me, or to the Australians, and he could simply be released.

The Law on Extradition of the Accused, Convicted Individual and Legal Cooperation Article (4)(2) was passed by parliament and signed by President Ghani in February 2016. This was a monumental victory not only for Rob but for any other foreigners incarcerated in Afghanistan in the future. We'd done it.

So was Rob released the following morning? Nope.

I knew after years of practising law in Afghanistan what a battle it can be to have a law enacted. In order to alleviate any discrepancies, a Presidential Decree was still going to be necessary. The Ghani administration tried to resist, but we persisted, and finally Ghani signed to release Rob.

In the decree, President Ghani agreed to the extradition, citing the new law that allowed for "the extradition of Robert Langdon to the Australian Embassy and his lawyer Kimberley Motley".

I never tell people they're going to be released until I know for sure that they're going to be released. Then I show up personally and say, "Let's go." That's how I have always done things because I've been working in Afghanistan long enough to know that prison officials aren't to be trusted. Often they will tell a prisoner they're going to get released on a particular day but there's just one more thing that needs to be signed . . . At that point, they'll demand a bribe. And then if it doesn't happen, they send the guy back to jail. It can make a person suicidal.

Often they'll continue to exploit that desperation, pressuring a prisoner into paying a bribe to grease the final cog. "Pay us $500 and you can go," they'll say. They never miss a chance for a shakedown.

I tell all my clients in Pul-e-Charkhi, "If you don't see me, you're not getting released. If I'm not there, don't believe what you hear. On the other hand, if you do see me, then it's time to bounce."

The night before Rob's release, he called me. I had kept him in the dark about everything we'd been doing to get him out.

"Hey, what's up?" I asked.

"I broke someone's nose," Rob said nonchalantly.

Silence.

"Kim?"

"What. Happened?" I spoke slowly, trying to hide my anger.

Rob had become fond of a cat who he named Shitty. It was his pet in prison and he took care of her religiously. Shitty became pregnant and had three kittens. For no apparent reason, a guard had stomped one of the kittens to death, so Rob broke his nose.

"Okay, I'm sorry that happened," I said when he finished explaining.

"I'm sick of this shit, Kim," Rob replied.

"Hey, when you get out, what is the first meal that you want to eat?"

"Why?"

"Just play along. What do you want to eat?"

"I don't know. Beer and steak?" Rob added, "What do you know?"

"Nothing. Listen, I get what happened, and that is fucked up, but I am begging you. Please. Be. Good."

The next day, I rocked up at Pul-e-Charkhi. Rob was sitting in the prison general's office. He seemed confused.

"It's time to bounce," I told him.

And with that, after seven years of imprisonment and torture, Rob walked out of the prison for the last time. He was a free man.

A week later, we were flying to Australia.

This kind of approach to the law can't be taught. Instead it was something that I was learning on the ground. I think often that the way I practise law is like DJ'ing, and I think it's funny that the thing I do professionally reminds me of the thing I do to relax. I had to adapt to the environment and change my playlist accordingly. The law isn't a straight road; it has twists and bumps and other traffic to avoid. You'll only get where you need to go as long as you're prepared to swerve a little along the route.

I had gotten to know a lot of people in Afghanistan and a lot of people were coming to me for various legal problems. I had people in the government seeking advice on legal issues. Everyone knew I wasn't playing games. And I knew how to get results.

Rob's case epitomised what I had set out to do in Afghanistan on so many levels. I'd won my case despite the bribes, the corruption, the cowboy security contractors and their shady companies. I'd had to adapt to all those corrupt distractions and work within the law. That was the box I had to work in. I felt that the laws that existed were enough to support Rob's release, but I still had to fight tooth and nail to get those in power to acknowledge those laws and exercise their power to release him.

I left Rob in Adelaide and boarded a flight back to the US. I was so tired I couldn't sleep, so I decided to put on a movie. I chose *Toy Story 2*, remembering it was the first movie I had taken Deiva to see when she was a little girl. I remembered how at the end of it the whole theatre gave a standing ovation. While on the plane, the movie had barely even begun before I just started crying. It had been years since I had cried. I had held so much in for so long that it just exploded out of me. I had been on autopilot, fighting for Rob and all my other cases, without a break, for too long. I was physically tired, and mentally exhausted. I knew that I needed to address some things within myself.

I knew that I was working too hard. I needed to check in with myself more often, I needed to exercise more, get more sleep, take better care of myself. I needed to pay more attention to what was going on inside me. From now on, things were going to change.

When I finally got home, Seoul was very happy to see me. He had looked up our names on a Wu-Tang Clan name generator website. Apparently his Wu-Tang name was Phantom Watcher, while mine was Wicked Ninja.

I must admit, I still marvel at all the legal gymnastics it had taken for Rob to be released. His journey began with three death sentences before they were commuted to a twenty-year life sentence. I had to fight to get over ten years in sentence reductions, then argue a pardon to two Afghan presidents, create a new law redefining the word "extradition" to mean release, get that new law passed through two Houses in Afghanistan's parliament, and then successfully fight for a specific presidential decree to effectuate Rob's "extradition" to me.

Wicked Ninja indeed.

18

CROCODILE TEARS

I failed.

Two months later I was back in Kabul failing to deliver on every promise I'd made to myself on the last flight home. I wasn't exercising. I wasn't taking care of myself. I was failing because, once again, I was back in Afghanistan and working all hours of the night. And yet I was happy to be failing. I rationalised that as long as I didn't watch any more Pixar movies, I'd be fine.

I had been back in my office one night in March, working late with the news on the TV in the background, when I first heard the name Farkhunda Malikzada. I heard her story in the same way as most people did: a news item about a young Afghan woman who visited the Shah-Do Shamshira shrine and did not come home again. I didn't realise it at the time but her story was one that I would come to know intimately.

A few weeks prior to Farkhunda's visit to the shrine, a sick female friend of hers had visited and bought an amulet from a market stall near the shrine. The stall owner told her that the amulet would help to get over her cold or he would give her her money back. These black magic cure-alls are common in Afghanistan. You can buy potions and amulets that are said to help you get well or pregnant; there're even ones that promise to ensure your next child is a boy. Farkhunda's friend bought her amulet confident that it would cure her.

Unsurprisingly, the amulet did not cure Farkhunda's friend, so four weeks later Farkhunda agreed to accompany her back to the shrine to ask for a refund. Farkhunda was well known among her friends as a devout Muslim. She had previously made it known to her family that she was appalled by the fortune tellers who peddled their charms at a holy place. She felt that they were not only being disrespectful to Islam but that they were exploiting women with their mumbo jumbo.

They found the fortune teller and Farkhunda demanded her friend's money back. The man was in no mood to hand over any cash; he refused, claiming that she must not have followed his instructions correctly.

Farkhunda jumped to her friend's defence. "You are abusing women," she said, "and you are charging them money for something that is not Islamic."[1]

The fortune teller tried to shoo Farkhunda away.

"Who the hell are you? Who are you to say these things?" he shouted at her.[2]

A crowd began to gather and Farkhunda warned them, "Don't buy anything from this man, he is cheating people!"

The stall was located just outside the shrine along the bustling stretch of the Andarabi Road that runs along the Kabul River. By now, it was near 4 p.m., prayer time, and the sidewalk outside the shrine began to brim with throngs of Afghan men, many of them unemployed, bored and looking for something to do. The riverbank is separated from the road by a low stone wall, which becomes a make-shift hangout for gangs of youths and homeless people.

As she continued to lambast the vendor, accusing him of fraud and being a bad Muslim, more people gathered around. Eventually, the illiterate man shouted back that Farkhunda had burned the Holy Quran. If true, this would be an egregious crime in an Islamic country. Of course, Farkhunda immediately denied the vendor's accusation and the two continued to argue.

By now, the confrontation had drawn a good-sized crowd. Some people were even starting to repeat the stall owner's accusation that Farkhunda had burned the Quran. Farkhunda continued to vehemently deny the accusation, but gradually she was drowned out by the ever-increasing number of men shouting her down.

Like pretty much anywhere else on the planet, where there's a public argument, there's always someone ready to start filming it on their phone. As Farkhunda and the fortune teller continued to argue, people began to get their phones out and film what was happening.

I can describe what happened next in detail because I have seen the footage.

Farkhunda is dressed head to toe in black. Her head-scarf only gives her a small slit though which to see her eyes, but you can still make out the look of defiance as men begin to gather around her. The footage shows her being backed into the corner of the store as the crowd becomes more and more angry.

"Why did you burn it?" one man demands.[3]

"I did not burn the Quran," Farkhunda insists.[4]

Another man shouts, "The Americans sent you!"

"Which Americans?" she replies.

The police arrive and an officer tries to take Farkhunda by the hand.

"No," she protests, pulling away. Being touched by a man, even a policeman, is still taboo in Afghanistan.

"She is an infidel," shouts another man from behind the lens, stirring up the tension.

"Do not call me an infidel!" Farkhunda can be heard to reply.

"Kill her!" shouts another man.

Following the order, the angry crowd of men grabbed hold of Farkhunda by the hair and dragged her into the street. Several more men gathered around her, pulling and pushing her around like a rag doll.

Farkhunda, now covered in blood, pleads for her life.

Then someone sucker punches her, knocking her flat out onto the ground. Suddenly a crowd of men begin piling into her, raining a barrage of kicks and punches down onto her head and body.

It seems impossible to comprehend it, but at least twenty people filmed this whole sequence of events on their phones and uploaded the footage to the internet. Later, fearing retribution, many took down the videos. But once online, always online, and the videos were later retrieved and subsequently logged as evidence.

The footage is a shocking example of the ignorance and brutality that permeates the culture in Afghanistan. The clips show a wild mob of angry men stomping on an innocent and educated woman as she writhes about on the ground, desperately trying to defend herself, screaming the whole time, "*Allahu Akbar. Allahu Akbar.*"

Over her cries you can make out the angry shouts from the mob: "Kill her. Kill her." This audio is just as disturbing as the heartbreaking images that accompany it.

The whole time, the camera footage wheels and spins around, capturing momentary images of her killers.

Finally, a police officer fires his gun into the air, dispersing the crowd. A bloodied Farkhunda, miraculously still alive, raises herself to a sitting position. Her veil has been torn from her head and her long black hair, soaked with her own blood, trails across her face. She raises a red, bloody hand to push it away. Dazed, Farkhunda stares up at the camera.

While she tries to get to her feet, another man can be seen pleading with one of the police officers to let him past. "Brother, please, let us have her," he implores.

The policeman pushes the man back. Another police officer, female this time, arrives and demands the crowd step back further, but the mob re-forms with renewed strength. Rumours have spread that a woman has burned the Quran and hundreds more people begin to scream and shout their disapproval.

Two police officers raise Farkhunda up and onto the corrugated-iron roof as the crowd surges again and more men scale the shrine walls, pouring into the area below. The officers try in vain to help Farkhunda escape, but the crowd below starts to pelt her with stones and rocks until she loses her footing and slides back down. A man reaches out and grabs hold of her foot, dragging her into the seething mass of bodies where the beating begins again all over.

Cries of "Defend Islam! Kill her! Infidel!" echo out.

At this point not one person attempts to stop the brutal attack on Farkhunda.

Eventually, the kicking stops and Farkhunda lies motionless on the sidewalk. Somebody appears to check her body before he announces to the crowd that she is dead. The crowd cheers. The police continue to stand, motionless.

The footage pans again and captures the size of the crowd: hundreds of men have gathered outside the shrine. But it doesn't stop there. Farkhunda's body is dragged onto the street so that more men can have a kick at her corpse. Then she is laid in front of a passing car and the crowd screams for the driver to run her over. Back and forth he goes until her body is dragged three hundred feet along the dusty street.

"Throw her into the river" are shouts that can be heard.

Around five hundred men had gathered by the time Farkhunda's body was thrown into the dry riverbed where still more men pelted her corpse with rocks screaming, "Whore, whore."

The horrific scene ends when they set Farkhunda on fire. Burning a Muslim body is the most extreme *haram*, expressly forbidden in the Holy Quran.

Two days later, the Ministry of Religious Affairs declared Farkhunda innocent of the charges of burning the Holy Quran.

Farkhunda's only "crime" was that she dared to confront an Afghan man and publicly humiliate him for being a crook. If she'd quietly accepted the vendor's refusal to return her friend's money and meekly walked away, she might be alive today. Instead she stood up for herself and refused to take no for an answer.

Farkhunda's case was a painful reminder that despite more than a decade of Western intervention and billions of dollars in international aid, Afghanistan remained a profoundly violent and volatile country.

So I was a little surprised to receive a call from a prominent Afghan woman a couple of days later asking if I would meet with Farkhunda's family to discuss their legal options.

My first reaction was to say no. I thought it wise to stay out of what was clearly going to be such a culturally divisive case. I also figured that with hundreds of eyewitnesses and so much videotaped evidence in existence it was the kind of case that could easily be handled by an Afghan lawyer. So I said, "Thank you, but I'm going to just stay out of it." But they insisted.

"Kim, the family needs your help."

"Alright, I will meet them tomorrow before I go to the airport," I said. The next day I was scheduled to go home and I needed a break.

It turned out that no Afghan lawyer would represent Farkhunda's family. Despite all the women's groups protesting, the UN's Human Rights Commission issuing statements and all the media coverage, every single Afghan lawyer had refused to get involved. Only one lawyer had told them he would consider taking the case, but only on the condition that the family guaranteed he would be able to get asylum in the United States. The other lawyers refused out of fear that they would be killed.

I met with Farkhunda's mother, Hajera, her father, Mohammad Nader, and her two brothers at their home. The house was a typical Afghan home in a nice district, not far, in fact, from where my first house in the city had been. I could tell right away that they were not poor. What stood out was that both of Farkhunda's brothers were armed. Guns are common in Kabul, but it's not the norm to see young men wielding them in their own house. They were scared, angry and on edge.

We sat down in their small front room, and while one of her brothers fetched tea Farkhunda's mother began to show me pictures of her daughter. She flicked through the photographs as she talked in a dry monotone.

"I spoke to her on the phone," she said, her voice expressing anger more than grief. "She told me, 'Mother, I'm on my way home.'"

The Malikzadas are a well-educated family. Farkhunda's father worked for nearly 40 years as an engineer for Afghanistan's public health ministry. Her older brother had a job at the finance ministry, while her younger brother was an engineer like his dad. But despite their education they were hopelessly unsure of their legal rights.

I had prepared a written cheat sheet and a roadmap of how the family's lawyer should handle this case.

"You have the right to a lawyer, which means that lawyer is able to represent your legal interests in court. You have the right to sue for money."

The father stopped me. "We don't want money," he said. "They should die for what they did to my daughter."

"Well, that is why it's important to have a lawyer because there are different types of murder charges. They can be charged for murder that has a legal death sentence."

I tried to impress upon them that while I certainly sympathised with their loss, this issue was now in a legal sphere. There was no vigilante justice that I would or could advise them on.

The police investigation began by heading off in a very troubling direction. Instead of rounding up the people who had killed Farkhunda, the police initially focused on investigating whether Farkhunda had actually burned the Holy Quran. It was absurd and infuriating. Farkhunda's older brother explained how officials had visited them the day after his sister's murder and attempted to coerce them into signing a statement that confirmed that Farkhunda suffered from a mental illness. The police said that if they stated Farkhunda's mental illness explained why she had burned the Holy Quran, they would be able to help the family and make the case go away. When they refused, the police told them they should leave Kabul for their own safety.

Sadly, I wasn't surprised. Farkhunda was brutally murdered in broad daylight and the police were focused on what she did wrong. I told her family that whether or not she burned the Holy Quran, that mob had no right to murder her.

"We don't have a lawyer and no women's groups have met with us. At the funeral, those women only picked up Farkhunda's coffin for a photo—just to try to be famous. They did not even ask," Nader said angrily before he left the room to hide his tears.

Her brother continued: "That was really disrespectful. They didn't ask anyone in our family for permission to carry her coffin. We wanted to stop them, but were afraid to say anything."

I felt bad for them. The photo of several young Afghan women carrying Farkhunda's coffin had been heralded by the international media as an iconic show of strength, when in fact it had simply further rubbed salt in the family's wound; a painful reminder of how, even after her death, they were still being disrespected.

Nader came back into the room.

"No one is helping us at all, except those at the Palace telling us to accept ibra', but I will never accept money for what happened to my daughter."

"And no lawyer will represent you?" I asked.

"No. They are too scared."

It was pathetic. The United States and the European Union have collectively invested over one billion in tax dollars to train Afghan lawyers to protect women; I had been part of that investment within the JSSP program. Yet despite all this investment, not one single Afghan lawyer was willing to represent the family.

"Can't you be our lawyer?" Nader asked.

"I am leaving for the US today but I'm coming back." I still wasn't sure. "But . . . here is my number in America. If you can't find anyone else, call me."

And, with that, I was off to the airport.

A few weeks later, the family contacted me asking that I represent them. Days later, I had flown back into Kabul and was on my way to meet with Farkhunda's father again. They hadn't found anyone else and I had agreed to represent them. Unbeknownst to the family, the trial had started the same day I arrived back in-country so there was no time to waste. I had already prepared the legal arguments that we planned to file in court, but I still wanted to go over what we'd discussed.

"We want you to go to court on behalf of our family," Farkhunda's father said. "I may not be able to control myself if I see them," he added diplomatically.

"I will kill them if I see them," Farkhunda's older brother seethed.

"No problem," I said, and with the relevant papers signed I was off to court.

News of my involvement had brought a new level of scrutiny to the case. Here I was, an American lawyer, fairly well known through my earlier cases, representing the family of a woman murdered for allegedly burning the Holy Quran. It gave the whole thing an interesting spin because it gave the impression that the US was somehow involved in the case. Of course, that was exactly what the Afghan government didn't want.

The trial against the police and Farkhunda's killers would be televised. I'm sure this, too, was the last thing the government wanted, but they were under so much national and international scrutiny to be open about the case that they didn't have much of a choice. A televised trial would be the first in Afghanistan. When I heard the news, I couldn't believe it. This was a remarkable development. For the first time in their history, there would be real transparency for the Afghan criminal justice system.

I assumed television meant the courts would have put on something that at least resembled a formidable trial. Police officers would have to testify, videotaped evidence could be subpoenaed, and I might actually get a proper witness list. I'd never seen any of these things in all the years I'd been practising in Afghan courts, so I could barely contain myself when I heard it. I was giddy that these basic rules of evidence were finally going to be followed in court.

Personally, I was thrilled, too, that the televised proceedings would finally allow everyone to see what I see. People often ask me what the Afghan court is like, but it is something I find very hard to describe. This time, they could see it all for themselves.

The courtroom was packed—it was standing room only. Judge Mujadidi filed in and took his seat, flanked on either side by two armed guards wearing sunglasses. Despite all of the international outrage, I was the only international in court. The only other women present were three MPs.

I knew Safiullah Mujadidi from previous cases. He had a fierce reputation. He was best known for a case in 2014 when seven Afghan men were accused of raping four married women in a rural area of Kabul Province. It was a high-profile case, and before the trial had even started the then-president, Karzai, had said publicly that he would approve a death sentence. Surprise, surprise, Mujadidi sentenced five of the men to death, even though they claimed in court that they had been tortured to confess. They were all executed, anyway.

In our case, Mujadidi again moved quickly. The prosecutors delivered their arguments, which included hundreds of pages of material, to the judges, and in May 2015 the trial began.

When the trial opened, there were two defence lawyers for the 49 accused. One lawyer represented a single defendant, and the other lawyer was there to represent the other 48. The lawyer representing the one defendant, Abdul Masood Khorami, a man I vaguely knew, later told me that he didn't even know the trial had started until he received a call from his client's father who was watching it on the TV.

Opposite the judge were the accused; 49 men of varying ages. The accused included eighteen police officers whom we had pressured the prosecutors to charge with failure to render assistance—a first in Afghanistan. The shoe was now on the other foot. While the police had initially been quick to accuse Farkhunda of wrongdoing, now they had to answer for their actions themselves. As the judge started to address us, the media crews cranked up their cameras and the show began.

Although the family had opted not to attend the trial, I was in constant communication with them over text, sending them updates, receiving questions in return. My role was to represent the family as victims, and the family had very specific questions they wanted me to ask in court, such as, "Was the person who ran Farkhunda over with a car present?" (He was not.) "Why not?" (Because the police had been unable to find him.)

In fact, many of the guys in the video footage had somehow avoided capture. A senior police officer I knew told me that he knew of at least three key suspects who'd just fled Kabul and were never picked up. This was a problem. Some of the men who had been arrested were later proven not to be present during Farkhunda's killing.

No doubt there were many other flaws in the trial, but, put in context, this was a huge legal leap forward for Afghanistan. Sure, Farkhunda's case highlighted the limits of the Western rule-of-law effort, but it suggested that there had been at least one significant achievement: Afghans could hold a trial and try to bring people to justice.

It took the prosecutor a while to finish reading the indictment. Each defendant was allowed to speak for two minutes, but only after the prosecutor had read the evidence against them. Many of these statements were pushed to the trial's last day, which meant they couldn't possibly have been taken into consideration by the judges, because the verdict was announced minutes after the last defendant finished speaking.

Despite these imperfections, the trial did at least allow people to get a semblance of what a genuine trial looks like.

My expectations of basic rules of procedure being followed were so low that I was delighted that evidence was even being presented. There was video shown of Farkhunda being beaten and I was pleased that many police officers actually testified against some of the accused.

The prosecutors were remarkably well prepared. One of the defendants spoke up.

"I was not there," he declared.

One of the prosecutors pushed play on the video.

"Is that you?"

Silence.

I was acting as a second prosecutor under the law that states the victim has a right to be legally represented in court proceedings. I was able to question members of the mob who were in court and be involved in the process just like a prosecutor.

One thing I wanted to prioritise was the conviction of the police officers who had been standing by and not helping Farkhunda during the attack. I had convinced the family that these officers were just as culpable as the mob and needed to be held to account. That type of criminal negligence on the part of the police had never been prosecuted in Afghanistan before, but I felt it was really important: Afghanistan is, by and large, a rural country, and often when women are attacked or abused the police just ignore them. Farkhunda's family agreed.

The judge delivered his verdict on the third day.

The four men directly involved in Farkhunda's murder, including the fortune teller, were handed death sentences. Eight more civilians were found guilty of major roles in the murder and were each sentenced to sixteen years in prison. The rest were found not guilty by lack of sufficient evidence.

Eleven police officers were also convicted for failure to render assistance. It was the first time police officers in Afghanistan were successfully prosecuted under a law that requires everyone to render assistance. This result showed everyone that not only do the police have a responsibility for the protection of the community and the protection of the women in it, but also that failure to enforce it will have criminal consequences.

After the trial it was a media frenzy. Everywhere I went I heard people talking about the case, and talking about Farkhunda. People had very strong feelings either for or against the verdicts.

I went to see Farkhunda's family at home. Her father, Mohammad Nader, told me that he was happy with what I had done for them. They were happy that I had been able to relieve the burden of them having to go to the court themselves.

We all sat down to have tea, but the mood soon darkened when Mohammad Nader got a call on his mobile phone. It was someone from President Ghani's office wanting to know why the family hadn't told them they had hired me.

Whenever I take a case in Afghanistan, it always gets a lot of media attention, but this time the president's office didn't want me part of that publicity. They didn't want people paying attention to this case for fear it would make Afghanistan look bad in the eyes of the international community. And since the international community was funding virtually every aspect of Afghan society, that perception was very important.

Then things got *really* strange.

A little boy I'd never seen before came into the room and started filming us on his phone. I was confused about the kid taping me, but I didn't stop him; instead I continued to run the family through the implications of the trial and began to prepare them for the fact that there would almost certainly be an appeal. They weren't out of the woods yet.

When Mohammad Nader got off the phone with the presidential palace, he began to relate how upset they were that I was representing them.

"I am sorry they are upset, but I don't understand why," I said to him.

"I don't either. But perhaps it is a good idea if you don't go to court anymore? Just represent us in the shadows."

There was no need for me to go to court again, anyway: the trial was over. I agreed to "represent them in the shadows". Over dinner, I advised them on how the appeal process would work. I told them that the appeal was still going to be very high profile and they needed to play it right.

A few minutes later, three black SUVs pulled up to the house and the room soon filled with Afghan guys carrying guns. They told us to follow them, forced us into the cars and we drove off. When I demanded to know who they were, the only reply they gave was that they were from the presidential palace.

Inside the car, a well-dressed Afghan woman in Western clothing who I didn't know was sitting on the back seat next to me. But she seemed to know who I was and she began to ask me how I was doing.

"What's this about?" I asked. I wasn't in the mood for chitchat.

"People are upset," she said cryptically.

"Yeah? Which people? Because the family seem pretty happy with what happened in court," I said.

"But you're representing the family. Now people may think the family isn't Muslim because you're an American," she said. "They may think the family are bad Muslims."

The penny dropped. Ghani's people wanted this case to go away as quickly as possible and that meant making *me* go away as quickly as possible. They wanted to negotiate ibra' for the family without my involvement and then get them out of the country. They figured I would get in the way of that plan.

The SUV convoy drove right up to the palace's front door. That's never happened to me before. Once we all got out, we went right up the stairs and into a room where we waited until a lawyer for the president joined by five other men came in.

A one-sided conversation began. The lawyer spoke to Farkhunda's brothers, appealing to their emotions, explaining that they should trust the president and that he was disappointed that I was representing their family.

Now I was starting to get angry.

"You guys come and kidnap me in the middle of the night. Then you force me to the palace. I want to know what I did wrong," I interrupted.

The lawyer addressed me. "Oh no, Kim, you didn't do anything wrong."

"Really? Because it certainly feels like I did something wrong. Why am I here?" I asked. "If you guys were so concerned about Farkhunda's family, why didn't you give them a lawyer? You work for the president, for God's sake."

Then Ghani's lawyer showed Farkhunda's brother a video on his phone. It was the footage taken earlier that night by the kid at Farkhunda's house. Slowly I began to work it out. They were trying to make out that this video had actually been filmed *before* the trial. They were trying to make it look as though what I'd said about the family not needing to go to court again was actually something I'd said weeks before. The implication being that I'd lied to them.

"See, here, you said you would represent them in the shadows. Why did you go to court?" the lawyer asked.

"That video was taken today. An hour ago. Which is why I have the exact same clothes on," I said.

I was furious. Right in front of me, Ghani's people were trying to make it look as though I'd told the family I wouldn't represent them—and had then tricked them into letting me represent them. They were trying to set me up. I also knew that if they sidelined me then no one would ever step in to represent Farkhunda's family.

"How many of you have ever spoken to the family until today?" I asked the room.

Silence.

"You know, instead of spending all your time and energy figuring out how to get me off the case, you should have been thinking about who you're going to get on the case," I said.

I was pissed. I was pissed that I was working so hard on a case that frankly I'd at first tried to avoid, only to have my motives challenged. I was pissed that not one Afghan lawyer had stepped up to the plate to take this case. I was pissed that I once again had left my family and cut my vacation short. Out of all the people in that room, I was most pissed at myself. I once again ran for the football that wasn't ever going to be there and dared to have expectations that were never going to be met.

It was clear that this wasn't going to end well, so I decided it was time to be magnanimous.

"Okay . . ." I laid my cards on the table. "Like I told the family, I am not going to court anymore. The family can appeal if they want, but that is up to them, and you should give them a lawyer."

"We will give the family a lawyer to represent them because Farkhunda is our sister," the lawyer said.

"No, you won't," I said, and that was it.

The palace called me the next day and again reassured me they were going to provide the family with a new lawyer. They never did. They lied right to my face and then went out of their way to call me to tell me the same lie. The family never received any further legal counsel, and no one represented them when the date was set for the appeal hearing forty-three days later.

From what I heard, the second hearing was the exact opposite of the first hearing. It wasn't televised, they didn't even tell the family when the hearing was, they had no legal representation and it was closed off to the public. No transparency. I would never have let them get away with that kind of stunt.

Secrecy is against the Afghan rules of criminal procedure. The defendants and their lawyers were called in for discussions with the judges in groups, depending on their sentences, and deals were done in back rooms where Farkhunda wasn't represented. I would have insisted that those meetings be transparent. I would have made sure I was in the room. If the family had wanted it, I would also have had the media briefed to keep up the pressure on the government.

I heard that the lawyers for the men condemned to death were arguing that because no one had ever determined exactly when Farkhunda died, the penalty should have been in relation to desecrating the dead body, rather than for murder, which would have had a far lighter sentence.

Despite its flaws, the first trial and the convictions felt like a huge victory in the struggle to give Afghan women their dues in court. For a while, at least, the case brought international attention to the plight of Afghan women. By and large, what happened after the first trial isn't known to the general public in Afghanistan. I guess in some ways that's a good thing. Afghan women saw a court trial, men brought to account and their subsequent convictions.

At the place where Farkhunda was killed, a memorial has been erected in her honour and the street is named after her. I've been told that it's the first and only street in Afghanistan named after a woman. Farkhunda has been officially declared a martyr, an honour that has only ever been bestowed on soldiers. Hopefully her legacy will further promote women's rights.

Farkhunda's story highlights, among other things, a continuing and pervasive misogyny in Afghan society. One of the most troubling things about her murder was that her killers were not religious extremists but ordinary Afghan men and boys.

What happened to Farkhunda is a painful reminder of how Afghan society has normalised violence, particularly towards women. It's a country where corruption trumps justice, and where Western money has turned corruption into a way of life. Programs like the one I worked for at the JSSP were too often designed with no regard for Afghanistan's own laws, and our best efforts to lift women's legal status has in some ways been used as an excuse by religious extremists to fuel the fires of resentment.

With any luck, Farkhunda's case has been a wake-up call for Afghan men who should now ask themselves, "What about my mother, sister, daughter? Is there a risk that they could be the next Farkhunda?"

At the time of writing this, Farkhunda's family has still not been afforded justice in the courts. No one has been executed and it is unclear if any of the original perpetrators are even still in prison.

19

WELL, YOU MUST HAVE DONE SOMETHING

Borders are important. We need them, right? Some believe that we need borders to keep people out—otherwise our countries would be flooded with immigrants. That's the conventional wisdom.

I actually think the opposite is true. I think we'd all be better off living in a world without borders, and I don't think it's right that people should ever feel imprisoned within their own country. I think people should live where they want to live because it doesn't seem fair that just because you are born in a certain country you can never make a life elsewhere.

Those who disagree with me argue that without borders everyone would just move to Europe and North America, but I don't think that's true. In my experience, people don't want to move away from their tribes; they prefer to live where it will be most comfortable for them. I deal with refugees who want to get to the US or to Europe all the time, but more often than not those people aren't running towards something but away from something.

The West falls into the trap of thinking that everyone wants to live where we do when what's really going on is that people are just desperate to get out of the dangerous mess they're living in now. And too often that's a mess we've helped to create.

Every refugee's story is of course unique, but I often find they share certain qualities. They tend to have a tale that describes a tragic plight in search of safety from rising levels of persecution and scorn and violence. A good example are Afghanistan's Sikhs.

There has always been a small population of Sikhs in Afghanistan. Traders by nature, Sikhs set up in Afghanistan hundreds of years ago, exploiting relationships with old Sikh communities in India and making money from the importing of popular goods. But their numbers have fallen steadily over the last 30 years as a result of oppression and persecution. One of the main problems Sikhs face is that traditionally they cremate their dead, but the act of burning a body is considered sacrilege in the Islamic faith (reserved only for the castigated, such as Farkhunda).

In the 1980s, during the war with the Soviets, many Sikh temples in Afghanistan were destroyed and thousands of Afghan Sikhs fled the country. A second, even larger exodus followed when the Taliban came to power in the early 1990s and the national policy towards Sikhs shifted from arbitrary oppression to violent persecution. By the time I came to Kabul in 2008, there were barely 10,000 Sikhs left in the country.

One of those Sikhs was Bikram Datta.

I had started representing another client, Michael Hearn, a British security contractor who'd been locked up, and I was now considered a specialist in representing foreigners. A few weeks earlier during a visit to the prison to see Michael, he mentioned that there was a nice guy from the UK locked up in the next cell.

"He's being abused," Michael said. "Some of the local guys are beating the shit out of him. He's being treated like the prison slave."

Michael said he'd been trying to stick up for the guy and asked me if I could take a look at his situation.

"Sure," I said, "I'd be happy to. What's he in here for?"

"That's the thing," Michael said, "I don't really know. He's not really being held for anything."

Bikram Datta was a young man, and haggard, bearded and thin. He eyed me curiously as I walked into his cell and asked if I could sit, replying in a soft voice. He was scared and timid as he began to tell me his story.

Bikram was born in Jalalabad in eastern Afghanistan in the late 1980s. Most Jalalabad Sikhs left the country long before I arrived. The Sikhs in the provinces outside Kabul were especially easy targets for the brutal Mujahideen leaders who emerged after the Soviets left. Outside of Kabul, many Sikhs were thrown off their land and removed from their jobs. The Taliban in the east also forced Sikhs to wear yellow markers on their clothes to identify them, just like the Nazis had done to the Jews in the Polish ghettos during World War II.

Like many other Sikh families, Bikram's had fled for India by way of Pakistan. Bikram had led a transient existence, spending his formative years bouncing from refugee camp to refugee camp in Pakistan, Bahrain and, finally, Egypt.

Bikram's family didn't stay in Egypt for long, instead deciding to try to make their way to Europe for a better life. Around this time, however, Bikram became estranged from his family. His biological father died when he was a boy and his stepfather was not fond of him. At the age of seventeen, Bikram was left with no choice but to leave his family in Egypt and set out for the UK alone.

In Britain, Bikram started a new life for himself, settling in Manchester, a hard, grey city in the north of England that's been a familiar landing spot for Asian refugees for decades. He immediately sought asylum with the immigration authorities in Manchester, and while his application was being processed he worked a string of menial jobs. At one point, he told me, he worked in a restaurant for meals. That's what he was paid: food, not money.

During his three years in England, Bikram had met an Indian woman who had also emigrated. They fell in love and were quickly engaged. Every Wednesday, Bikram was expected to go and sign at the immigration office to show that he was still in the area and staying out of trouble. On his way to sign on one week, Bikram was met by the police who told him that he was going to be deported back to Afghanistan. Just like that. They refused to even allow Bikram to use his phone to call his fiancée. He was put on a UK-government chartered plane and flown back to Kabul.

To make matters worse, the money he had been carrying to pay the couple's bills disappeared after he was taken into custody. That was still haunting Bikram: he worried that his fiancée would think that he'd run off with all their money. Since he'd been in prison, he'd never been allowed to contact her to tell her what had really happened.

"I begged them not to deport me, ma'am," he said. "I told them, 'I am Sikh, they will kill me if you make me go back to Afghanistan . . .'" He trailed off and looked at the floor.

"But they ignored you," I finished the sentence for him.

"Yes, ma'am." He nodded in sad resignation.

"But what did you do?" I've heard the "I'm innocent" schtick too many times to believe people get locked up for nothing.

"Nothing, ma'am. Nothing."

"Hmmm," I mused. Then almost under my breath, "Well, you must have done something."

When Bikram was returned to Afghanistan in July 2010 on a chartered plane full of Afghan refugees, he was the only Sikh onboard. The plane landed in Kabul and the refugees were met by the Afghan police, who took one look at his turban and arrested him on sight. Everyone else on the plane was free to go, but Bikram was detained for having no documentation to prove he'd been born in Afghanistan.

What's supposed to happen when Afghans are deported from Britain is that the UK government, the Afghan government and the International Organization for Migration should be there to receive people off the plane. This allows for the provision of basic information regarding housing and other services. However, when Bikram was deported, the only people waiting for him at the Kabul airport were the police.

People deported back to Afghanistan from the UK are supposed to be free on arrival. They're not supposed to go to jail.

Bikram had been sitting in jail for a year and a half when I first met him. As Michael had told me, he was being regularly abused by other inmates, as well as guards. The guards forced him to sleep outside in a courtyard next to the bathrooms. He showed me some of the bruises on his body where the other inmates routinely kicked him on their way past him to the bathrooms.

Shortly after he arrived in Tolkeef, a group of inmates forced Bikram to convert to Islam. They surrounded him and held him down, while they ripped off his turban and cut his hair, an important tenet of his Sikh faith. Then they made him repeat the few phrases a convert must say to proclaim his Islamic faith. Bikram didn't really understand what was happening. He only repeated the words because he was so scared they would beat him up again. Afterwards, the mob lifted Bikram onto their shoulders and carried him around the detention centre, celebrating his "conversion". The guards videotaped the spectacle and leaked it to the local news, where it was televised.

News that a Sikh had converted to Islam inside the Kabul detention centre reached two Sikh members of the Afghan parliament, who paid Bikram a visit just to let him know he was a disgrace to their religion and that the Sikh community would not help him. Bikram had no remaining family ties in Afghanistan. He was truly isolated and alone.

Despite having been mistreated by everyone in Afghanistan, he seemed to bear no malice. As I sat and listened to Bikram's story, I thought that if I'd been him I'd have been angry at *everyone*. But he remained composed, polite, almost compassionate towards those who had mistreated him. I'd never heard anything like it before. I wanted to help him.

After our conversation, I went to see the director of the prison to get a copy of Bikram's file. He didn't want to show it to me, however, which was unusual as the prison authorities were usually pretty cool about that. This time, though, he seemed annoyed that I was even asking. The more people I asked about Bikram, the more I realised that no one could tell me what he was in prison for. I started to wonder if he had indeed been locked up for nothing. Maybe it wasn't that unbelievable after all.

I started asking the prison guards if they knew what the charge against Bikram was, but even off the record they claimed not to know. One guard, on the promise of anonymity, did tell me that I should talk to someone at the Attorney-General's office.

I added Bikram's case to the list of things to raise when I was there next. My contact at the Attorney-General's office was a middle-aged prosecutor, bearded and a haircut straight from a 1970s John Travolta movie. I decided to bury Bikram's case in among a pile of other issues so as not to make it look like the main reason I was there. Then I just bided my time until I could casually raise it.

"Oh, yeah, another thing," I said walking out of the room as though I'd almost forgotten to mention it. "I wonder if I could see Bikram Datta's file?"

He looked surprised to hear Bikram's name.

"There is no file," he said.

"Really? That's weird. Do you know what it is he's been charged with?"

No answer. He shook his head.

"Well, I'm gonna need to see that file," I said, ramping things up a little.

"We already spoke to the Indian Embassy." His voice suggested he was becoming a little irritated. "But they won't come to get him."

"He doesn't have any family or friends in Afghanistan," I explained.

"And his guarantor needs to own a business," Alako added.

Really?

"Okay. So he needs a guarantor, in Afghanistan, and that person needs to own a business? Despite the fact that Bikram has not committed any crimes?" I wanted to make sure I was hearing right.

"Yes."

"Okay. Then I'll guarantee him."

They couldn't argue with that. I was a person, in Afghanistan, who owned a business.

So Bikram was released and came to live with me. For six months. It was like having a child staying with me. He had been deported from the UK with only the clothes on his back. He had no money, no clothes, nothing. I arranged to get everything for him. I didn't want him to just sit around while I was working all day, so I gave him books to read. I told him, just like I would tell my kids every summer, "You're not going to sit in the house all day doing nothing." I reached out to male friends, too, who brought over all kinds of stuff that he needed like clothes and shoes. It was really great. A community of people all working together to rebuild a broken young man. I was determined that we could get him back on his feet and reintegrate him into Afghan life.

Pretty soon, however, it was time for me to return to the US to see my family. I had been home for two weeks when I got a call from a friend in Kabul who was keeping an eye on Bikram. Bikram had called her in tears. He was really upset. He had gone out to get a loaf of bread and one of the guards from across the street had asked him for ID. Since he didn't have any, they beat him up.

The day I got back in-country I walked Bikram over to the same guards and I made him point out which ones beat him up. Bikram didn't want me to do anything, but as far as I was concerned what they'd done was not only disrespectful to him, it was also disrespectful to me. I was furious.

"Did you hit him?" I asked the guard.

He clutched his AK-47 close. "What?"

"Did. You. Hit. Him?" I repeated.

A small crowd was gathering around us, curious about the scene. The guard didn't answer, but looked at me coyly. I had my answer.

"Let me tell you something. Don't you ever *ever* disrespect me like that. He is my guest and when you hit him you are disrespecting me. Do you understand?"

"He should have ID," he said.

"Oh yeah? I don't have ID, do you want to hit me?"

I was ready for a fight. He looked at me blankly.

"You apologise to him right now."

Silence. But I just kept looking at him.

"Sorry," the guard said quietly.

"Thank you," I said.

It felt meaningful, but I knew deep down that Bikram just wasn't safe to walk the streets of Kabul on his own.

I decided to go to the Sikh temple in Kabul. I wanted to approach its members and encourage them to support Bikram. There are only a handful of Sikhs remaining in Kabul, and while they were open and polite it was obvious that their survival tactic has been to remain as invisible as possible. They wanted to keep it that way—and that meant they weren't going to stick their necks out to help Bikram.

He had even been abandoned by the people who should have helped him the most.

It was clear that there was no way for Bikram to stay in Afghanistan. He wasn't safe around ordinary Afghans and he wasn't wanted by the Sikhs. I had to get him out of Kabul.

I went back to the British Embassy to explain that the Bikram problem wasn't over. The right thing to do next was for them to contact immigration back in the UK. In order to be awarded asylum in a new country, you have to be outside the country in which you were born. If you're in your home country then immigration officials don't consider your application because the threat must not be that bad. But even though Bikram was in his "home" country, he wasn't safe. Because the British had illegally deported him in the first place and put him in such danger, I argued that they didn't have a choice but to take him back.

A few months later, Bikram was in the UK.

Bikram's situation may have been unique, but his plight is the same as millions of other refugees. People too often find themselves in another country, fleeing war or persecution or disease and starvation, and then wind up living in the shadows like nomads trying to get to the promised land. They risk their lives to get there, often travelling without any ID. Refugees can't be on the radar. They have to stay off-grid and that makes them vulnerable.

From Bikram I learned the reality of the experience of a global refugee; what it's like to live as a stateless person. Bikram's nightmare might be over, but for millions of other refugees—those pouring out of Syria, for example—it's just beginning. According to the UNHCR, over 65 million people have been forcibly displaced globally. Europe and the rest of the Western world are only starting to come to grips with this vast new wave of immigration.

The current pervasive attitude is that refugees aren't to be regarded as human anymore. People have become desensitised to the issue and don't seem to understand the terrifying choice made by refugees. The vast majority of people who are fleeing from places like Syria and Afghanistan are literally fleeing for their lives. They are fighting for their basic human right to exist.

The politics of this issue has changed dramatically as the number of refugees has grown, especially from Islamic countries where connections to fundamentalist Islam raise the fear of terrorism. Unfortunately, many people from the West tar all refugees from Islamic countries with this brush and it has perpetuated a racist fear that *all* refugees are coming to do us harm. It's become frighteningly easy to discriminate against Muslims and label them all terrorists.

Bikram fell through the cracks. Because he didn't matter.

We need to put the humanity back into our immigration practices because we're treating immigrants like monsters. They're people. Just like us.

20

HIGH FIVES

I've been asked before if I would ever consider becoming a judge. Short answer? No way. Sitting there all day listening to other people talk? Judging them? No, thank you. Not for me. I enjoy the fight too much, and there's not enough action in judging. Having said that, I'm also of the belief that you should try everything once.

I doubt many other lawyers with whom I graduated from Marquette Law School back in Milwaukee ever sat as a judge, let alone as a judge on an Afghan jirga. In fact, I'd bet good money on it. And if they have then I feel for them because it's hard work.

The case I was judging concerned a little girl named Naghma.

Naghma lived in the Charahi Qambar, a camp for Afghans who have been internally displaced. The camp is located on the outskirts of Kabul. Naghma lived with her parents and eight brothers and sisters. They shared a small, dingy one-room tent, one of hundreds at the camp. Years of war and poverty had forced her father, Taj, to take the family from their home in the southern province of Helmand in search of a better life elsewhere. People are sometimes surprised to discover that there are thousands of Afghans who return home, often after decades of being away, due to the fact that they were not able to make a better life for themselves elsewhere.[1]

Like most refugees, Taj had only ever worked menial farming jobs, but in the camp, where they had no land, these skills were useless. So he went to look for work as an unskilled labourer. Every morning he woke up at the crack of dawn to go in search of whatever paid work he could find that day. When the work was steady, he could make around US$50 in a month. But work was scarce, especially during the winter months, and the jobs got fewer and farther between. Most days he would come home empty-handed.

The camp is a dirty, dusty, open block located in a very dangerous part of the city. It's filled with people who've fled rural areas to escape the fighting between the government and the Taliban or IS-led insurgents. As more internally displaced Afghans came in, it became even harder for men like Taj to find jobs. To make matters worse, insurgents hung around looking to recruit desperate refugees. It's not a good place for anyone to grow up. It's not a good place for anyone to live.

During one winter Taj's wife fell ill and was hospitalised. At the same time, their three-year-old son froze to death.

Desperate, Taj borrowed $2500 from a neighbour to pay for his wife's medical bills and other family expenses like firewood and food. He borrowed the money in good faith, promising to pay it back, but when his son died he fell behind on his payments and slid deeper into debt.

Then the neighbour demanded the money back.

When Taj explained that he couldn't pay back the loan, the neighbour insisted that the tribal elders intervene and a jirga was called. The elders and religious leaders decided that the best way to satisfy the debt was for Taj to marry off his six-year-old daughter, Naghma to the neighbour's 21-year-old son.

To the more cynical of you, this story may not seem particularly shocking given Afghanistan's reputation as a lawless nation where women are routinely treated as property and the practice of marrying off child brides for money is still widespread. But even in the refugee camps the rule of law still exists—and this was illegal.

Naghma's story made international news. The BBC, CNN and the *New York Times* ran pieces expressing outrage at the violation of a child's human rights and soon several well-meaning NGOs became involved. A couple of Afghan women's charities were so outraged that they contacted the Ministry of Interior Affairs in Afghanistan to intervene. Because child marriage is a violation of Afghan law, they reasonably expected the decision to be quickly overturned. But nothing happened.

I had already heard about Naghma's story when I received a call from the UK. The person on the other end of the line introduced herself as a representative of the billionaire entrepreneur and philanthropist Richard Branson. He had first contacted the BBC, who in turn had put him in contact with me. This was a rather surreal moment in my life as a total stranger explained to me that Richard Branson wanted me to represent him. He wanted to pay off Naghma's father's debt.

It was a kind gesture, but I had to make it clear that it wasn't that simple, and just because he had the money to pay, that did not mean the problem would disappear. Unfortunately, that has never worked in Afghanistan. A cash payment didn't address the larger issue, either: laws had been broken. Naghma's life could only be made whole again if those mistakes were acknowledged and accepted by all sides. To do that, I'd have to get everyone involved to agree.

I decided to visit Naghma's family first.

The Charahi Qambar refugee camp was a mess. Kids running everywhere, open sewers, rats—it looked worse than the inside of the prisons in Kabul. The walls of Naghma's family house were made from mud. The ceiling was crafted from blue and white woollen UN blankets. No electricity and no running water.

At first I wasn't sure what the best way was for me to engage with the situation, but I knew that this being Afghanistan they would at least be willing to talk. Everyone always wants to talk in Afghanistan. I just needed to convince them to trust me and tell me the story. I'd read all the media coverage, but no matter how great the reporting, there's always something inaccurate in a story. I never rely on the media. I have to gather the facts for myself.

I needed to know who was involved in the first jirga, how things had played out, and what discussions there had been about the alternative outcomes.

Taj and I talked at great length so I could get an understanding of what had happened and how Naghma found herself in this situation. Without hesitation, he said that he didn't want his daughter to be sold. He was very protective of Naghma. I asked him if he would be interested in having a second jirga? He said yes.

The first sticking point was that, from the point of view of those who had participated in the jirga, the resolution was still a good one. It may have shocked the world, but as far as they were concerned it solved the problem. However, in order for *me* to solve this problem, a second jirga had to be called, but we also needed the neighbour, his son, the village elders and the religious leaders to agree to take part. We needed to convince everyone to look again at potential solutions that meant Naghma didn't have to be sold.

The man who intended to marry the six-year-old had already started showing up at Naghma's house to instruct the family on how he wanted her to be raised in preparation for when she was to be turned over to him in a few weeks' time. First, he told her family that he didn't want her going to school. It was a waste of her time, he said, as she certainly would not go to school when they were married. Then he warned them that she better start learning to cook and clean, that his new little slave bride better learn to make herself useful. He didn't exactly ingratiate himself with his prospective in-laws.

After hearing all of that, I was looking forward to meeting him.

I went to see the neighbour who lent the money. He told me he was reluctant to agree to a second jirga because his son was really looking forward to owning Naghma. Since he seemed to genuinely not care about what was best for the little girl I decided to appeal to his common sense. I told him that Naghma was a liability. She is going to get sick just like her mother, I said. She's going to cry and be homesick and miss her family. You're going to have to pay for her clothes. It's going to be a lot of work for your family, and especially for your son, to take on this six-year-old girl.

By that time, I knew Branson was offering to pay the $2500, but without mentioning the Branson money directly I hinted that there might be another way to get his money back. It would need to be discussed at a second jirga, I explained. Finally, after about 30 cups of tea, he agreed. We were going to have a second jirga.

The final clincher for me was that if I was going to influence the decision in Naghma's favour then I would have to preside over the proceedings. While I was making visits to the camp, the Taliban were becoming more and more aware of my activities there. When I began to feel that it was no longer safe to meet inside the camp we started to meet on the outside. I spent hours meeting and talking with the elders as well as the families all over Kabul. I finally got all sides to agree that I could be the judge.

The first jirga had taken place inside the camp. Naghma was a pretty little six-year-old girl with big eyes, a nose piercing, and a crooked baby front tooth that looked like it was ready to come out. While the elders decided her fate inside a tent, she was playing outside on the ground with her toys. When the first jirga was over, one of her brothers had started to tease her, saying, "Ha ha, you're a bride now." I'm sure she had no idea what he was talking about.

Usually, when the bride is as young as six in Afghanistan, she starts off in her new home as a house slave. Naghma was probably too young to be sexually exploited at that point. Probably. Sometimes girls who are turned into domestic servants at a very young age are sexually abused too. Either way, it usually graduates to a sexual relationship very quickly.

The idea of giving away your six-year-old daughter to pay a debt seems insane to the average Westerner, but in Afghanistan females are collateral, chattels, pieces of property to be traded, bought and sold. That's how the men in the jirga saw it. Taj had fought hard against the decision but, with no other assets to cover his debt, he had no leverage. He had tried to save Naghma, which is something that the media seemed to miss.

Let me emphasise this point, and I can't emphasise this enough: it's illegal to sell your six-year-old daughter under Afghan law. It's illegal to sell your six-year-old daughter under Islamic law. It's illegal to sell your six-year-old daughter under international law. There's absolutely nothing legal about it. Unfortunately, it still persists as a cultural practice and it happens all over Afghanistan. I had to impress upon the second jirga that what had happened at the first jirga had been illegal. Not just wrong, but illegal.

I organised to have the second jirga at Babur Gardens, a park on the outskirts of Kabul. It was an ideal location: I wanted it to be outside and I knew that there would be security and that guns would not be allowed into the park. It's a public space, kind of like Central Park in New York. I didn't want to get caught up doing this in the refugee camp since I'd heard about the Taliban taking an interest in us. It was much too dangerous in there now. But the park seemed neutral. Nothing bad had ever happened there in all the years I'd been in Kabul.

I'd heard some of the women's groups were still buzzing around the case. Once something gets in the paper, people come out of the woodwork professing to want to help out.

The problem for me was that their idea of help was more of a hindrance: many of them wanted Naghma's dad arrested. That was going to be very unhelpful to my strategy of finding a workable solution. Quite apart from my belief that they were targeting the wrong guy, I also knew that without Naghma's dad involved we couldn't make my plan stick.

I was also afraid that if Taj was arrested he wouldn't be able to provide for his seven other kids, his mother and a sick wife. No one would be better off if he was arrested. So we needed to get the jirga settled before that happened.

It was a hot day. In the park, we found a patch of grass where we all sat in a circle. There were ten people: eight older men, my translator Khalil, and me. My driver Kadar was in the background keeping a lookout in case anything shady happened. I had brought my portable printer because, if we agreed to a settlement, I wanted to draft a legal agreement and get it signed right away. The BBC came along as well to record the whole thing.

For many of the guys in that jirga—uneducated Afghan men living in a refugee camp—it was the first time they'd ever sat down with a foreigner, let alone a foreign woman. It was probably the first and last time, too. But their willingness to do it showed a certain amount of open-mindedness. I'm a glass-half-full type of person. I was gambling that because they'd agreed to meet at all, they might be willing to listen to my arguments.

It was pretty funny. The second the jirga started and we were on a roll, I got a call from Cherish back home. She and Seoul were having an argument about whose turn it was to take out the garbage before they went to school. I needed to excuse myself from the Afghan jirga to deal with a jirga in the US. I had to ask the elders to pause deciding the fate of a six-year-old for a moment while I arbitrated on my seven- and twelve-year-old's household duties.

We got going again and the jirga lasted nearly two hours. It never felt formal or forced; instead I tried to keep the tone conversational so that everyone felt comfortable. I hadn't told anyone that I had Branson's $2500 in my back pocket, but knowing that I did meant that I could project an attitude that said, "I can solve this."

I think the men could feel that confidence coming from me. That was the one thing that was missing from the first jirga—the leverage. I knew if everything else fell through that at least I had the money, but I felt first that there was an opportunity to impress upon everyone the legal aspects of the situation. For the sake of every little Naghma coming after her, I had to make them see that forcing this engagement was illegal under Afghan law as well as Islamic law.

I did not want to be too preachy, either, but I did my best to make it clear to the men that it wasn't just me telling them what they'd done was wrong and immoral. No one wants to hear it, but the Holy Quran says a female should not be given away because we women are all precious gifts. All humans, for that matter. We're all gifts. You don't just give us away. That's not why we're here.

Then I turned to the neighbour who had lent Taj the money and addressed him on a practical level.

"What do you think this six-year-old is going to do for you? What is she going to be capable of?"

He shrugged as though he'd asked himself the same questions.

Then I turned to his 21-year-old son.

"What's wrong with you?" He looked surprised. "You

shouldn't buy little girls. Can't you get a wife your own age?"

All the elders started laughing as Khalil translated. I was teasing him, kind of.

"You're too old to be buying children."

When I talk about the law, I try to talk about it in a language that everyone can understand because otherwise it doesn't mean anything. I had my work cut out convincing a group of religious leaders, however. They believed that because Taj owed the neighbour the money, and because he couldn't pay, they'd made the best decision under the circumstances. I absolutely don't agree with them, but I do understand why they made this decision. They had been making decisions like this one unchallenged for their whole lives. They still thought it was fine.

Don't get me wrong: I'm all for finding the best solution to a horrible situation. I was used to it. In fact, you could say that kind of attitude is fundamental to my whole legal style. But this solution wasn't fine.

Let's call it what it was: Naghma had been sold into slavery. Slavery is never the solution. It should never have been contemplated. If the jirga had felt like they were up against the wall, other solutions should have been explored first. They could have gone to the court, Naghma's father could have been given a payment plan, the neighbour's debt could have been written off. Whatever happened, the life of a child should never have been on the table.

I tried to explain the legal situation to the elders in human terms. I didn't waste my time citing specific sections of the penal code; that wouldn't have meant anything to them. I told them that, according to the law, a girl has to be sixteen to be married. And Islamic law says that a woman needs to agree to the marriage. Naghma didn't even know what a bride was; if this were to go ahead, she would have no idea what was happening to her.

The "What if this was your daughter?" argument doesn't always work with everyone. I knew it wouldn't work with this crowd because they would have simply said they'd have done the same thing—given up their daughter to pay off the debt. So I decided to take a different approach.

I began to appeal to the elders by asking them, "What if it was your six-year-old son and what does your six-year-old son know?" He knows about as much as Naghma knows. So what value can he really add to the situation? A six-year-old will be more of a burden than a help. The men weren't so comfortable with that thought. Shifting the scenario from a daughter to a son was resonating with this crowd.

Eventually, my arguments were finished and it was time for me to listen. The men spoke in turn, each one mostly agreeing with what I had said. Each made the point that none of them had the right to sell their daughters, and that it was their daughters' choice to decide who they wanted to marry. They also stated that, legally, all their daughters had the right to an education and that using females as collateral is morally and culturally wrong in Afghanistan, as well as being illegal. I could barely contain my emotional response. It felt like suddenly I was sitting among the most progressive group of men in Afghanistan.

I typed on my laptop as the men spoke, putting down the salient points in a document, and then I asked everyone to listen while I read it back to them. I wanted everyone to sign to show that they agreed to the following:

I agree and understand that receiving a female in lieu of payment is illegal in Afghanistan; I also agree and understand to not ask for human beings in exchange for any other past, present or future debts owed; I also agree to allow my daughters to go to school as long as allowed by law; I agree that I'll protect my daughters in all future endeavours; I also agree that my daughters will have the freedom to choose the husbands that they want to marry when they become adult women.

In Western culture, this all seems like a no-brainer, but remember this is Afghanistan. Even if all of those terms are in accordance with Afghan and Islamic law, the laws just weren't being followed. One man after another signed the paper, some with their thumbprints because they couldn't write their own names. But, in the end, I got every one of them to agree to adhere to those laws and in the process overturn the fate they'd handed down to Naghma.

On one condition.

Even though Taj, his neighbour and the son had agreed to all the terms and signed the agreement, they still needed the money. The engagement could only be terminated as long as the debt was financially repaid.

Kadar went to the car and brought over the $2500 that Richard Branson had donated. He strolled over, sunglasses on, money in a bag, and handed it to me like it was a drug deal. I gave it to the neighbour, who showed no surprise. I think he knew all along that he was going to get his money. Maybe that's why he agreed to the terms. I'll never know for sure. I made him count it out and state for the record that he was sure he had been repaid in full. I also had him sign a receipt saying Taj no longer owed him anything.

This was the end of the debt. I never told anyone where the money came from.

One of the elders then started asking me for more money. I guess he figured I had a lot of it to go around. He was asking me for cash and I was like, "What?" I raised my hand in the air and told him to do the same. He didn't understand.

"Like this," I said, demonstrating.

He raised his hand and we high fived.

"That's what you get," I laughed.

He looked confused, which cracked me up.

It's vital to find the right tool in your box to solve a problem. In Naghma's case, we were able to satisfy the debt and deal with this problem in an unconventional way, but we still used the law. We prevailed because we were able to bring in both local laws and religious laws, and we used those laws to protect her. It was very important to me that these men all understood that Naghma had legal rights that protected her.

The second jirga was a gamble. It could have gone really wrong, really fast. You don't know how any trial is going to turn out, but it was a gamble worth taking.

I was very happy that Naghma was able to stay home with her family and I still stay in contact with her father. He calls me every year on the holidays just to thank me for helping him to keep his daughter.

21

ARTICLE 71, I THINK

Women's shelters in Afghanistan are packed to the rafters with female victims who have survived horrendous, torturous abuse, usually at the hands of their own family members. Every single day more women are admitted to these safe places and their stories are hauntingly familiar. According to a United States Institute of Peace (USIP) report from 2014, at least 87 per cent of women in Afghanistan have experienced some sort of domestic abuse, while a staggering 62 per cent admitted to having suffered multiple incidents of violence in their own home.

Women's cases weren't really on my agenda when I first arrived in Afghanistan, but after a few years I realised that women's lack of protection was increasingly impossible to ignore. It almost felt irresponsible for me *not* to get involved in women's cases. I'm not talking about marching

ARTICLE 71, I THINK

or campaigning, more a responsibility to get involved legally. I didn't want to be thought of as a women's rights lawyer necessarily, but I knew I had the skills to help women, and when you know you can help, how can you not? Especially when nobody else is.

I first met Sahar Gul shortly after she arrived at a women's shelter in Kabul amid a firestorm of international outrage and press coverage. She stood in front of me, a meek fourteen-year-old, struggling to maintain eye contact while she spoke barely above a whisper as she told me her story.

A few months earlier, Sahar had been rescued from the cellar of her home in Baghlan in the northern mountains of Afghanistan, hundreds of miles from the rural province of Badakhshan where she was raised. When she was eight years old, Sahar had been sold by her brother to a 30-year-old stranger for $5000 and was promptly shipped off to serve as his second wife.

For years Sahar was enslaved in her husband's house, cooking, cleaning and performing domestic chores. While child brides are below legal age, they are often put to work by their in-laws. Unfortunately for Sahar, her new mother- and sister-in-law were particularly cruel and she regularly received beatings for "poor behaviour".

Around the time she turned twelve, her husband started grooming her, planting the seed in her head that she could earn money for the family by working as a prostitute. His calculation was that she could make him lots of money if he sold her virginity. His mother and sister backed him up, and soon the whole family was exerting huge pressure on her to sell her body for money. Despite her tender years, Sahar, raised as a devout and religious girl, refused. Angered at her resistance, the beatings from her in-laws became more severe, until eventually her husband and his family began torturing her daily.

Sahar was chained to the wall of a windowless basement and starved for long periods. Her husband would visit her in the night to burn her skin with hot metal rods. Several times he pierced her skin to the bone. Her mother- and sister-in-law would routinely kick and punch her, ripping out handfuls of her hair, or beat her across the face with sticks. Sahar's fingernails were individually ripped out with pliers. She was struck over the head with a hammer. Electric rods were forced inside her body.

Once, Sahar managed to escape, only to be discovered by a neighbour who immediately dragged her back to the house. The punishment she received for her defiance was even worse.

Thankfully for Sahar, her uncle came by the house unannounced one afternoon and saw what was happening to his niece. He immediately informed the police. When they went to investigate, the police found Sahar chained in the basement lying on top of a pile of animal shit. She was barely alive, and was so weak that she had to be carried out of the house in a wheelbarrow. She spent three months in hospital being fed through a tube because her jaw was too badly fractured to chew. It would be months before she would walk or eat solid food again. The doctors said it was a miracle she had survived.

And now, months after her rescue, as she stood in front of me, the blotchy scars on her face and hands remained. Sahar was also developmentally delayed for her age, another direct result of the abuse she had endured.

Sahar's story generated a media storm in Afghanistan. Her mother-, father- and sister in-law were all arrested and charged. They were all convicted in July 2012 and sentenced to ten years in prison. Sahar's husband, however, was never questioned, let alone arrested or prosecuted. Despite the failure of every governmental justice department in Afghanistan to go after him, the other convictions were widely heralded as a huge victory for women's rights, and Sahar became the poster child for the cause.

Many of the Afghan women I represent live in women's shelters and I had become involved in Sahar's case when I got a call from Manizha Naderi, the director of one of those shelters: Women for Afghan Women, one of the largest and most successful shelters in the country. Manizha is someone I wholly respect. She has been the architect of the most progressive approach to women's shelters in Kabul. Her philosophy includes allowing women to go to school and work while they live at the shelter. Manizha is a visionary and has saved thousands of lives. She was calling to let me know that Women for Afghan Women had taken in Sahar after she was discharged from the hospital while she continued to recover from her injuries.

Manizha told me that she just found out by happenstance that Sahar's mother- and sister-in-law had been released from prison. She explained that the appeals court had met in secret without informing Sahar and had decided that the in-laws had been punished enough. Their sentences had been reduced to one year, which they'd already served, so they were set free. Sahar was understandably terrified and upset.

"Is there anything that you can do?" Manizha asked.

The timing of Sahar's appeal couldn't have been better for me. I had been successfully involved in many controversial cases for the country by now, but this was a chance to make an even bolder impact on women's rights in Afghanistan.

I'd had an influx of enquiries from Afghan women and children who were being railroaded in the legal system. This case would be a good test of what we could achieve.

I told Manizha that of course I'd take the case.

Despite the fact that Afghan law allows a female victim or her family to be represented in court, not a single Afghan lawyer wanted to represent her. There wasn't a precedent for it. Added to this, in cases of rape and sexual abuse, Afghan judges would often blame the unrepresented female victim and then send them to prison. In Gulnaz's case, the judges behaved more like matchmakers, forcing the young mother to marry her cousin's rapist husband so as to make the problem disappear. I was determined to take on this corrupt and morally reprehensible practice, I just needed a client who was on the same page as me. Sahar, I felt, could be that client.

The court had freed Sahar's in-laws 28 days prior to our first meeting. When I realised this, I knew we had a problem: under Afghan law, an appeal to the Supreme Court has to be made within 30 days of the appellate court hearing.

The maddening thing about the Afghan courts is that they often have no problem violating due process rights of victims and defendants, but when the cases involve women as victims of sexual or domestic violence then they can become super technical. So it was fine for them not to notify Sahar of the proceedings while at the same time allowing no flexibility around the rules of appeal. I only had two days to get a case together for a potential client who I had only just met.

During the initial court hearing, Sahar hadn't been physically capable of attending: she was still in hospital recovering from her injuries. No one was there to question why her husband and her brother had been absent from the proceedings. It appeared to have been silently accepted and brushed under the carpet. The record reveals that, according to the prosecution, the men could not be found. The prosecutors, meant to uphold the law and investigate this travesty, failed to address how she had been violated. Nobody even took a statement from her. Sahar had no idea that, as the victim, she had certain rights; or that laws existed to protect her.

I met with Sahar again, this time on the day before the appeal documents were due. Sahar was understandably scared, worried that her in-laws would come looking for her. I needed her to trust me, to trust the law, and see that I would represent her without reservation. I wanted her to understand that she also had agency over the process, but I needed her to first tell me that she wanted to appeal. I didn't want to pressure her, so I just laid it out for her to consider. If we went to appeal, we had a chance to put her in-laws, as well as her husband, behind bars, but only Sahar could make that decision as she would also need to physically go to court. She was the client and in order for her to get justice she would need to confront her abusers in court. It was a big decision for a teenager to make and I didn't want to rush her, but she had only twenty-four hours to make the decision for herself.

The next day, she asked me to put in the appeal.

I pulled out my standard letter of engagement and carefully explained it to Sahar. It outlines the terms and conditions of my representation. I was representing her pro bono, but I wanted her to have our agreement down in writing. I tried to explain it in the most simplistic way.

"I am your lawyer, which means that I do what you want. I am your voice. I work for you. You are my boss."

She looked confused. Nobody had ever spoken to her like this before.

"If I do anything that you don't like, you can fire me at any time."

Sahar smiled at that idea. It was the first time I ever saw her smile.

"Is there anything you would like to change?" I asked.

She shook her head. "Nothing."

"Do you have any questions?"

"No."

"So, everything makes sense?"

"Yes."

"Okay . . . I need you to sign the contract."

Sahar studied me carefully as I signed the document. I suspected she couldn't read, so I added my thumbprint.

"Are you ready to sign?"

She smiled and held up both hands, offering me her thumbs.

As I guided Sahar's hands to make her mark, I was reminded of Gulnaz and how in that same moment her life had changed, and how big a deal this act actually was. For many of my clients, this is the first big decision that they make. And it is potentially the most important one of their lives.

I now only had a few hours to file the paperwork with the Supreme Court. Like pretty much everything in Afghanistan, a simple procedure was made complicated. An hour later, I found myself arguing with the court administrator. He didn't want to accept Sahar's appeal since such an application had never been made before.

I held up the application in defiance. "Pursuant to Article 71 of the Interim Criminal Procedure for the Courts 'the victim . . . can lodge a recourse to the Supreme Court if the complaint refers to: a) violations in the applications of the law or wrong interpretation of the law'."

Since Sahar had not been informed about the initial appeal court hearing, we could use this as the minimal basis for this appeal. However, it seemed Sahar's very right to appeal was the issue with the administrator.

"Only the prosecutor or the defendant can appeal," the clerk told me. He wasn't going to budge.

"Yes, that's true," I said, flashing him my friendliest smile. "However, according to Afghan law, a victim may appeal as well."

No dice. He shook his head.

"I cannot accept it because you cannot represent her."

I tried to reason with him, but no matter what I said or what law I pointed to in the statutes, he simply wouldn't budge. Finally, he dismissed me. I would need to get special permission for him to accept me as Sahar's lawyer and file the appeal.

It's always been my experience that pervasive corruption in Afghanistan sometimes makes people even more paranoid when doing their jobs. People are often so terrified of being accused of doing something wrong that they can't do something right. Out of fear that he would be viewed as corrupt, this clerk was afraid to make a decision, even one clearly following the law. Instead he decided that it was safer to not act at all.

As I sat there in his office, I hoped that he wouln't call on Deputy Chief Justice Baha. He wasn't someone I enjoyed engaging with. No matter how friendly I was, how polite, this guy was not having it. He was always super rude, super nasty and downright disrespectful. I don't think he had the ability to smile.

"Please don't be Baha. Please don't be Baha," I thought.

The clerk came back a few minutes later and told me that Baha wanted to see me. *Perfect!* As I slowly walked down the hall to meet Baha, I felt like I had been sent to the principal's office.

"Good afternoon, Judge," I said with a beaming smile as I handed over the paperwork. "I represent Sahar Gul and we are just trying to put in this written appeal."

Baha sat silently and read over my documents.

"You can't appeal," he said flatly without looking up and handed back the documents.

"Great," I thought. He's going to absolutely love me schooling him on the law.

I said, "Well, I believe Sahar can. If I understand the law correctly, a victim can also appeal?" I was half-telling, half-asking the question to which I already knew the answer.

"You can't appeal," he repeated. "This is not America. This is Afghanistan and *in Afghanistan* this is not possible."

"I thought in the Code a victim can appeal. I have a copy right here that I carry around." I handed him the book. He took it and started reading it over.

"Article 71, I think . . ." I said as quietly as I could.

Baha glared at me. It seemed like it took him hours to read the article I'd directed him to. He must have read it ten times.

"I will take the paper and let you know," he said.

"Thank you."

I passed him the two-page appeal document, one in Dari, the other in English. This was typical of how I would file court documents. A lot of legal words do not exist in Dari so an English version is always mandatory. Baha simply tossed the English page in the garbage.

"Alright, mother fucker," I thought. "I'll be back."

I thanked him and left. I could at least be satisfied that the appeal was lodged before the deadline to file had passed.

It was important for me to know as much as I could about what had happened to Sahar in order for me to represent her to the fullest. I'm quite obsessive about detail, so it's important for me to know not only what she went through but also to understand what she felt, what she smelled, what she saw—everything that happened in that basement where she was kept in chains.

When I take testimony from clients, it often gets very, very uncomfortable for them, but it helps me get more emotionally invested, which is a big part of my litigation style. It's also quite time-consuming; getting people to open up requires a lot of trust, and trust doesn't come quickly.

Initially building trust with Sahar involved many hours of talking together about nothing important. Like, what does she like to do? (I learned that she likes to jump rope.) Typically visitors are not allowed in the women's shelter for security reasons, but I insisted on seeing Sahar's room. I think you have to give trust to earn trust and so I shared a lot about my own life with Sahar. I talked to her about Deiva, Seoul and Cherish, and showed her pictures of them. I took any opportunity I got to visit her for nearly a month, spending many, many hours chipping away at the barriers until, at last, she started to trust me.

As she opened up, Sahar began to explain exactly what happened during her time in the basement. I played a game I call "red light–green light". It's something I do with a lot of my clients. It's a stop-and-go game that helps me get information. If they're going off message, I say "red light" and they know I've heard enough. If I want more detail, I say, for instance, "green light on the floor" to encourage them to focus on the floor and keep going. The technique helps us both to focus on small details that could eventually prove vital in court. I find it especially helpful in cases involving sexual and physical abuse because the clients can call a red light, too, if ever they start to feel uncomfortable.

It wasn't easy for Sahar to talk about her abuse. There were times when she would call "red light" instantly and shut down, get really upset and leave. I was getting her story in bits and pieces, and along the way I was educating her slowly about the law, impressing on her that her in-laws had no right to do what they had done to her. I told her over and over, "What they did to you was wrong. You did not deserve this. They should still be in prison."

Unfortunately, Sahar was not of sound mind. She was so badly damaged that she'd been left with mental health issues. Sahar would often rock back and forth shaking while we talked. She would avoid eye contact and her face still had visible scars. It was not unusual for us to meet and for Sahar to get so upset that she would walk out of the room. It was a very meticulous yet swift process, as we had to get through it because court was coming up. Talking with her, I learned that the first wife had been prostituted by the husband and also horribly beaten. But when the first wife managed to escape, the husband turned his focus to Sahar.

My aim was to argue that Sahar's in-laws should not have been released and the reduced sentences were too light. It was important, too, that her husband be prosecuted. I also wanted her brother, who had sold her in the first place, to be prosecuted. I wanted to challenge the forced marriage laws that had never been challenged in an Afghan criminal court because it was time that women being bought and sold like cattle came to an end. I knew that I had not only the law but also the Holy Quran on my side.

If the convictions stood then I felt that we'd also be in a strong position to sue for civil damages. Again, this had never been done before. The important thing, of course, was our message and not the money, but still, whatever happened, Sahar was going to have a difficult life when this was over and money would help her.

All the laws I would cite in court had existed for years. The problem was that they'd just never been used. But now, in the Supreme Court, the highest and most credible court in Afghanistan, we had a chance to make those arguments for the first time. A decision from the Supreme Court matters so much more than it does in other courts.

Some of the laws I would be using had been re-codified in the Elimination of Violence Against Women legislation passed by presidential decree in 2009. But some of the more conservative Afghans were questioning the legality of this law as it still hadn't gone through parliament. I knew they were going to argue that the law was invalid.

Misogyny is alive and well in Afghanistan. Very few lawyers would even advocate for a woman in court. The legal system is not viewed as a viable way to protect women. In fact, it's quite the opposite, with the system more often used to oppress women. Time and again I'd seen women charged with "crimes" like running away or adultery. More often than not, it seemed like the Afghan legal system was more designed to ensure that Afghan men weren't humiliated by a woman.

In an adversarial system like we have in the United States, it's one side against the other side, but Afghanistan's legal system is, in theory, inquisitorial, meaning the prosecutor, judge and defence lawyer are supposed to work together to come to the truth of the matter. The reality, however, is that I've seen it get really adversarial in the Afghan courts, especially when the defendant or victim is a woman.

The hearing before the Supreme Court was held in July. It was hot and sweaty in the courtroom and none other than Judge Baha was in charge. He was rude, as usual. While I was sitting there in silence, he and eight other Supreme Court justices walked into the courtroom. Sahar had been brought along from the shelter and was sitting next to me, dressed in black. She looked nervously at the floor the whole time.

This occasion was truly amazing for me personally and professionally. I've never seen nine Supreme Court justices in the same building, let alone in a single courtroom. The fact that they all showed up demonstrated that they were taking Sahar's case seriously. It also showed a certain level of respect, and I was pleasantly surprised. Arguing in front of nine of the highest judges in any country is quite an experience.

I knew that I needed to tell Sahar's real story and not just rehash what had been written in the media. Most of all, I needed to turn Baha. If I convinced him, the other judges would follow. These judges might have heard stories of abuse a thousand times before, but I needed Sahar's story to be the one that they remembered. To do that, I needed to put all the judges in that basement with her. So I told her story.

We walked into Sahar's house of horrors together. I told them about Sahar being a terrified little girl whose father had died only to be sold by her brother who was supposed to protect her. I described her torture in excruciating detail. I described the burning hot rods that pierced her skin. I explained how dark, cold and lonely that basement had been. I told them about the filth and the shit. I asked them to imagine a little girl, constantly in pain, hoping for some food or water. I told them how she screamed while her mother-in-law tore at her hair, and how her father-in-law used pliers to rip her fingernails out. I asked them to close their eyes and think what it sounded like as she begged for them to stop, pleaded for mercy . . .

I showed the court pictures of Sahar taken after her rescue. You could have heard a pin drop.

"They beat her." *Bam!* I showed the judges a picture of the bruises all over her face.

"They cut all over her body." *Bam!* Pictures of the cuts and the scars.

One thing that makes people extremely uncomfortable in Afghanistan is when you talk about sex, especially if there are women in the room. I needed to shove my point down the judges' throats.

"They wanted her to have sex. They wanted this little girl to have sex with strangers."

That made everyone squirm.

Sahar's in-laws had said they would stop the torture if she agreed to prostitute herself. But Sahar didn't agree. I asked the court to acknowledge that.

"This child, faced with a way out of all that pain and suffering, remained moral, courageous, as well as pious, and lived her life by the word of the Holy Quran."

At last, I could see that I was getting through.

"Almost every adult in Sahar's life has failed her miserably. Almost every adult she has known has treated her like an animal. You have the power to protect Sahar in ways that the other adults have failed. You have the power to treat Sahar like a human being."

Sahar continued to sit there in silence. That's when I turned to her.

"Did they chain you in the basement?" I asked her.

"Yes."

"Did they beat you?"

"Yes."

"Did they beat you with their hands and hit you with a stick?"

"Yes."

It was as though all the judges were invisible to her. She was talking to me. We were playing the red light–green light game in real time inside that courtroom. She told her story. Just like we'd practised at the shelter.

When I was done, Sahar did something that will forever surprise me. She looked up and addressed the judges directly.

"I want them dead," was all she said.

This was pretty much the first coherent, independent thought I had ever heard her utter.

When Sahar spoke up, the power in that courtroom completely shifted. The judges listened. I noticed that a couple of them were wiping away tears. There are so many stories of abuse in Afghanistan that people can become immune to suffering, but in telling her own story with such courage Sahar got to their souls.

The hearing had been going for four hours. It is extremely rare to have a court hearing in Afghanistan last more than fifteen minutes. The judges asked everyone to remain seated while they deliberated, and they started talking openly to each other in front of the court.

To my surprise, Baha was the first to speak.

"This is horrible, this is our daughter, this is our sister. This happened to our sister."

They all agreed that the in-laws should have their prison sentences reinstated. They agreed that Sahar was entitled to financial compensation. They said the marriage should be annulled. They also agreed that Sahar's brother should be prosecuted for selling her and that her now ex-husband should be prosecuted for his role in the abuse. They referred their decision to the prosecutors and directed that the ex-husband and brother be located and arrested.

This response was tremendous. I really think if Sahar's ex-husband had been in the courtroom, they would have whooped his ass right there. They were really angry and determined to find them right at that moment. I was really proud of the judges. I felt as though they wanted to become part of the solution and with this there was an acceptance that Sahar's case was no longer just another statistic.

The court rejected the notion that day that beating and torturing a woman is culturally acceptable in Afghanistan. They could have ruled that the original sentences had been overturned and not heard our appeal. But they didn't. They could have reinforced the notion that female victims in Afghanistan don't get compensated for their suffering. But they didn't.

But, for me, something even more important happened that day in court. The second Sahar spoke up for herself in front of those judges, no matter what the outcome, she had won. The judges saw her and, most importantly, *heard* her. And it was at that moment that she saw herself. The shackles from that basement had finally been broken. Sahar was freed the second she started speaking up for herself and it will always be a very special memory for me.

Aside from the birth of my kids, this was one of the most beautiful experiences I have ever had in my life. Sahar, an illiterate teenage girl who went through the most horrible experience imaginable, spoke up for herself in the presence of elderly men. Nine Supreme Court justices, no less. That is a huge victory for Afghan women.

Sahar is one of the strongest people I've ever met. It's remarkable that at age twelve she refused to sell her body knowing what extreme torture awaited her. I didn't teach Sahar to stand up for herself—that was in her DNA long before I met her.

At the end of it all, I believe I learned more from Sahar than she learned from me. I realised that as much as I was standing up for her, she was standing up for herself because the law had empowered her to do so.

22

OH . . . *THIS* IS AMERICA

Anniversaries often make us reflect on how things have changed. It's hard to describe how much Afghanistan has changed since I first arrived here more than eleven years ago. My job has definitely become harder, and the security situation has worsened. There's a cloud on the horizon and any day it could blow into town, bringing an almighty storm with it. No longer is the threat simply the return of the Taliban or Al Qaeda but now also IS and numerous other violent splinter groups, spouting their own twisted ideology. Who knows what will happen next?

And yet cases keep finding their way to me. As I write this book, my latest case, Mary, is a great example of why I still won't leave, and of just how much more work is still to be done here.

I first met Mary when I was doing some consulting for Save the Children in Herat in the west of the country. Mary was assigned to me as a translator and she caught my attention immediately because, despite the traditional clothing and the fact that she spoke Dari like a native, she looked more like she was from South-East Asia than Afghanistan. Then when she spoke English, she did so with a soft Texan accent. I was suddenly intrigued to hear Mary's story. How did this girl end up speaking Dari and Texan English? Her explanation was one of the most remarkable stories I'd heard in my time in Afghanistan.

Mary's Afghan mother left the country in the 1980s, and made her way as far as Bangkok. Unfortunately, she fell in with Mary's father, a Thai pimp, who put her to work as a prostitute. Together they turned tricks on the streets of the city until Mary's mother became pregnant and gave birth to a baby girl. It took Mary's mother another three years to decide that prostitution was no longer for her and she took Mary to Karachi, in Pakistan, to live within an Afghan community. These were Taliban times and many Afghans were living in exile over the border. To this day, Mary does not know her father's name, or if he's still alive.

Mary explained that her grandmother would come from Afghanistan to visit her daughter in Karachi but that their relationship was often fractious. Her grandmother would turn up and demand money from her mother's new boyfriend. "There were always fights," she said. Eventually, tired of the relentless drama, the boyfriend kicked Mary and her mother out, and they had no choice but to return to Afghanistan. The whole family—grandmother, mother, Mary, her two uncles and two aunts, barely a few years older than Mary—moved into a single-room house in Kabul.

"My mother was a beautiful woman," Mary told me, and it wasn't long before she drew the attention of another man. Pretty soon, a local from Kabul had come knocking and asked for her hand in marriage. There was only one problem: in Afghan culture, it is virtually unheard of for a man to marry a woman who isn't a virgin. Mary was an unfortunate and very clear piece of evidence in that regard. So her mother and grandmother came up with a plan.

"My grandmother took me into a room and sat me on the bed. My mom was there, too. She said to me, 'You can't call her Mommy anymore. Call *me* mommy. Call her Susan.'"

I tried to imagine if one of my own kids were told that they couldn't ever call me "Mom" anymore, but I just couldn't.

"How did that feel?" I asked.

"It was weird for me because I'd never called my mom by her name before." Her voice cracked. "But I had no choice."

Mary's mother married again and moved out of the house to a new home with her new husband. Mary stayed behind to live out her new identity as her grandmother's daughter, treating her aunts as though they were sisters, sworn to secrecy for all time.

"Sometimes I would cry and ask them to take me to my mommy," Mary recalled. "But they wouldn't most of the time. I saw my real mother again maybe two more times."

In fact the last time Mary saw her mother was during her only visit to her mother's new house. Her mother had arranged it in secret while her new husband was out. She led Mary into the bedroom and sat her on the floor.

"I remember she gave me a red apple," Mary said. "Then she hugged me and said, 'Baby, I'll miss you so much,

I wanted to come with you, but I couldn't. But you're gonna be okay with my mom, she will take care of you.'"

"And then what happened?" My heart was breaking for the little girl in the story.

"And then she wiped my tears and we went back in the other room. I sat next to my grandmother like nothing had happened."

The next day Mary left with her grandmother and her aunts to go back to Pakistan. She was six years old.

Her grandmother had filed an application for asylum when she had been in Pakistan. In order to apply for asylum you have to be out of the country you were born in. Since the grandmother was born in Afghanistan she put in an application for herself and the three girls. It stated that she had three daughters, including Mary. They were granted asylum and arrangements were made for them to travel to the US. Mary arrived on a UNHCR flight in New York in 2000 with her grandmother, who she now called Mom, and her two aunts, who she now called sisters. They were eventually housed in Houston, Texas, and they were taken in by a local Catholic charity, which provided them with basic food, clothes, and support to fit into the community. Mary and her "sisters" were enrolled in the local Islamic school.

"It was really weird because we had this picture of America that was all white people because all we ever saw was American movies. But there were Spanish people, African-Americans, all these different kinds of people." She laughed. "So we were like, 'Oh . . . *this* is America.'"

It was Mary's grandmother who had enrolled the girls in the Islamic school. Mary said it was a sign of her grandmother's reluctance for the girls to behave like "other Americans". She was receiving public assistance and food stamps, and their tuition at the school was funded by donations from the mosque.

Then, in 2001, they got a call from Afghanistan. Mary's mother had died. Unbeknownst to anyone, her mother had contracted HIV from her new Afghan husband. Apparently, he wasn't a virgin either.

The family went back to Afghanistan for the funeral and remained there for a few months before returning to Houston. By now, Mary was fluent in English and her grandmother agreed that she could attend public school when they returned to Texas. Mary said that she felt like she was finally becoming more American: "I was wearing jeans, T-shirts, talking to American people. Boys as well as girls."

But her grandmother became increasingly unhappy with Mary and the attention that she was getting. She especially did not like Mary talking to boys.

"She would say, 'Don't talk to boys, don't talk to that black girl, don't wear those clothes, don't eat that food . . .' Over and over she'd say it. Only to me, never to my sisters."

It was a sign of things to come.

As Mary became more "American", her grandmother became more and more abusive. Soon she became violent, often beating Mary when she came home from school.

"She would make up stories," Mary said. "She'd say, 'This girl had a friend and then her brother came and raped her', or 'This other girl had an American friend and then her father came and raped her.'"

The stories were always designed to frighten Mary. To dissuade her from mixing with American kids.

Her sisters were mean to her, too. Mary was an academically gifted child and graduated in Advanced Placement classes with a 4.0 Grade Point Average. The sisters would pick on her and express their jealousy by telling tales and encouraging her grandmother to punish Mary. It was like a straight-up Cinderella story.

"Whatever music I listened to they'd turn it off and say, 'Don't listen to that! That music is for black people or that music is for Hispanic people.' If I talked to a Hispanic person, they'd say, 'Hispanic people are prostitutes.' If I talked to a black person, they'd say, 'Black people are gang members.'"

Mary said that she was scared to confide in her teachers about what was happening at home for fear they'd tell her grandmother. She couldn't talk to the other kids either as she was afraid they'd make fun of her. Although Mary was well liked at school, she had only one close friend—a Hispanic boy named Mario—who she trusted with her secrets.

Mary confided in Mario, who encouraged her to run away to his house. Mario's family offered to help and took her in, but eventually, after the police became involved, Mary had to return to her grandmother. Back at the house, her grandmother began to beat her more severely. During one particularly violent episode, the neighbours called the police, who instead of protecting fifteen-year-old Mary, arrested her and charged her with battery. When she returned home, she had reached the end of her tether.

"I used to put a pillow over my head at night so my grandmother wouldn't hear me crying," she said. "I was worried she would beat me again if I woke her."

As the summer approached, Mary's grandmother told her that her cousin was going to get married in Afghanistan. The wedding had been arranged by the respective families and would take place in Kabul that summer. Preparations were made, tickets booked.

Mary's grandmother was uncharacteristically nice to her. "My grandmother took me shopping; she'd never done that before," said Mary. "She bought me shoes and dresses. She was like, 'You know what, we're going to go to the wedding, but when we come back you can talk to Mario. You can go hang out with Mario. It's fine. I don't care anymore.'"

When 15 May came around Mary, her grandmother and sisters went to the airport to fly back to Afghanistan for the first time in many years. Once they reached the gate, however, it became clear that not everyone was going. Mary's older sister, Wranga stopped at the gate. She didn't have a ticket.

"She said that she had to stay behind to look after some of the details of my arrest," said Mary. "But I could tell she was lying. There was another reason she didn't want to go."

A much more sinister reason.

When they returned to Afghanistan, Mary's grandmother's attitude immediately changed and she became abusive again. Most days Mary was left behind at her uncle's house looking after his younger children while her grandmother and sister went out shopping. Mary assumed they were buying things for the wedding. Finally, a trip was arranged to visit her cousin.

"It was normal at first," Mary said. "We were drinking tea. He was there, so I said to him, 'Congratulations, when are you marrying your fiancée.' But he just went quiet. Everybody went quiet."

That was when Mary realised there was no wedding.

Two days later, Mary's grandmother and sister began loading their suitcases into the back of a taxi. They were returning to America without her.

"Everyone just pretended that nothing weird was happening," Mary said, "and I was too scared to say anything."

It must have been excruciating for the sixteen-year-old.

The whole thing had been a trick. There was no wedding. Her grandmother had come up with the story as a way to imprison Mary in Afghanistan so that she could leave her there. As her grandmother and sister drove away, Mary was left alone on the street. Tricked and abandoned in Afghanistan.

Unfortunately, the abuse didn't stop there. Mary was forced to live with her conservative uncle and was put to work as a translator, administrator and secretary for the family business, an NGO funded by US-taxpayer dollars. Mary wasn't paid for her work, despite putting in long, six-day weeks. She felt even more trapped now, not allowed to go to school or outside unescorted, not allowed to have a telephone or even to make friends. An American teenager had been kidnapped and enslaved in Afghanistan.

After almost a year of living in Afghanistan, a young, uneducated Afghan man who worked as a driver for the family business began to show interest in Mary. It's a sad truth in Afghanistan that a single woman has no power until a man comes along. The man made an approach to her family. She'd never actually met him, but she knew that he had asked her aunt for permission to marry her. Mary objected to the marriage, so her uncle and aunt beat her. Shortly thereafter, Mary was married off to the stranger.

"Did you feel like you had no choice?" I asked.

"Yeah, because I was really stuck and I wanted to get out. But after getting married to him I told him the whole truth."

"Why did you do that?"

"Because at first my grandmother told him that I was a bad girl. She told him that I was not a virgin and that he should not let me work because I would run away. She told him that he should beat me a lot."

"And what did he say?" Most Afghan men I've met would have run a mile.

"At first, he was very strict with me," Mary said. "He would not let me work, he would beat me, he would not let me leave the house, he even stood outside the door when I went to the bathroom. But once I became pregnant, he realised that I was not going to run away."

Now they have three children.

Mary is a remarkable person. I have met many people who have been through hardship during my time in Afghanistan, but I have never met anyone who has remained as positive in the face of relentless adversity as Mary. Certainly she has been helped by her considerable intellect but, still, it suggests an extraordinary strength of character that you don't encounter very often. If Mary were still in the US, I have no doubt that she would be thriving.

After I had sat down and heard her story, I was determined to help her. As I mentioned earlier this is exactly the sort of miscarriage of justice that keeps me coming back to Afghanistan year after year. It's the Marys of this world who need the law the most.

Ever since her grandmother abandoned her, Mary had been trying to retrieve her passport and Green Card number. Mary never received a reply from her grandmother. Similarly, Mary has written to the US Embassy in Kabul asking for help but, again, to no avail.

I started representing Mary soon after I met her. My aim was to help her get her Green Card number because without that it would be impossible to obtain her file with the US citizenship and immigration office. I contacted Mary's old high school, but her file no longer existed. I contacted the Catholic charity that helped her family all those years ago, but again they initially found no information. I contacted the UNHCR, but received no answer. I contacted Mary's grandmother, who refused to help. Finally, I continued to talk to the Catholic charity and was able to get someone at its headquarters to dig for her file. After weeks of investigation, they finally found her Green Card number.

Coincidentally, a few months later in April 2018, Mary's grandmother returned to Kabul. She had bad news: one of Mary's sisters had committed suicide in the US. Maybe out of guilt, maybe as a final act of spite, her grandmother had returned to Kabul to give Mary her paperwork. I say spite because when Mary examined her newly returned Green Card she saw it had expired the year prior.

I was determined to set about getting the Green Card reinstated. As far as I was concerned, Mary had been a trafficked minor, brought to Afghanistan against her will. Retaining passports and IDs is a classic technique of human traffickers, but now that Mary had the expired paperwork and knew her Green Card number, we could make a case to the US Embassy for her to be issued a new immigrant visa.

Unfortunately, with the influx of refugees and changing political ideologies, it's harder to get a US visa than ever. Add to that, Mary is now a married woman and mother of three children which further complicates her case. Getting Mary's visa will be the first of many mountains we will have to climb in the hopes of getting her back to America.

Thankfully, the US Embassy had recently asked me to give a seminar to them about legal issues in Afghanistan. The timing was great. I mentioned Mary's case and requested an interview with the Consulate. A week later, they gave us a date.

The night before our interview, Mary and I met.

"I am so nervous because I have been waiting so long to speak to them," Mary said to me.

"You'll do fine," I said. "All you need to do is go in there and tell the truth. That's the best you can do."

The next day, after nearly ten years after she was trafficked from the US, Mary walked into the embassy. Back onto American soil. We took our number, sat down and waited our turn.

"What do you think will happen?" Mary asked me for the hundredth time.

"I don't know," I said. "But I won't stop fighting for you until things are made right."

Finally, Mary's number was called. She walked nervously alongside me towards a private interview room reserved for cases that the embassy considers highly sensitive. Clutching the few documents that she had managed to salvage, Mary entered the room with me and sat opposite a window. Slowly, she began to tell her story to the consular.

At the time of writing this, we are still awaiting the decision from the US government. Time will tell what adventures and obstacles lie ahead for Mary. But, for now, I remain optimistic.

23

MOTLEY'S LAW

Mary's situation is still far from perfect, but now she has a fighting chance to make her life better. I think it's a good example of how I feel about the law: that practising law is an art and not a science.

For me, litigation is a very creative process. While it's my craft it's also art. It's how I express myself. I have come to realise that I can blend my two passions: law and music. I've always felt that laws are like songs in a playlist, and that being a great DJ isn't just confined to music. Practising law, especially the art of litigation, is a process of not only getting people to understand what you're saying but, more importantly, getting people to *feel* what you're saying.

I realise now that even way back when I was still at the Public Defender's Office in Milwaukee I saw the practice of law in much the same way. That day, when I was defending

David in Milwaukee, I didn't stick to the rule book, I didn't follow the prescribed playlist, I didn't play the obvious track. Instead I read the mood of the court and used the letter that he'd written to the victim's mother to defend him. Planted within those first playlists lay the seeds of justness.

I did something that day that defined how I would act for the rest of my career. Just as a DJ sets the ambience in a club by picking the right songs to get a room on its feet, I selected what I felt was the right song for the courtroom. David's letter resonated with the court much more than any sentencing arguments I could have made.

Over time, I've come to understand something about justice. It may be a vaguely abstract idea, meaning different things to different people. To some, justice is about retribution, to others it's about compensation or even revenge. But to me justice is something different. I don't believe that justice is ever *achievable*. This is something I thought even as a kid. When you grow up surrounded by crime and chaos, justice seems as make-believe as the tooth fairy. Now, instead of fighting for justice, I prefer to think about my clients' needs in terms of "justness".

Justness represents the imperfect but realistic outcome that suits an imperfect situation. There is no one-size-fits-all verdict, or sentence, or punishment for any crime or misdemeanour. People are imperfect; they come in all shapes and sizes and so they mess up in ways that are often unique and particular to themselves. How could we ever expect to find remedies for those infinitely complex mistakes? We can't. It's impossible. My job requires me to be the voice that's fighting for realistic solutions within the bounds of the law for my clients. That's what I call justness.

Justness for me entails a common-sense approach to the law. It's about practical thinking rather than theoretical constructs. I try at all times to take a 360-degree view. The first question is always, "What's going to move this situation forward?" I've grown to sometimes appreciate the Afghan approach to the law. Sure, the legal system still has a long way to go and it desperately needs more fierce advocates to be a part of it, but for now, I can appreciate the Afghans' openness to discuss. Call a jirga if need be, just as I did in the case of Naghma, find some way, some arena, some means to talk things out.

Misogyny is a disease that pollutes our global society, but in very few places as much as it does in Afghanistan. I think America and its allies made a fundamental mistake when they arrived here in 2002, when they accepted deeply entrenched Afghan misogyny in the name of "cultural sensitivity". We've been swimming against that tide ever since. However, many of the things we have achieved over the years have gone some way towards fighting this cancer. The convictions of the men who murdered Farkhunda, the prosecution of the men who traded and then tortured Sahar Gul, the overturning of Naghma's potential forced marriage—these individual victories could have huge significance. I am hopeful that one day Afghanistan can be a society where men and women will stop turning a blind eye towards culturally oppressive practices and stop treating women as second-class citizens.

My concept of justness may have fully taken shape in Afghanistan, but it didn't begin there. It began to grow and evolve when I was in Milwaukee. Right from the get-go, I sought to match my personality, litigation tactics and stylistic skill set to the people I represented while spinning the most effective playlist of laws to represent them.

What I've learned in Afghanistan has also affected things further afield, too. As a result of our success in recovering the kidnapped British kids, I've been involved in more cases with similar circumstances and have applied a blueprint to these investigations to assist in finding other missing children.

As a lawyer, I try to understand the beat of the court. As I mentioned, there is a huge creative aspect to being an effective litigator. It requires understanding the court's genre. Some courts prefer house music, some prefer hip-hop, other courts prefer rap; it is my job to understand what the court wants to rock to on any particular day and drop the right track that flows. When I go to court, I want the judges to walk in my client's shoes, I want them to feel what I'm saying—in their souls. Like they're listening to Adele or Marvin Gaye. When I go to court, I want to use the laws in the most effective way possible, and give them something to dance to. Give them a bit of law for their soul. That's being a DJ in law.

When I took on the cases of Irene, Bevan and Rob, I had to create a brand-new genre of music. I used Islamic law and mixed it with some of the obscure Afghan traditions, to reduce their sentences and ultimately secure their releases. That's the creativity of what I love about being a lawyer: the law often provides another way.

The way I practise law is about improvising, trusting my instincts and understanding my audience. It's not about being prideful or selfish, but about setting realistic expectations while also taking calculated risks. To achieve that, I have to be honest about my mistakes, accept them and learn from them. It's about fighting. Fighting intelligently, strategically and, most importantly, effectively. It's about being true to yourself, true to your clients and true to your audience. Trial and error. That's what has worked for me in courtrooms from Milwaukee to Kabul.

While I was sent to Afghanistan to capacity-build, I have realised that it has capacity-built me. I'm always learning, and Afghanistan has educated me in a way I would never have been at any law school. What I've learned here will shape how I practise law and who I am for the rest of my life.

EPILOGUE

THE AFTERMATH

While having my philosophy of "justness" realised in Afghanistan was satisfying, it opened my eyes to the reality that the world is full of Robs, Bikrams and Sahars, and that my work was only just beginning. Before leaving the United States in 2008 I had never travelled out of the country. I met the world in Afghanistan. As a result, my growing reputation has led to other high-profile cases, including an opportunity to represent the *New York Times* in a case that had broad ramifications for freedom of the press in that fledgling democratic nation. In the summer of 2014, *New York Times* reporter Matthew Rosenberg was expelled from Afghanistan for writing critically about the government. I was able to convince the court to overturn this illegal expulsion and Rosenberg was allowed to return.

What started as an *Alice's Adventures in Wonderland*–style journey in Afghanistan has allowed me to branch out to other countries and take on other cases. The media profiles are alright, but the opportunity to deploy my global vision of justness has been the true reward. In Cuba, where I was illegally arrested, I had the opportunity to represent a world-renowned graffiti artist, Danilo Maldonado, who was jailed for celebrating the death of Fidel Castro. He was eventually released and testified in the US Congress on his illegal detention; in Malaysia, I represented the former Deputy Prime Minister Anwar Ibrahim, who was imprisoned on politically motivated trumped-up charges of sodomy—he has now been released on a pardon and is set to become the Prime Minister of Malaysia; in the US, I was able to successfully argue for asylum for Niloofar Rahmani, the first female Afghan military pilot whose goal is to join the international fight against terrorism; and I have my sights set on taking a few cases in a few countries in Africa, South America, and also countries in Scandinavia.

Thanks to Afghanistan, I learned that there's more to lawyering than simply representing your clients. It's about lifting and empowering people. That's justness. That's been my mission in Afghanistan and will remain so moving forward. I'm not content to contribute solely as some sort of American "capacity-building" trainer. There are enough people capacity-building in challenging places around the world. My role is to spread justness, to fight, and to help those seemingly buried in a society in which they think they have no voice to stand up and be heard.

I have experienced many highs and lows. A few months ago I was asked to provide training to several defence lawyers on DNA testing in Afghanistan. This was a remarkable development considering where the legal system was in 2008 when I first arrived. It is my intention to share my knowledge and to make these young, ambitious, smart Afghan lawyers the premier advocates for women's rights and other legal avenues. What can we do to get DNA evidence to protect my client who was raped? That is a question that I was asked. In 2008, I had to convince lawyers to show up to court.

However, what Afghanistan giveth, Afghanistan taketh away. I left the DNA training feeling inspired, happy and hopeful. On the way home, we drove through a neighbourhood past a young Afghan boy who looked no more than fourteen years old. After passing him, he violently struck the back of our car. This was during a period when magnet bombs were regularly being stuck to vehicles. We drove for nearly twenty minutes in silence, praying that the boy did not put a bomb on the car, until we stopped at the nearest checkpoint to have our car sniffed by bomb dogs.

As frustrating and soul-wrenching as this work can be it's worth it because my clients are worth it. Thankfully Laila did get in the fucking car and I reflect on the importance of my work while boarding a plane with her to Vienna. Just as she is off to new and indescribable horizons, I can also appreciate the adventures that fighting for justness has taken me on and I am excited about where it will push me to go.

ENDNOTES

CHAPTER 1

1   Bayatpour, A.J., "Unwanted label: How did Milwaukee become known as 'America's most segregated major city?'", Fox6Now, 17 August 2016 https://fox6now.com/2016/08/17/unwanted-label-how-did-milwaukee-become-known-as-americas-most-segregated-major-city/

2   Joseph, G., "How Wisconsin Became the Home of Black Incarceration", Citylab, 17 August 2016 <https://www.citylab.com/equity/2016/08/how-wisconsin-became-the-home-of-black-incarceration/496130/>

3   Speri, A., "Black Students in Milwaukee Are Demanding Changes to Racist Discipline in Public Schools", The Intercept, 12 April 2018 <https://theintercept.com/2018/04/11/school-to-prison-pipeline-milwaukee/>

CHAPTER 2

1   "Providing Mentorship to Reform the Afghan Justice System", Inside PAE, 28 October 2016 <https://www.pae.com/news/pae-news/providing-mentorship-reform-afghan-justice-system>. According to the website JSSP claims to "employ international and Afghan advisors to:
   • Train Afghan official
   • Build capacity
   • Improve and expand access to the state justice sector
   • Provide technical assistance to Afghan ministries and institutions

- Develop a safe, secure and humane Afghan corrections system that meets international standards and Afghan cultural requirements
- Reduce corruption"

CHAPTER 3

1   Pursuant to Article 3 of Afghanistan's Constitution codified in 2004: "No law shall contravene the tenets and provisions of the holy religion of Islam in Afghanistan."

2   Furthermore, according to Afghanistan's Constitution Article 130 states in cases under consideration, the courts shall apply provisions of this Constitution as well as other laws. If there is no provision in the Constitution or other laws about a case, the courts shall, in pursuance of Hanafi jurisprudence, and, within the limits set by this Constitution, rule in a way that attains justice in the best manner.

3   Pursuant to Afghanistan's Constitution, Article 2 specifically states that, "Innocence is the original state."

    Furthermore, according to the 2004 Interim Criminal Procedure Code for the Courts Article 4(1) entitled Presumption of Innocence specifically states: "From the moment of the introduction of the penal action until when the criminal responsibility has been assessed by a final decision the person is presumed innocent. Therefore decisions involving deprivations or limitations of human rights must be strictly confined to the need of collecting evidence and establishing the truth."

    It is important to note that the Presumption of Innocence was reconfirmed in Afghanistan's Criminal Procedure Code Article 5.

    In addition to this, the UN Convention on Human Rights (which Afghanistan is a signatory to) Article 11 states that "everyone charged with a penal offence has the right to be presumed innocent until proven guilty according to law in a public trial at which he has had all the guarantees necessary for his defence."

    The UN Covenant on Political and Civil Rights (which Afghanistan is a signatory to) Article 14(2) states that everyone charged with a criminal offence shall have the right to be presumed innocent until proved guilty according to law.

4   According to the Holy Quran and Sunna one is to prohibit any infringement upon their personal life. Evidence must be built upon truth and obtained through legal means otherwise this would violate the privacy rights protected by Islamic Shari'a Law. Furthermore, another important aspect of Islamic Shari'a law is the right to confront the evidence against him or her including confronting the victim.

    UN Covenant on Political and Civil Rights Article 14 states that "All persons in criminal matters have the right to examine, or have examined, the witnesses against him and to obtain the attendance and examination of witnesses on his behalf under the same conditions as witnesses against him."

5   In the Special Inspector General for Afghanistan Reconstruction (SIGAR)
    report released July 2015, they "determined that DOD, DOJ, State, and
    USAID have spent more than $1 billion on at least 66 programs since 2003
    to develop the rule of law in Afghanistan". They further determined that the
    rule of law strategy had been impaired because DOD is unable to account
    for the total amount of funds it spent to support rule of law development.

CHAPTER 5

1   Pursuant to Afghanistan's Interim Criminal Procedure Code for Courts
    codified in 2004, Article 4 entitled Presumption of Innocence states, "From
    the moment of the introduction of the penal action until when the criminal
    responsibility has been assessed by a final decision the person is presumed
    innocent. Therefore, decisions involving deprivations or limitations of
    human rights must be strictly confined to the need of collecting evidence
    and establishing the truth." This article was later endorsed in Afghanistan's
    Criminal Procedure Code signed into law on 23 February 2014 as Article
    5(1) of the newly enacted code and it states, "Presumption of innocence
    is the original state in which accused persons are innocent unless they are
    convicted by a final decision of a competent court."

CHAPTER 6

1   According to the Interim Criminal Procedure Code for Courts ratified in
    2004 Article 81 entitled Cases of Revision states:

    1. It is permitted, at all times, the revision, in favor of the person
        sentenced for misdemeanors or felonies, of the final decision in the
        following cases:

        a. When the facts on which the sentence is based cannot be recon-
            ciled with the facts established in another final decision;
        b. When a judgment drawn up by a civil Court upon which the
            sentence is grounded has been quashed;
        c. When facts, circumstances or documents, demonstrating the
            innocence of the sentenced person, which were not known
            before the sentence, are newly disclosed or emerged;
        d. When it turns out by means of judicial assessment that the
            sentence was based on false testimonies, forged documents or
            any other fact of criminal nature which have been assessed by a
            final judicial decision;
        e. When after a sentence for murder new evidentiary elements
            supervene or emerge according to which results that the death
            of the person did not occur;
        f. When the sentence was adopted at the end of a process conducted
            without informing the accused by regular notifications or not
            giving him the possibility to appear so to deprive him of the
            right of defence or when a real impediment for appearing was
            not known or disregarded by the Court.

ENDNOTES

2   Pursuant to Afghanistan's Counter Narcotics Law Article 16(1) states specifically: Whoever commits a drug trafficking offense involving the following quantities of heroin, morphine, or cocaine, or any mixture containing those substances, shall be sentenced as follows: (vi) Over 5kg, life imprisonment, and a fine of between 1,000,000 Afs and 10,000,000Afs.

3   According to Afghanistan's Interim Criminal Procedure Code for the Courts enacted in 2004 Article 81 entitled Cases of Revision states:

1. It is permitted, at all times, the revision, in favor of the person sentenced for misdemeanors or felonies, of the final decision in the following cases:

   a. When the facts on which the sentence is based cannot be reconciled with the facts established in another final decision;

   b. When a judgment drawn up by a civil Court upon which the sentence is grounded has been quashed;

   c. When facts, circumstances or documents, demonstrating the innocence of the sentenced person, which were not known before the sentence, are newly disclosed or emerged;

   d. When it turns out by means of judicial assessment that the sentence was based on false testimonies, forged documents or any other fact of criminal nature which have been assessed by a final judicial decision;

   e. When after a sentence for murder new evidentiary elements supervene or emerge according to which results that the death of the person did not occur;

   f. When the sentence was adopted at the end of a process conducted without informing the accused by regular notifications or not giving him the possibility to appear so to deprive him of the right of defense or when a real impediment for appearing was not known or disregarded by the Court.

   It should be important to note that in 2014 a new Criminal Procedure for Courts was passed and the right to revision is codified in Article 282.

4   Abdul Salam Azimi (Pashto: عبدالسلام عظیمی, born: 1936) in Farah Province) was the Chief Justice of Afghanistan and, as such, the head of the Afghan Supreme Court from May 2006 to October 2014, when he resigned his position <https://en.wikipedia.org/wiki/Abdul_Salam_Azimi#cite_note-1>.

CHAPTER 7

1   Motley, K., "An Assessment of Juvenile Justice in Afghanistan", Terre des Hommes, January 2010 <https://childhub.org/es/system/tdf/library/attachments/tdh_10_juvenile_0710.pdf?file=1&type=node&id=19019>.

CHAPTER 11

1   Bush, G.W., "Remarks at the Signing Ceremony for Afghan Women and Children Relief Act of 2001", US Department of State <https://2001-2009.state.gov/p/sca/rls/rm/6816.htm>.

2   Afghanistan's Advocates Law was signed into law by President Hamid
    Karzai on 25 November 2007. Pursuant to Article 5(1) of the Advocates
    Law, an advocate is defined as a person who is included in the Roster
    of practising advocates and is entitled to defend and represent the rights
    of his/her client before a court of law, other authoritative tribunals, or
    initiate judicial proceedings, in accordance with the provisions of the law.

3   Presidential Pardon 84 dated 22/09/1390 states: "Taking into account,
    the provisions of constitution Article (64) paragraph (18) and penal
    code article (171) and based on the decision of the Legal and Judicial
    Committee of Islamic Republic of Afghanistan, made on Thursday date
    10,09,1390 (01 Dec 2011), the clemency is granted to Gulnaz D/o Abdul
    Ahad who pursuant to article (427) of the penal code is charged with
    forced adultery and sentenced to three years of imprisonment by the final
    decision of the Criminal Division of the Supreme Court numbered (2826)
    dated 30, 07,1390 triggered with time of arrest 06,03,1389 out of which
    she has served one year seven months and thirteen days in prison. The
    Ministry of Justice and the Attorney General's Office shall take required
    legal actions to reinforce the decree."

4   Presidential Decree 107 Article 2 entitled Forgiveness of Punishments states
    that convicted women who have reached the age of 60 or if more than two
    of their children are living in prisons and detention centres or if they ran
    away from their parents' house in order to marry their ideal person or if
    they married their ideal person shall be forgiven unconditionally.

5   The Attorney-General's directive number 92/202 dated 11 April 2012.

CHAPTER 12

1   Afghanistan's Constitution Article 32 specifically states: "Debt shall not
    curtail or deprive the freedom of the individual. The method and means
    of recovering debt shall be regulated by law."

CHAPTER 14

1   The National Directorate of Security was founded as the primary domestic
    and foreign intelligence agency of the Islamic Republic of Afghanistan in
    2002 and is considered the successor to KHAD which was the previous
    intelligence organisation before the Afghan Civil War (1996–2001)
    <https://en.wikipedia.org/wiki/National_Directorate_of_Security>.

2   The British National Crime Agency is an agency consisting of 4200 officers
    in locations worldwide whose role is per their website "to protect the
    public from the most serious threats by disrupting and bringing to justice
    those serious and organised criminals who present the highest risk to the
    UK". <http://www.nationalcrimeagency.gov.uk/>.

3   Afghanistan's Civil Coded Article 218 states: "Any child born as a result
    of a marriage belongs to the husband provided that the least period of
    pregnancy during the marriage contract expires and that intercourse and
    full privacy between the parties are proved."

ENDNOTES

4 Afghanistan's Civil Code Article 249 states: "The care period of a mother to a male child shall be ended when he attains the age of seven, and the care period of a female child shall be ended when she reaches the age of 9."

CHAPTER 17
1 "Afghan executions: Five hanged for Paghman gang-rape", BBC News <https://www.bbc.com/news/world-asia-29537738>.
2 Pursuant to the Criminal Procedure Code Articles 350(2) and (3) state:
   "(2) Imprisonment punishment for the convict of the following crimes may not be pardoned:
   1–Intentional murder
   2–Kidnapping for receiving property or benefit
   3–Taking hostage
   4–Administrative corruption
   5–Drug trafficking
   6–Repetitive criminals
   7–Other crimes as determined by the president
   "(3) Commuting the imprisonment punishment of the convicts of the crimes set forth in subparagraphs (1 and 2) of paragraph (2) of this article may be commuted if, in murder crime, the inheritors of victim waive the convict's punishment and, in kidnapping crime, the property or benefit obtained is returned to the victim."

CHAPTER 18
1 Rubin, Alissa, "Flawed Justice After a Mob Killed an Afghan Woman", 26 December 2015 https://www.nytimes.com/2015/12/27/world/asia/flawed-justice-after-a-mob-killed-an-afghan-woman.html.
2 ibid.
3 ibid.
4 ibid.

CHAPTER 19
1 *The Refugee Convention, 1951*, UNHCR <https://www.unhcr.org/4ca34be29.pdf> ARTICLE 33. PROHIBITION OF EXPULSION OR RETURN ("REFOULEMENT") 1. No Contracting State shall expel or return ("refouler") a refugee in any manner whatsoever to the frontiers of territories where his life or freedom would be threatened on account of his race, religion, nationality, membership of a particular social group or political opinion.

CHAPTER 20
1 *Afghanistan: A Country on the Move*, International Organization for Migration (IOM), Geneva, 2019.

ACKNOWLEDGEMENTS

I am humbled to have been helped on my journey by so many people in many amazing ways. My work has always involved the assistance of good people—it by no means has been an individual endeavor. I would first like to thank the various men, women and children clients in Afghanistan and beyond who have shown unbelievable strength, humility and courage. It has always been a great privilege to be trusted enough to be the voice to represent you. So many clients have taught me in so many different ways, but collectively, especially for those who were imprisoned, I have learned the terrifying beauty of vulnerability. You have all made a lasting impression on my life. Thanks for letting me show up.

Very rarely have I been afforded the opportunity to thank the countless unsung heroes in my life—particularly Kadar and Khalil, who are not only my colleagues but family. Thank you for having my back, especially in some of the tough situations we have been in. It has been a great honour to fight together side by side. I would also be remiss if I did not give a big shout out to all the amazing journalists, diplomats, documentarians and photojournalists who I have befriended and who taught me about the intersection of good investigative reporting, diplomacy and lawyering, which has been invaluable.

Very special thanks are due to Claude, Deiva, Seoul and Cherish for your love, support and general patience with me in life, and particularly with this book. To my kids, who often tell me that I am crazy, you're right. Crazy can be good, and would you really want me any other way? To Claude, thanks in particular for your love and support. I certainly hope that moving forward we can figure out our balance. I also want to thank my baby sister Jade, my brother Jay-sun, my cousins Joyce, Janeen, Rene and Bryan, and my beautiful nieces and nephew Kennedy, Joshua, Zoe, Skylar, and the baby to come. I would also be remiss if I did not thank my parents Kim Chongyon Bowman and Credell Bowman who instilled so many things in me, but most of all perseverance and the value of hard work.

And thank you to my great friends and family who I have picked up along the way. In particular, Jennifer Glasse, Eva Schworer, Payvand Seyedali, Mihaela Moldoveanu, Laila Nazarali-Fedida, Tameeza Alibhai, Cedric Fedida, Tammy Flantroy, Charles O'Malley, Manizha Naderi, Tom Freston and so many others who have helped and encouraged me. Also thanks in particular to Rod Nordland who was has always been a wonderful friend and an especially great sounding board for this book. You all have been very positive influences in my life and your support is appreciated.

There are so many others whom I would like to thank but I will save that for the next book.

One of the great privileges of this project that I thoroughly enjoyed was working with an amazing team. This book would not have been made possible without my amazing agent at Curtis Brown, Gordon Wise. Gordon, thank you for being more than an agent and for being the catalyst for this memoir. I would also like to thank my co-writer, Dunstan Prial, who was instrumental in completing the book. Thank you for your endless hours and tireless efforts. You helped pull out a lot of my personal experiences that at first I was scared to share. Thank you for creating a safe space. I also am sorry you almost got arrested in Afghanistan. However, I knew that I would be able to get you out! A huge thank-you also goes to my editor, Conor Woodman. Thanks for pulling out my personality and I appreciate your time, effort and friendship. I'm looking forward to more projects down the line. I also want to thank Tom Bailey-Smith, Rebecca Starford, Tom Gilliatt and the other team members at Allen & Unwin who edited and laid out this book. Thank you for believing in this project and for your constant professionalism.

I am so excited at continuing the fight for justness around the world, and I cannot wait for the what the future holds. I'm just getting started. To all the amazing lawyers, advocates, and general superheroes who I have met all over the world: keep fighting, the universe needs you. And to those who are inspired to tango in our legal dance party and who would like to join forces with the Justness League, we would love to have you.

"Well he is Afghan, not Indian, so it would make sense that they wouldn't get involved."

"No, no, he's not Afghan," came the reply.

"Yes, he is. You may not like it, but he is one hundred per cent Afghan."

"Well, Afghan or not, you need permission to see his file."

"Why would I need permission to see a file that you said doesn't exist?" I asked innocently.

All of this might have been mildly comical if Bikram's freedom hadn't been at stake.

Over the next weeks, I haggled with the guys in the Attorney-General's office to explain exactly what law Bikram had broken until eventually they told me he'd been imprisoned because he didn't have any ID when he arrived. He couldn't prove he was Afghan, which they said was a crime in Afghanistan.

Of course that was crazy. Bikram had been forced by the British government to return to Afghanistan and he'd left the country as a small child without Afghan ID.

I asked if anyone had called the British Embassy.

No.

I went back to see Bikram and apologised for doubting that he was being held for no reason. I'd had so many other prisoners tell me they'd been locked up for no reason that I'd become hardened to it. But in Bikram's case I had to concede it was true.

It felt like his whole life had fallen through the cracks. I think he's one of the unluckiest people I've ever met. He's a person who never really had a country, never had a place he could safely call home. He's lived his life under the radar. Yet somehow, despite all the difficulties, he's managed to end up very well educated. He found the time to learn several languages and could speak Urdu, Dari, Pashto and English. Now, despite being a law-abiding citizen and a gentleman, he was imprisoned in Kabul and being regularly abused.

I decided the best route was to set about tracking down Bikram's paperwork from the UK. The Brits are great record-keepers; I figured if anyone had documentation I could use it would be them. A few enquiries led me to a paper trail from Bikram's application for asylum. From there, I was able to obtain the name of his barrister in London and his petition to marry his fiancée. It wasn't a lot, but it was a start.

Unfortunately, Bikram's barrister over in the UK wasn't very helpful. According to the file, after Bikram's initial application was turned down he had been entitled to appeal, but no appeal was ever filed. Instead of informing his client of that fact, the lawyer gave Bikram the impression that he was only waiting for an appellate hearing. So it came as a complete surprise when he showed up at the immigration office and was deported.

That was Bikram's life in a nutshell. It seemed like everyone who was in a position to help him along the way had missed the chance to see the good in him and instead focused on the problems. It made me sad to think how much of his life had been taken away from him. But that made me even more determined to help because that's what the law exists for: to help people who need it.

According to international law, a host country can't return an asylum seeker to another country if there is a reasonable belief that their life or freedom will "be threatened based on their race, religion, nationality, membership of a particular social group or political opinion".[1] That meant the UK government had broken the law by deporting Bikram to Afghanistan because there was a reasonable belief that, as a Sikh, his freedom and safety were in jeopardy, along with the fact that he had no identifying documents.

I decided to set up a meeting at the British Embassy. I was still appointed as Her Majesty's Legal Representative to the United Kingdom's Ambassador and Embassy so I was already representing the embassy on a bunch of other legal matters. I had a really good relationship with the senior staff right up to the ambassador. I decided to raise Bikram's case with the ambassador and appeal to him on humanitarian grounds, while gently hinting at the lack of due process on the Brits' part. I asked if he could set up a meeting with the Afghan Attorney-General, Alako. If I could get those guys in a room together then they couldn't pass the buck and we'd have to find a common way forward.

This time when I went to meet with Alako I didn't speak to him in German.

His office was full of Afghan men, who just seemed to be hanging out. I'd learned a long time before that even though I'd scheduled a meeting with one person, often it was about convincing everyone else in the room. I didn't like it, but there was no way around it.

"Good morning, Alako," I said, shaking his hand. "I represent Bikram Datta. A man who has been illegally imprisoned in Afghanistan for almost two years. He has not committed any crimes. He has no family. He was deported from the UK to Afghanistan without a *tashkira* [Afghan government–issued document] illegally."

"He has not committed any crimes?" he asked, half-talking to me, half to the other men in the room. None of them seemed to have any idea.

"Rameen and Abdul are the prosecutors handling this matter," I said.

A few minutes later, Rameen and Abdul were summoned to the room.

"Bikram is from India and illegally entered Afghanistan," Rameen explained.

"No, that is not true," I said.

For months the prosecutors had claimed Bikram was from India because he was Sikh. Numerous times I told them that this was simply not true. They were punishing him because he was not Muslim. They knew it and I knew it.

"He is not from India," I continued, "and there is absolutely no proof that he is from India. Here is a letter from the British Embassy, which acknowledges his deportation."

Alako took the letter. "Did you know about this?" he asked his prosecutors.

"He told us he is from India," Abdul lied.

"I think this is a 'lost in translation' issue," I said. "Because it's a fact that he was deported from the UK to Afghanistan without any legal documents nearly two years ago and he's been in jail ever since. It is not his fault that he does not have the correct documentation; that letter from the British Embassy confirms it. And he hasn't committed any crimes, so he should be released immediately."

Alako sat quietly. The whole room waited for his response.

"Bikram should be released immediately," he said, "but only with a guarantor."

A guarantor is essentially a person who vouches for an imprisoned person and "guarantees" that the person under investigation will cooperate with the government. If at any time the person does not show up when the government wants them to then the guarantor can be arrested.